A HISTORY OF THEATRICAL ART

Portrait of Molière as a young man.

Fig. **12.**

A History of Theatrical Art

In Ancient and Modern Times by

Karl Mantzius

Authorised Translation by

Louise von Cossel

Volume IV

Molière and his Times

The Theatre in France in the 17th Century

GLOUCESTER, MASS.

PETER SMITH

1970

First Published, 1905
Reprinted, 1937
Reprinted, 1970

PREFACE

THOUGH the book which is here presented to English readers chiefly deals with Molière, and includes a sketch of the life of the great dramatist, the author does not wish it to be considered as a biography properly so called. It is at the same time something more and a good deal less. It supplies more of the background of theatrical history and of the *milieu* in which the great actor-manager lived than is found in the ordinary biographies of Molière; whereas the reader who looks for detailed information about Molière as a poet, and desires an æsthetic appreciation of his works, will not find what he seeks in these chapters.

KARL MANTZIUS.

COPENHAGEN, 1905.

CONTENTS

LIST OF ILLUSTRATIONS

I

AT the close of the sixteenth century theatrical affairs
in France were still on a very low level. While, about
the year 1600, London possessed no less than six large
permanent theatres, a class of uncommonly efficient and
generally esteemed professional actors, and a dramatic
literature which has never yet been equalled in power
and splendour ; while Italy was sending forth its brilliant,
well-trained companies to all civilised countries ; Paris as
yet possessed but one poor play-house, with a class of
actors hardly superior to common jugglers, and a
répertoire of scarcely any literary value.

It is not difficult to find the reason of this poverty in
a nation otherwise endowed with great dramatic talent.
In Paris, which was then, as now, the heart of France,
all theatrical business was by royal privilege in the
hands of a dramatic society of artisans, called the
" *Passion-Brothers*," who had the power of preventing
all theatrical performances of which they did not reap
the profits "in the city of Paris as well as in its suburbs
and the surrounding country."

The first privilege of the Passion-Brothers dated from
1402, the last—which was confirmed by all the kings

successively, and was still in force at the beginning of
the seventeenth century—was granted in 1548. As the
Brothers were at the same time forbidden to perform
Passion-plays and Mysteries, and as, moreover, they no
longer appeared on the boards in person, it might be
thought that the privilege had lasted long enough, and
that there would have been good reason for intimating
to the dramatic artisans that in future they had better
content themselves with keeping to their professions.

Privileges, however, as we know, are an obstinate
evil, and the France of the seventeenth century
offered a particularly favourable soil for this parasite.
So the Brothers did not actually lose their old prerogative till 1677, though, indeed, their monopoly had
been violated many times in the interval, and though
their connection with theatrical art during this period
had been limited to constant litigation with the actors
with whom they had had to deal. To these lawsuits,
however, posterity owes some obligation, inasmuch as
they present a few points of support to the historians
of this otherwise obscure period.

As it was, at the beginning of the seventeenth
century the Fraternity [1] was in possession of the only
established theatre in Paris, and no company was allowed
to act in any other place. This theatre was called " The
Hôtel de Bourgogne," as it was built on a site on
which in former times the Dukes of Burgundy had
had their castle, and which had been acquired by the
Brothers in 1548 with the purpose of building their play-

---

[1] For its earlier merits and other details of its work, see vol. ii., *Middle
Ages and Renaissance*, pp. 113-118.

house there. The Hôtel de Bourgogne theatre was situated at the corner of the Rue Mauconseil and the Rue Française in the Saint Denis quarter, not far from the present *Halles Centrales.*

We have no detailed description of the outward appearance of this theatre. Originally it was destined for the performance of Mysteries, for the decree which forbade this kind of plays was not issued till after the house had been built, and in spite of the prohibitions, the old ecclesiastical plays, disguised as tragedies or historical plays, were performed throughout the whole of the sixteenth century. In accordance with its original purpose, the stage, no doubt, consisted of the usual large platform or tribune extending towards the auditorium, and affording sufficient space for the multitude of decorations required. The auditorium was long, narrow and low, with two galleries running along the walls. So far as can be judged from the scanty contemporary evidence, the Hôtel de Bourgogne was a rather gloomy and not very festive spot, and during the first period of its existence the public which visited it was on a level with the place—a gang of idlers who met in the theatre before the beginning of the entertainment to drink, gamble, and fight, and to whom the play only offered additional opportunities for quarrels and disturbances, so that the enemies of the theatre had indeed some justification for calling it "a den of iniquity and a house of Satan, named the ' Hôtel de Bourgogne.' "

But times changed and so did the theatres. The Italian and Spanish companies, which from the close of the sixteenth century frequently visited France, brought lessons of other styles of theatrical art very superior to the dramatic entertainments that had hitherto satisfied the Parisians. The Italians in particular introduced a perfectly developed theatrical technique, a refined and formally complete style of acting and a peculiar and varied, répertoire which, notwithstanding the foreign speech of the performers, enchanted the French public. The Spaniards, it is true, offered plays of much higher value than the Italians, but the Spanish language was much less known to the public than the Italian, and the Spaniards could not compensate for this drawback by the brilliant and expressive gesticulation and the vivid facial play, in which the Italians were, and are, unsurpassed.

The clumsy amateur art of the old artisans had become a laughing stock. It became evident now that they could neither speak nor move properly, and though, no doubt, it was hard for them to give up their pretentions to being artists, they had to submit to the irresistible demands of their age.

As early as 1578 they had let their theatre to professional actors, and these formed the first French company which acted in Paris under the management of Agnan Sarat, "the first," says a somewhat later author, "who won fame in Paris."[1] How he did so, what his répertoire was, and what his style, we are absolutely ignorant. A remarkably dense obscurity prevails with regard to all French actors at the close of the sixteenth and beginning of the seventeenth centuries, and this proves more conclusively than anything else that the national art was still of very slight

[1] *Les historiettes de Tallemant des Réaux*, vii. 170.

importance, and its effect quite insignificant compared with that of contemporary art in other civilised nations.

During the later decades of the century, the Hôtel de Bourgogne was used for performances by French, Italian, and English companies in turn. Now and then the Passion-Brothers themselves mounted the boards, and it was not till the new century that they definitely gave up acting, and contented themselves with being present at the performance and criticising the foreign companies from the two principal boxes close to the stage, which they continued to claim for themselves, besides a very considerable rent.

Henceforth the Hôtel de Bourgogne was a real theatre, managed and let by the Passion-Brothers, something in the manner of a company of privileged shareholders, who interfered each time any company except the one renting their play-house attempted theatrical performances in Paris.

As yet this single Parisian theatre was not permanently occupied by one established company; it was used in turn by the best provincial troupes and by foreigners. In the spring of 1599 two companies arrived in Paris, one French, under the leadership of Valleran Lecomte, and one Italian. Both these troupes acted at the Court of Henry IV., which, of course, the Brothers could not forbid; but when they attempted to give performances in the town, in some tennis-court or other suitable place, the Passion-Brothers at once stepped in with their privilege, and both troupes were compelled to hire the Hôtel de Bourgogne, where for a short while they played alternately. Valleran Lecomte called his company "The French Actors in Ordinary to the King," a title which was afterwards transferred to the company of the Hôtel de Bourgogne.

But neither of these companies remained for long. The French troupe could not stand against the competition of the Italians, and had to retire. Then the Italians left. A new French company arrived, under the leadership of the celebrated fat comedian, Robert Guérin, nicknamed Gros Guillaume; after remaining there for some years, it was succeeded by a third troupe, the distinguished Italian company *i Gelosi*, with Francesco Andreini and his beautiful wife Isabella as the most prominent elements, who acted for some months in the year 1604, just before the death of Isabella.[1] Then Valleran Lecomte returned. In short, there was perpetual restlessness and change, with no sign of order and stability in theatrical matters.

About ten years of the seventeenth century have to pass before at last we find a stationary company at the Hôtel de Bourgogne. This company was Valleran Lecomte's. Its performances took hold of the Parisian public; its actors became popular; the *ensemble* of the three comic actors, Gros Guillaume, Gaultier Garguille, and Turlupin,[2] was the standing wonder to be seen by

---

[1] On this company see vol. ii. *Middle Ages and Renaiss.*, p. 281 ff. I take this opportunity of correcting a mistake. The statement on p. 284 that "after a sojourn of three *years* in Paris" Isabella was to return to Italy, should read three *months*. The performances of the company began in December 1603 and ended in March or April 1604.

[2] These early actors of the Hôtel de Bourgogne have also been mentioned in some detail in vol. ii. *Middle Ages and Renaissance*, and I again take the opportunity of correcting some of my statements. Opposite p. 194 is an illustration, which had hitherto escaped the attention of historians of the French theatre. It shows, among other things, a hitherto unnoticed actor

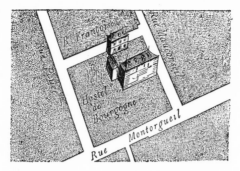

I

3

1—Situation of the Hôtel de Bourgogne.
3—Guillot Gorju.

everybody; the répertoire, provided by permanently engaged authors, mostly by Alexandre Hardy, hit the general taste; in short, the proper conditions for the success of a theatre in the modern sense of the word were now at hand.

It is obvious, however, that this one little theatre could not supply the needs of so large a city, or of the numerous actors then in France. In the provinces

named Michau, whom I supposed to have been a forerunner of Gaultier Garguille. However, Professor Eugène Rigal, the greatest modern expert on the theatre of this period, has convinced me that he was more likely a successor of that comic actor, whose costume he wears ; and both of us have come to the conclusion that he may possibly have been identical with Jacquemin Jadot, who also appears in the costume of Gaultier Garguille. In that case Jadot—like Garguille and others—would have borne three names : Jacquemin Jadot in private life, La France as a tragedian, and Michau as a farce-player. (Comp. Rigal : *Le Théâtre français avant la période classique*, p. 330 ff.). Moreover, since I published the volume containing this portrait, I have seen this same Michau mentioned in a way which proves that he belonged to the company of the Hôtel de Bourgogne. On the occasion of the sojourn in Paris of Christina, Queen of Sweden, Loret, the chronicler of the time, writes in his *Muse historique* for March 2nd, 1658 :—

> . . . La dite Majesté
> A, trois ou quatre fois, été
> Au fameux Hôtel-de-Bourgogne ;
> Non pas pour voir Dame Gigogne,
> Turlupin, Garguille ou Michaud ;
> De telles gens il ne lui chaud,
> Ains plutôt les méprise, parce
> Qu' elle n'aime farceur ni farce ;
> Le comique ne lui plaît pas . . .
> Mais elle aime la tragédie.

(Her said Majesty has been three or four times to the famous Hôtel de Bourgogne ; not to see Dame Gigogne, Turlupin, Garguille, or *Michaud* ; for such folks she does not care ; nay, rather she dislikes them, because she loves neither farce-player nor farce. The comic she does not like . . . but she loves tragedy.)

In 1658 Gaultier Garguille was dead, but his name lived, and its being mentioned here in connection with that of Michau shows us the right chronological relation between them, at the same time proving beyond doubt that in 1658 Michau was a farce-player at the Hôtel de Bourgogne.

several smaller companies were travelling about, longing to go to the capital, but unable to satisfy their desire except at the times of the fairs ; for, in spite of all their resistance, the Passion-Brothers had not been able to drive away the actors from the large fairs of Saint Germain and St Laurent.

King Henry IV., who was very fond of visiting the fairs, where he gambled and amused himself in different ways, granted a special license for the performance of plays there, of which the actors were not loth to avail themselves.

Some of them were engaged by the great travelling quacks, who used them to advertise their remedies. We must not understand by this that one or another of them was paid to play the mountebank, to beat a drum and shout witticisms from a platform. Far from it ; the quack doctors were great and mighty people, who grudged no expense in advertising. Here is a contemporary description of their proceedings : " They are wont to parade through the streets on horseback in superb and magnificent raiment ; from their necks hang gold chains, which have, perhaps, been borrowed from some goldsmith. They are well mounted on Spanish jennets, Neapolitan palfreys or German hacks, followed by a large train and caravan of hangers-on, idlers, jugglers, actors, farce-players, and harlequins. Thus, in gorgeous procession, they visit the cross-roads and public places of towns and villages, where they set up their platforms or theatres, from which their buffoons and cunning rogues amuse the people with a thousand tumblings, buffooneries, and conjuring tricks, while they advertise and sell

2—The Fair of St Laurent.

their goods, or rather, their quack remedies, to the crowd."[1]

These quacks would engage whole companies of actors, even of the better sort. Thus, for instance, the "miracle-doctor," François Braquette, hired the distinguished Italian troupe, *i Gelosi*, to give performances for him in Lyons. Several of the Hôtel de Bourgogne actors are said to have won their spurs on the improvised stages at the fairs, in the service of so-called "operators"; Jean Farine, for instance, who is supposed to have been a travelling doctor himself, but who afterwards mounted the boards of the Hôtel de Bourgogne in Gros-Guillaume's branch of the art ; Deslauriers, surnamed Bruscambille, who gained fame by his comic prologues, which he composed for himself; and Bertrand Hardouin, whose name as a farce-player was Guillot-Gorju, and who ridiculed professional physicians in the character of the pedant, which was his class of part.[2]

Others never rose to be more than mountebanks ; such was Jean Salomon, whose theatrical name, Tabarin, was as well known as the Pont-Neuf, where he played his farces for the benefit of the pills and ointments of the quack Mondor.

How close was the connection between the jugglers and the actors properly so called, may be seen, for one thing, from the fact that a daughter of Tabarin was married to Gaultier Garguille, one of the leading actors of the Hôtel de Bourgogne. It may be supposed, on the

[1] *Satyre contre les charlatans et pseudo-médecins empyriques.*—Paris, 1610, quoted by E. Rigal : *Le Théâtre français*, p. 19, n. 2.

[2] Vol. ii., *Middle Ages and Renaissance*, pp. 206, 207.

whole, that neither the public nor the actors of the time made any distinction between the art of the fair and that of the theatre. And, indeed, the only difference lay in the localities; the répertoires and the style of acting were the same, for even at the fairs plays of a higher order might be seen, like those which formed the répertoire of the Hôtel de Bourgogne, together with the farces.

The theatre in France was still very far from occupying the central position in literature and society which it was to acquire under Louis XIV., when actors of independent means and fashionable actresses vied in gorgeousness with their aristocratic public of nobles, wits, and great ladies. Under Henry IV. the theatre was nothing but a very popular place of amusement, and the actors a flock of impecunious jugglers, who lived by their wits, and had to pocket the insults of the nobles, together with the few *sous* charged for admission— sometimes even the former without the latter. This, at least, seems not unfrequently to have been the case. We can imagine how exceedingly humble were the arrangements of the theatre, when we hear that the manager himself stood at the door with his cash-box, and received the admission fee. To what insults this function might expose him may be seen from the following little story, which relates to Battistino, an Italian actor.

In the year 1608, when in Paris with his company, he was standing one day at the door of his theatre receiving the money for admission, when a nobleman of high rank stopped and gave him, not money, but a blow, then pushed him aside and entered the theatre. Battistino followed him, complaining of the insult to which he had been subjected, and repeating his request for the fee. The nobleman replied : " I have paid you in the coin you deserve." Upon which, the Italian flew into a rage, and answered : " If that is so, I will certainly pay you back your due," and, so saying, he struck him a violent blow straight in the face, which made his blue blood stream freely from his nose. The nobleman then drew his sword against the actor, and some of his friends did the same ; but by the assistance of some of his countrymen the Italian succeeded in escaping. A few days later, however, the nobleman came back with a band of armed attendants, and killed poor Battistino.

If the Italians, who enjoyed especial favour in France, and were patronised by the Court with Marie de Medici at its head, could be treated in this way, we can scarcely doubt that their French colleagues, who were held in very low esteem, had to accept a blow as an honour.

Their morals, of course, were on a par with the treatment they received. " They were nearly all rascals," we read in a contemporary author, who knew a good deal about theatrical affairs,[1] " and their women lived in the greatest licentiousness ; they were common property, even among the members of the company to which they did not belong."

These are hard words and perhaps unjust, but the accusation seems to have been common, since the actors frequently defend themselves against it. Thus in Scudéry's *La Comédie des Comédiens*, Mlle Beausoleil

[1] Tallemant des Réaux : *Historiettes*, vii. 170.

says, in speaking of the importunate admirers who crowd in the wings : " They think the farce is a picture of our life, and that we act on the stage only what we do off it ; they think the married women amongst us must needs belong to the whole company, and as they imagine that we are common property like the sun and the elements, there is not one of them who does not fancy that he has a right to annoy us with his importunities." [1]

Slander may to some extent have exaggerated the facts, but it was seldom through virtue that French actresses won their fame.   This, at least, is certain, that during this period the men and women had their tiring-room in common, and also received visitors in it, an arrangement which neither was a sign of rigid morals, nor tended to produce them.

However, though the progress was slow, time improved matters for the actors in this as in other respects. The reign of Henry IV. was in so far propitious to the theatre, as the country found leisure and means for amusement.   The popular Vert-Galant himself did not despise the pleasures of life, but to actors he was not liberal in money matters, and though the company of Valleran Lecomte called themselves " The King's Players," this title did nothing to swell their purses.   It was, as a nobleman says in the play quoted above, on reading the play-bill of the Hôtel de Bourgogne : " The King's Players ! Ho ! I understand.   This rank and the title of Gentleman-in-Waiting are cheap nowadays, but then the salary is not large either." [2]

[1] Scudéry : *La Comédie des Comédiens*, i. 3.
[2] *La Comédie des Comédiens*, i. 5.

The Parisian actors were constantly quarrelling with the proprietors of the theatre, the Passion-Brothers, whom they wanted to give up their claim to receive rent for the use of it ; they seemed to think that having acted in it for so many years, they might now have acquired the right to consider it as their own property, and be dispensed from paying rent.   They sent in one petition after another to the Government, but Parliament could not adopt their views, which, it must be admitted, were anything but businesslike, and the Brothers continued to enjoy their rent.

The company, moreover, was divided by internal quarrels.   In 1607 a leading actor, Mathieu le Fèbvre, called Laporte, separated from the royal troupe, and with his wife, Marie Venier or Vernier, went elsewhere, probably to the provinces ; nothing certain is known about it.   She—as Mlle Laporte—was the first French actress who may be said to have won a name.   A few years later Laporte succeeded in gaining permission to act in a house called the " Hôtel d'Argent," which was situated close to the old Place de la Grève, the present Place de l'Hôtel de Ville.[1]   But he had to pay a tribute of sixty sous a day to the Passion-Brothers ; and if it had been his intention to establish another permanent theatre in opposition to the Hôtel de Bourgogne, this plan, at any rate, failed, for we find that only in the

---

[1] Not in the Marais quarter.   So the Hôtel d'Argent is not the same as the Marais theatre, as all earlier historians of the theatre have supposed. It is Prof. Rigal who, in the book quoted above, has cleared up these hitherto very obscure matters with admirable sagacity and thoroughness. He has proved, in particular, that the Marais theatre, the existence of which all earlier authors had dated from the year 1600, belongs to a much later period.

following year the Laporte family and their company left the Hôtel d'Argent, and the Brothers remained in unshaken possession of their privilege.

For some years the relations between the Royal Company and the Passion-Brotherhood seem to have been tolerably peaceful; the Hôtel de Bourgogne theatre gained a firm footing in the favour of the public, and in the eyes of the Parisians became a feature of their town. But the quarrels about the theatrical prerogative broke out afresh, and in 1622 the relations became so strained that a rupture was inevitable. The Royal Actors left the Hôtel de Bourgogne, and shortly after left Paris altogether; the Brothers then made a venture with another company, but without success. That troupe also went to the provinces, and for more than a year Paris was left entirely without theatrical entertainment.

> Tout divertissement nous manque;
> Tabarin ne va plus en banque,
> L'Hôtel de Bourgogne est desert,[1]

writes a chronicler about the year 1622.

At last the Italians, under the leadership of Giambattista Andreini,[2] brought comfort to the Parisians; but it was not till 1625 that a French company again made its appearance at the Hôtel de Bourgogne—not the old Royal Actors, however, who continued to be constantly at war with the Brothers—but a new company calling itself "The Players of the Prince of Orange," which was then probably already under the management of the actor

---

[1] We have no amusements left us : Tabarin no longer plays the fool, and the Hôtel de Bourgogne is deserted.

[2] Comp. vol. ii., *Middle Ages and Renaissance*, p. 284.

Lenoir, and included as its foremost actor Mondory (Guillaume Desgilberts). This company seems to have been able to compete with the Royal Players; the latter, at any rate, became uneasy, and tried to injure their rivals as much as possible ; so much so that the magistrates had to interfere and to forbid them to disturb the company of the Prince of Orange, or to act near the Hôtel de Bourgogne.

The new company included, besides Mondory, who played the heroes, a number of comic actors, who became very popular, such as Jacquemin Jadot (under his stage names La France and Michau), a successful imitator of Gaultier Garguille ; Alizon, who represented comic old women, and above all, Jodelet (Julien Geoffrin), whose nasal twang and performance of the typical cunning servant became immensely popular.

For the first time after a long period we can speak of an actual competition with the Royal Company, and the establishment of another permanent theatre in Paris becomes possible. It was soon to become a reality.

In 1628 the contract between the Passion-Brothers and the Prince of Orange's Players expired, and the Royal Actors made haste to return to their old theatre, where they now settled down for a long period.

However, the Prince of Orange's Players had gained too great favour with the Parisians to lose their hold of them so soon. It seems that they parted in peace and friendship from the Brothers, and began acting on their own account in the tennis-court of Berthault (Rue Berthault, formerly Rue des Anglais, not far from Porte St Martin).

The company was most fortunate in being able to begin their performances with a new play by a new author, which became an extraordinary success. On its journeys through the provinces the troupe had visited Rouen, and there its leading actor, Mondory, had made the acquaintance of young Pierre Corneille, who had given him his comedy, *Mélite*, to be performed by the company. Now, when they were going to make a fresh start in Paris, under the official leadership of Lenoir, they chose for their first appearance this work by a beginner, and its performance actually became a turning-point in theatrical history.

Mélite took the Parisian public completely by surprise, but in a peculiar and quiet manner. Nobody knew its author, and no noisy advertisements had paved its way. "I wonder to think," Corneille himself exclaims, "of the slight sensation it produced in Paris, coming from an unknown author,—so unknown, that it was an advantage to keep his name secret; I wonder to think, I say, that the three first performances put together did not draw so large an audience as the least profitable of those which followed in the winter of the same year."

The fact was, that *Mélite* did not afford the kind of farcical amusement to which people had been accustomed. It had none of the stock characters of farce, such as the foolish servant, no Gaultier Garguille or Gros-Guillaume; and at first people were rather puzzled. Soon, however, the wiser judgment of the few was accepted by the many, and the rush to see the play became enormous. "Its success," Corneille goes on, "was startling. It established a new company of actors in Paris, in spite of the merits of that which had hitherto maintained itself there alone."

Corneille's *Mélite* was performed in 1629, and thenceforward the company of Lenoir and Mondory never more left Paris, though they changed their quarters several times. In 1632 we find them acting in the Fontaine tennis-court, Rue Michel-le-Comte, also in the Quartier Saint-Martin; but the actors were driven thence by the inhabitants, who complained that the working of a theatre caused too much disturbance in such narrow and inconvenient streets. Finally, two years later, the company settled down definitely in the Marais tennis-court, which stood in the Rue Vieille du Temple, between the Rue de la Perle and the Rue des Coutures St Gervais (fig. 4). The play-house adopted the name of the tennis-court, and called itself the Marais theatre.

II

Two Styles in Dramatic Art—Bellerose and Mondory—First Performance of *Le Cid*—Richelieu and the Theatre—*Mirame* on the stage of the Cardinal.

IN 1634, therefore, Paris possessed two permanent theatres, the Hôtel de Bourgogne and the Marais, each with its fixed company : the Royal Players, who now, under Louis XIII., found some protection and support in the King, and the Marais company, the leadership of which had naturally by degrees passed into the hands of its leading actor, Mondory, a man of exceptional ability both on and off the stage.

The management of the Royal company was no longer in the hands of Valleran Lecomte. At the close of the twenties a new man had joined the troupe; Pierre le Messier, surnamed Bellerose. Hitherto the Hôtel de Bourgogne had excelled in the old, coarse farce and in the popular plays of Alexandre Hardy, but the taste of the time began to require something more refined; the Court, and consequently the people, demanded a more polished style and a more careful delivery, and Bellerose, according to the very scanty information we possess, seems to have been the very man for his time. Good-looking, rather affected and insipid, but impudent and bold, he became the gallant lover and hero, whom the public wanted, and whom the average woman admired.[1] With good reason the title-rôle in Corneille's *Le Menteur* is specially associated with his name, for in this part his very faults must have been advantages. Otherwise it was as a tragedian that he won his greatest fame through the sentimental style of his acting, and the position he acquired through his talent, combined with his rhetorical gifts, naturally assigned him the leadership.

His style of art contrasted strongly with that of Mondory, the manager of the Marais theatre, and undoubtedly each of these two artistic individualities impressed his own particular stamp on the style of acting of the two theatres, at all events in tragedy. Mondory, too, was a tragedian, but his manner was as

---

[1] Evidently he was not equally seductive to all women, for we are told in the Memoirs of Cardinal Retz that Mme. de Montbazon could not fall in love with la Rochefoucauld because he resembled Bellerose, who was too vapid for her taste. *Mémoires du Cardinal de Retz* (Les grands Ecrivains de la France), ii. 485.

4

5

4—Situation of the Marais Theatre.
5—Pierre Corneille.

coarse and violent as that of Bellerose was affected and
sweetly sentimental.   As long as its management was in
his hands he seems to have conducted the Marais
theatre with immense energy.   Though Cardinal
Richelieu valued Mondory highly, and patronised his
company, the latter had to struggle with great difficulties.
For the King, who had to yield to the Cardinal in all
important questions, frequently revenged himself by
annoying his severe master in small matters.   Knowing
Richelieu's predilection for Mondory's company, he one
day suddenly ordered six of its best actors to be transferred to the Royal Troupe.

In this way Mondory lost Lenoir and his wife, Jodelet
and his brother l'Espy, Jacquemin Jadot and Alizon.
This happened very shortly before the company moved
to the Marais.   But Mondory did not lose courage ;
he engaged new members, among them the two Barons,
the parents of the afterwards famous Michel Baron, and
" ere long his troupe was even better than the other, for
he alone was worth more than all the rest." [1]

The theatre of Mondory had a powerful support
in Pierre Corneille.   Mondory had given him his first
start, and Corneille, in his gratitude for the success
which his *Mélite* had gained through Mondory, put his
subsequent plays into his hands.   Nor could the author
at that time have found anyone more capable of understanding the great fermenting powers of his genius, than
this robust, violent and somewhat bombastic actor.

During Mondory's management we find Corneille
producing first a series of comedies, such as *La Veuve*,

[1] Tallemant des Réaux, *Historiettes*, vii. 173.

La Galerie du Palais and *La Place royale*, which were
all successful, new and fresh in both subject and form ;
then the tragedy of *Médée* which, by the bye, met with a
rather cold reception and later (in 1636) *L'Illusion
comique*,[1] which was much admired, especially on account
of its amusing principal part, "Matamore" probably
written for Bellemore, the splendid Capitano-actor, whom
Mondory had acquired for his theatre. This play,
according to Corneille's own account, maintained itself
on the boards for more than thirty years. Finally, at
the close of the same year came *Le Cid*, the performance
of which was to be one of the greatest theatrical events
of this period.

[1] E. Rigal, in his *Théâtre français avant la période classique*, thinks
he can prove that Corneille's *L'Illusion comique* was played at the Hôtel de
Bourgogne from the very beginning.   For once I cannot agree with
the excellent author.   His opinion, which differs from that of earlier
historians, is based on a statement in the "memorandum of decorations" by Mahelot, the machinist of the Hôtel de Bourgogne, the MS. of
which is preserved in the National Library in Paris.   In that book, however, *L'Illusion comique* is not mentioned, but another play bearing the
same title as the first comedy by Corneille, viz., *Mélite*, to which a later
hand has added the name of Corneille.   The description of the decoration
however does not agree with that belonging to Corneille's *Mélite*, but may
with some ingenuity be made to suit *L'Illusion comique*, and has been
supposed to belong to this play by Perrin, a former manager of the Théâtre
français.—I think it more reasonable—until better proofs are forthcoming
—to abide by the earlier opinion that Corneille gave this play, like his others,
to the Marais theatre during Mondory's management, especially as the
Capitano-player of that theatre was actually called Matamore, like the
principal character of Corneille's play, while the Capitano of the Hôtel de
Bourgogne went by the name of Fracasse.   Tallemant des Réaux says of
Mondory : " It was he who acquired Bellemore, called *capitan Matamore*, a
good actor.   He left the theatre, because Desmarets (the well-known
dramatic author) in a fit of temper dealt him a blow with his stick behind
the theatre in the Hôtel Richelieu (the private theatrical hall of Richelieu,
afterwards the Palais Royal).   Later he became a commissary of artillery and
held this post till his death.   He dared not revenge himself on Desmarets
for fear of the Cardinal, who would never have forgiven him."

Mondory himself, in a letter written shortly after the first performance, gives a vivid description of the success which this masterpiece of Corneille's gained for his theatre; "It is so fine," he says, "that it has inspired even the coldest ladies with love, so that their passion has sometimes broken out in the public theatre. People have been seen in the boxes, who seldom leave their gilded halls and fleur-de-lis covered arm-chairs. There has been such a rush at our doors, and our space has proved so small, that the remotest corners of our theatre, which usually serve as resorts for the pages, have been converted into places of honour for the Knights of the Holy Ghost, and every day the stage has been adorned with the crosses of these knights."

We find an even more convincing proof of the enormous success of this wonderfully fresh and powerful play in the jealousy of the other dramatic authors. The petty wits of course found that, in our modern, critical jargon, it was not "literary." It was a success, of course; that, unfortunately, could not be denied; but its success was due solely to the excellent acting. The piece was absolutely not worth reading. A kind-hearted colleague, whose name nowadays is known only to historians of literature and of the theatre, suggested to Corneille, that if he decided to have *Le Cid* printed at all, he should try to find means to represent in print the gestures, expressive tones, good looks and fine clothes of the performers as well. Another writes: "You must remember that . . . the skill and good-will of the actors both in playing well and in setting off the play to advantage by inventions of their own, an art in which M. de Mondory is no less experienced than in his profession, have been the chief ornaments of *Le Cid* and the principal cause of its undeserved reputation."

In short the poetasters were furious, and the public enthusiastic. But the fury of the former and the enthusiasm of the latter served to spread the fame of the theatre and the actors: the poets exalted the performers in order to lower the merits of Corneille, and the public gave them their due in acknowledging their share in the work which had called forth such raptures of delight.

It is difficult to say what position the Marais company might have won in the history of the French Theatre, whether the energy of Mondory and the support of Corneille, combined with the patronage of Richelieu, would have raised it to a similar importance to that which the company of Molière was destined to enjoy at a later period, if after the success of *Le Cid* another momentous event had not deprived the infant stage of its chief strength and the real instrument of its work.

It is evident that during the few years he had been acting in Paris with his company, Mondory had staked an extraordinary amount of energy and hard work on raising his theatre to honour and dignity in the eyes of the Parisians. Of course he did not limit himself exclusively to the plays of Corneille; others were produced as well. Thus at the beginning of the year 1636 he had had a great success with Tristan's *Mariamne*, in which he himself played the part of Herod with the untamed violence which was the most prominent feature of his acting, and which carried away the public to frantic enthusiasm.

But the excessive strain of his double work, as manager and as actor, had probably undermined his constitution, for one day while exerting himself to the utmost in the part of Herod in that play, his strength failed, and he was seized by an apoplectic fit, which paralysed his tongue in particular. After some months' rest he seemed to have partially recovered his strength, enough, at least, to believe himself able to appear at a great entertainment given by Richelieu in his palace, on February 22nd, 1637, to which the Royal family and a brilliant circle of princes and nobles had been invited. A new play was performed : *The Blind Man of Smyrna*, written, by order of the Cardinal, by a company of five poets, and it is not improbable that this performance was intended by Richelieu to eclipse *Le Cid* of Corneille, whose glorious success had been a thorn in the flesh to the vain statesman. The play was to be acted by select members of both the Parisian companies, and the Cardinal particularly wished his favourite actor to appear in it.

Mondory complied with the desire of his patron, but the effort proved too much for him. He had barely succeeded in getting through the second act, when another fit came on, and this was his last appearance on the stage, though he lived till 1651.

It must be added that Richelieu did not abandon his favourite, but at once allowed him a pension of 2000 francs, an example which was followed by several other great persons, so that Mondory at all events had the satisfaction of possessing, so long as he lived, an income of from 8000 to 10,000 francs, which would correspond to the value of about five times that sum nowadays.

But to the Marais theatre the loss of Mondory meant the loss of the reputation it had acquired during the last few years.   Nothing shows more clearly the great importance of this man, than the helpless decline of his theatre when he became an invalid.   Under his management it had become the central and most interesting stage in the city of Paris, on which Tristan l'Hermitte and Pierre Corneille had won their first laurels and their sensational victories ; it now sank down into sad obscurity and inferiority, and the Hôtel de Bourgogne took the lead.

Probably soon after the collapse of Mondory, three of the best actors left the Marais and joined the Royal company : Baron senior, an excellent actor, both in tragedy, in which he played kings, and in comedy, in which peasants were his speciality, and the two Devilliers, of whom the husband, besides being a useful actor—his name as farce-player was Philippin—possessed some small talent as an author, while his wife had become popular, especially as fellow-player to Mondory.   Mondory's own parts and his function as " Orator "—a very important one, which consisted in making all direct communications to the public—were undertaken by d'Orgemont, and after his death a little later by the excellent Floridor.   Floridor might have supplied the place of the old " star " at the Marais theatre ; he was, in fact, a much finer actor than Mondory ; but he soon tired of working in conjunction with the old, bad players, and he too joined the Hôtel de Bourgogne.   In short, the rats left the sinking ship, and soon, as we read in Tallemant,[1] "the Marais theatre did not possess a single good actor or a single good actress."

The theatre, moreover, was situated in a remote quarter of Paris, in that part of the present Rue Vieille du Temple which in those times belonged to the out-skirts of the city, and in a narrow and dirty street—none of which was calculated to attract people, "especially," as Chappuzeau says, " in winter, and before the estab-lishment of the fine institution of having the streets well lighted till midnight, and of cleansing them everywhere from dirt and villains."[2]

As long as Mondory was on the stage, people forgot the long way and the dirty, dark and dangerous streets, in their eagerness to see his acting and the splendid new plays he produced.   But after his retirement they noticed at once that the place was remote and gloomy. The patronage of Richelieu vanished together with Mondory ; Corneille went to the Hôtel de Bourgogne with his plays ; and the Marais theatre took up the old-fashioned popular farces, which were no longer appreci-ated by the more refined public, and which had to wait for Molière to be raised to a new sphere of honour and dignity.

The Hôtel de Bourgogne, on the contrary, now took up tragedy.   The three old farce-players, Gros-Guillaume, Gaultier Garguille and Turlupin, were dead,[3] and though, as we have mentioned, they had found

---

[1] Tallemant des Réaux : *Historiettes*, vii. 178.
[2] Chappuzeau : *Le Théâtre François*, Brussels, 1867, p. 100.
[3] Gros-Guillaume in 1634, Gaultier in 1633 and Turlupin in 1637.

imitators, these never rose as high in public favour as the originals. It was necessary to retain the farce in the répertoire, for the sake of the less select public; but the taste of the leading spectators tended towards tragedy and the higher comedy, and it was along the line of tragedy, above all, that the Hôtel de Bourgogne specially developed. During the whole of this theatrical period it maintained its superiority in the eyes of the public as the tragic stage.

The staff was naturally constituted with this end in view, and a tragic school was formed, after the model of Bellerose, an artificial and thoroughly affected school, which, however, suited the taste of the time and gained great celebrity for its adherents. Of Bellerose, who was, so to speak, the inventor of this sweetly sentimental style, Tallemant says maliciously : " Bellerose was an affected actor, who looked where he was putting his hat for fear of spoiling the feathers. Sometimes, he indeed succeeded in telling stories and reciting certain love-passages well, but he did not in the least understand what he was saying." [1]

Montfleury, who was engaged about 1637, came from the provinces and his fat body and bombastic delivery occupied the stage of the Hôtel de Bourgogne for many years, to the horror of men like Molière and Cyrano de Bergerac, but to the admiration of a less critical public and the delight of dramatic authors. Nobody equalled him in calling forth rapturous applause at the close of a scene—Molière called it "brouhaha"—when he thundered out the last verses without regard to their sense, and in a

[1] Tallemant des Réaux : *Historiettes*, vii. 175.

voice that shook the theatre.   We shall have an opportunity later of mentioning the relation of Molière to the
art of Montfleury ; that he was hated by Cyrano is a well-
known fact.   Cyrano said of him : " Because that rascal is
so fat that he cannot be thoroughly drubbed in one day,
he thinks he can give himself airs."   It is well-known,
too, that once, after quarrelling with Montfleury, Cyrano
forbade him to appear on the stage for a month, saying
that if he did, he would make him pay for it.   Two days
later Montfleury was seen acting again ; but Cyrano, who
was in the theatre, cried to him from the pit to leave the
stage at once, and Montfleury obeyed.[1]

It was Bellerose and Montfleury who impressed their
stamp on the Hôtel de Bourgogne ; and to a certain
degree, in spite of all their absurdities, they raised the
theatre above the somewhat tainted atmosphere in which
the old farce-players had kept it, to a higher, if not
altogether a pure sphere.   Even contemporaries saw
clearly that the theatre was beginning to rise to importance.   Thus Chappuzeau, the naïf historian of the
seventeenth century theatre, who, by the bye, tells us
nothing about the characteristic features of these two
men, writes as follows : " They [the actors] only
began to obtain celebrity during the reign of Louis
XIII., when the great Cardinal Richelieu, patron of the
Muses, showed that he was fond of comedy, and when
one Pierre Corneille put his stately and tender verses
into the mouths of a Montfleury and a Bellerose, who
were finished actors."[2]

[1] This actual occurrence has been used by E. Rostand in the introduction
of his celebrated play.
[2] Chappuzeau : *Le Théâtre François*, 1867, p. 95.

To the same generation and the same school belonged Beauchâteau and his wife, against whom also
Molière had a grudge, but who were highly commended
by the writers of the time.   Of the bewitching Beauchâteau, or François Châtelet, as his real name was,
whom no woman was able to resist, it was written,
though after his death :—

> C'est en vain que Molière tâcha jouer son rôle,
> Il irait longtemps à l'école,
> Avant que d'égaler un tel original.[1]

The lines allude to the fact that Molière in his
Impromptu de Versailles had parodied the manner of
Beauchâteau.   Nor did he spare the wife.   In the same
little satirical play he says of her acting : " Don't you
see how natural and full of passion that is ?   Look what
a smiling face she keeps through her deepest afflictions." [2]
She represented princesses in tragedy and love-parts in
comedy.   Both husband and wife ranked for many
years among the pillars of the Hôtel de Bourgogne, and
both won a considerable circle of admirers by their
sweetly affected manner of acting.

For the higher drama there were also Lenoir and his
wife, from Mondory's company ; but of these two we
hear nothing after their transfer to the Hôtel de
Bourgogne.   Very likely they had a difficulty in adopting the new tragic style and were gradually forgotten.

---

[1] In vain did Molière try to play his rôle.   He might go to school for
ever without being able to equal such an original.

[2] This and many other translations of passages from Molière are taken
from *The Plays of Molière in French, with a new translation and notes by
A. R. Waller* (London 1902, etc.).

Among other actresses, by the bye, Mlle. Bellerose,[1] Mlle. Beaupré and Mlle. Valliot were the most distinguished.

Of the comic actors of the company we have less to say, especially after Jodelet, the best of them all, had left the " Hôtel " and returned to the Marais, which had chosen farce as its chief line.   There was Michau or Jacquemin Jadot, but he was only an imitator of the unique Gaultier Garguille ; Dr Boniface, who copied the Italian Dottore Boloardo, the comic woman, Alizon, and the " Zanni," Philippin,[2] but none of these seem to have gained great popularity.   They were eclipsed, apparently, by their tragic brethren.

It was different at the Marais.   Here Jodelet became very popular, and authors like Scarron, d'Ouville and Thomas Corneille, wrote a whole répertoire for him. Tallemant was right in saying : " There is no longer any farce except at the Marais, where they have Jodelet, and it is due to him that it exists there at all."

With the increasing artistic importance of the theatres their economical condition considerably improved. When it had become fashionable in the higher classes to go to the play, the actors could raise the admission fee, spend more in the mounting and arrange the stage according to the more modern principles which they had learned from the Italians.[3]   The time seemed very

---

[1] Bellerose's wife.   Only ladies of quality were called madame, and actresses were always mademoiselle, though they might be both married and noble.

[2] Comp. vol. ii., *Middle Ages and Renaiss.*, facing pp. 194 and 196, two prints representing these four farce-players.

[3] For the development of the stage, see vol. ii., *Middle Ages and Renaiss.*, pp. 333-349.

far removed, when the manager stood at the door in person and received the small coins which flowed sparingly enough into his cash-box.   The revenues had now increased so as to allow of engaging a whole staff of functionaries — *officiers*, as they were called—to perform all the non-artistic work, among others an armed door-keeper, whose difficult duty it was to stop refractory play-goers who refused to pay, an office which frequently cost that functionary his blood, and sometimes his life.

Whereas hitherto both royalty and nobility had been very liberal of promises, but sparing of money, under Louis XIII. the Hôtel de Bourgogne, at any rate, received a considerable subsidy.   From 1641 it was fixed at 12000 francs annually, and this pension to the Royal French Actors was continued also under Louis XIV.   The Marais theatre does not seem to have received any subvention ; at least we have found no definite information to this effect.   It is true the actors sometimes speak of themselves as " supported by their Majesties," but it is not improbable that they had to content themselves with the honour and prestige which was then, as now, attached to the mere name of royalty, without pecuniary gain in addition.   The Italian company continued to be the most favoured ; it received an annuity of no less than 15,000 francs out of the royal exchequer, besides having the theatre for nothing, as the King had granted it permission to use a hall in one of the wings of the Louvre, called the Petit Bourbon, for this purpose.

There can scarcely be a doubt, that this sudden and

abundant growth of the theatre in France, from the
vagrancy of a juggler with no artistic or material centre,
into a fixed indispensable institution with, at any rate,
promises of great artistic and literary value, was—
like all other development in France at this period—
essentially due to Richelieu. During the first twenty
years of the century, as a matter of fact, very little
happened in the theatrical world. Though we should
have supposed Henry IV. to be the very man to
promote national dramatic art, he did nothing for it.
The Queen, Marie de Medici, only interested herself
in the Italians ; scarcely anything was too good for
them ; and while the business of bringing them from their
own country to Paris, was a task of diplomacy treated
with as much care as the most important affairs of state,
their French colleagues stagnated, and nobody thought
of considering their plays as anything different from or
superior to the performances of rope-dancers or con-
jurors. The first actors of the time, Valleran Lecomte
and Laporte, are constantly mentioned in public documents as *bateleurs* (mountebanks).

But during the eighteen years which Richelieu spent
in making France an absolute monarchy, and himself
the absolute master of the monarch, this man of genius,
who seemed to find time for everything, managed also
to direct theatrical affairs into the right groove.

It is a well-known fact, that the Cardinal took a great
interest in literature, and that the drama in particular
had a strong attraction for him. He was fond of
suggesting ideas to dramatic authors ; he even wrote
fragments of plays himself, and formed a kind of literary

staff, consisting of five poets, to work out his subjects.[1]
His lively interest in Mondory, who was probably the
most distinguished actor of his time, has been mentioned
before.   In Richelieu's   Palace—the   present   Palais
Royal—he   had   his   own   theatre   which   at   first   was
comparatively small, but during the last years of his
life was rebuilt most magnificently and at enormous
expense.   "As to decorations and 'machines,'" says
Pellisson, the historian of the French Academy, "he was
their sole inventor, and they cost him no less than
200,000 to 300,000 *écus.*"[2]   That no expense was spared,
we can well believe, when we hear that for the ceiling
the builder ordered eight oak beams of such colossal
dimensions, that the carpenters laughed on receiving
the measurements.   The trunks, however, were furnished
by the royal forests of Moulins ; the beams were hewn
on the spot, but each of them cost 8000 francs in
carriage.

It must not be concluded from these statements that
the theatre of the Hôtel de Richelieu was of enormous
dimensions.   This was by no means the case.   Originally the hall had only room for six hundred people ;
when rebuilt, it was certainly enlarged, but still did not
exceed medium size, and was considerably smaller than
the Marais theatre.   But it was fitted out to fulfil
all modern exigencies in the way of machinery on the
stage and of comfort and elegance in the auditorium ; it
became, so to speak, the first play-house in France which
approached the modern idea of a theatre.

[1] These five poets were : Boisrobert, Corneille, Colletet, de l'Etoile and
Rotrou, and sometimes Scudéry and Claveret took part in the work.

[2] Pellisson : *Histoire de l'Académie française.*   Paris 1729, i. 90.

6

7

6—Jodelet.
7—Stage of Richelieu—Third Act of *Mirame*.

The hall was a long parallelogram, with the stage at one end ; the floor ascended gradually in the opposite direction by means of twenty-seven low, broad stone steps, on which stood wooden seats. The steps did not curve, but crossed the whole breadth of the hall in a straight line, and ran up to a kind of portico at the back of the hall formed of three large arcades. Along each side two gilded balconies ran from the portico to within a short distance of the proscenium. The actual stage did not occupy the whole breadth of the hall, but formed a kind of large, flat arch (fig. 7) supported by two pillars of masonry, which on the sides facing the audience were decorated with Ionian pilasters, while the sides that faced each other contained each two niches with allegorical statues. From the stage six steps led down to the seats on the floor, and at the top, in the middle of the arch, was Richelieu's coat-of-arms.[1]

All that could possibly be contrived in the way of machinery was of course introduced on this little model stage, which none of the best Italian stages with all their marvels—conjuring tricks, characters snatched from the stage up into the air, flying dragons, gods in the skies, and the rest of it—could excel. And indeed the theatre of Richelieu inaugurated a new era in the history of French theatrical art, by arousing a taste for the *pièces à machines*, as they were called, spectacular plays, and plays of magic. But his stage was not to become the proper home of such performances ; it was destined for a more glorious fate. It was the Marais theatre, which

[1] The hall of the King's private theatre in the Petit Bourbon palace was arranged in a similar way, so far as the stage was concerned, but not so with the auditorium. (Comp. fig. 8.)

had long been struggling hard for the favour of the
public, that scored on this new speciality, for which its
spacious dimensions were particularly adapted, and which
set it on its feet again for a time.

Richelieu's theatre was opened with great solemnity
on January 14th, 1641, with a show-piece *Mirame*, to
which Desmarets had lent his name, and which Richelieu
himself had in part composed for the occasion. The
audience invited by the Cardinal was of course most
select, and had been chosen according to rank and
position with the minutest regard to etiquette. Every·
body wanted to see the magnificent new theatre and the
ingenious machinery ; there were rumours afloat of a
sunset and a moon-rise, not to speak of a distant sea with
ships sailing on it. But it was exceedingly difficult to
gain admission. So strict were the regulations that the
Abbé de Boisrobert, though on very familiar terms with
the Cardinal, was excluded because he had procured
admission for two ladies of doubtful reputation. The
King and Queen were present in the box nearest the
stage, and Richelieu himself followed the performance
with strained attention. According to a contemporary
report, when the audience applauded he was delighted
and would rise and lean forward from his box to show
himself to the assembly ; at other moments he would
hush the spectators when they made a noise, and call
their attention to some particularly fine passage.

The play was neither better nor worse than the
majority of the serious plays of the time ; but in spite of all
that had been done to make its performance a glorious
event, it had no enthralling power, and the polite

8—Louis XIII. and Richelieu in the Petit Bourbon Theatre.

applause with which it was greeted was nothing in comparison with the roars of cheering that hailed the pieces of Corneille and others in the ordinary theatres. Richelieu was aware of it, and it annoyed him. The author, Desmarets, glibly put the blame on the actors ; they had all been tipsy, he declared, and had not studied their parts properly. This accusation, however, is emphatically contradicted by other witnesses, and one of them, the Abbé de Marolles, actually attributes his failure to the very thing that had been counted on to secure success, viz., the mounting, the "machines," as it was called at the time ; it diverted the attention from the acting and the words, which to the sensible Abbé were the essential things. "All the rest of it," he says, "is only a useless hindrance, which gives false ideas by making people look like giants, who by the laws of perspective ought to look unnaturally small in the distance, in order to create the right illusion."

Yet *Mirame* possessed only one piece of fixed scenery, a colonnade and a terrace with a view over the sea. We can imagine how modest the outfit of public theatres must have been, if this one scenic picture, however lavishly executed, could disturb the attention of the spectators.

At the subsequent performances of the play a "Rhinoceros-ballet" was introduced, which had a greater success than the Cardinal's verses. Still, it was not till much later, that this theatre was destined to obtain real importance in theatrical history. Richelieu had no opportunity of continuing his experiments in dramatic technique. He died the following year, and under his will his palace, with the theatre and all that belonged to it, passed into the possession of the King.

How it went on to become the stage of the most glorious period of the whole history of French theatrical art will be shown in the following chapters.

III

First Steps of Molière in his Theatrical Career—The Béjart Family and the Illustrious Theatre—Molière's Family and Education—The Struggle to conquer Paris—Failure of the Company—Molière and the Béjart Family go to the Provinces.

On June 30th, 1643, a small company, who had hitherto been acting as semi-amateurs under the name of *Les Enfants de Famille*, made a contract to maintain their partnership, thus founding a new company, to which they gave the pompous title of *L'Illustre Théâtre* (The Illustrious Theatre). The " better class persons " of whom it was composed, were ten in number, and their names are given in the contract in the following order :—

> Denis Beys
> Germain Clérin
> J. B. Poquelin
> Joseph Béjart
> Nicolas Bonenfant
> Georges Pinel
> Madeleine Béjart
> Madeleine Malingre
> Catherine Desurlis
> Geneviève Béjart.

The little company hired a tennis-court which stood in the old moat near the tower of the Hôtel de Nesle— where nowadays the Institut de France assembles the celebrities of its country—and so speedily converted it into a theatre that it could be opened on January 1st, 1644. They played under the patronage of Gaston, brother of the late King Louis XIII., who had died shortly before, and tragedy was their chief study.

Though the " Illustrious Theatre " did not at once correspond to its glorious name, some of the members of this "band," as it was called at the time, deserve a special mention.

The leader of the " band" was Denis Beys, no doubt an older and more experienced actor to whom the other young "amateurs" had attached themselves when they became professional actors. His task, doubtless, was to be the solid support in business matters, of which the young and inexperienced members stood in need. Of his art as an actor we know nothing.

It will have been noticed that the name of Béjart is represented by no less that three members of the small company, two sisters, Madeleine and Geneviève, and one brother, Joseph, and, no doubt, it was this family which originated the plan of forming the company; the contract indeed was signed in their house. The three Béjarts were children of a recently deceased forest officer, who was destined to enrich the French dramatic world with altogether five members ; a second son, Louis, and a third daughter, the much discussed Armande, subse- quently increased the number of the troupe.

The late Béjart and his wife Marie Hervé, lived in

poor circumstances and had many children—fifteen, it is supposed.   Of these, Joseph was the eldest, but Madeleine the most distinguished.   At the time when the Illustrious Theatre was founded, she was twenty-five years old, tall and robust, with red-gold hair, not actually handsome, but lively and intelligent and very attractive to men.   In fact, her life had already had its adventures. Seduced at twenty, she had given birth to a child, whose father, a nobleman, M. de Modène, remained her friend through all the vicissitudes of her life.   She wrote verses, and at a later period also plays, besides being a good actress and having much practical sense.   No wonder that she was the main support and the chief organiser of the company.   In fact, we read in the contract mentioned above that, whereas, as a rule, the author of a new play has the exclusive right to distribute its parts, and no member shall complain thereof, Madeleine Béjart shall have the privilege of choosing any part she pleases.

To one member of the company, the one in whom we are most interested, she became of great and lasting importance.   We are speaking of young Jean Baptiste Poquelin.   In his enumeration of the most distinguished actors in Paris, old Tallemant des Réaux, whose lively, though not always trustworthy information we frequently quote, says of Madeleine Béjart : " She belongs to a provincial company ; she has acted in Paris, but with a third troupe that remained there only for a time [the Illustrious Theatre].   A youth, named Molière, left the benches of the Sorbonne to follow her.   For a long time he was in love with her, became the adviser of the company, then a member of it, and at last married her."[1]

Our friend Tallemant is mistaken. Molière never married Madeleine, though she became his mistress, but, much later, he married her little sister Armande, who, at the time when the *Illustre Théâtre* was founded, was not yet one year old.[2]

The youth Molière was not born with that name at all, but with that of Poquelin. He was of an old and substantial family of citizens ; his father, Jean Poquelin, was an upholsterer, an industrious and enterprising man, who knew how to increase his fortune in different ways. That he was highly esteemed in his profession is sufficiently proved by the fact that he was appointed upholsterer to the King and Court, a much coveted and lucrative position, which even entailed personal nobility. But he does not seem to have been a very attractive character. He is supposed to have conducted money transactions not unlike those by which Harpagon enriched himself, and of higher interests he possessed none. There is good reason to assume on the other hand, that his first wife, Marie Cressé, the mother of Molière, was a lady of taste, of some culture and of a certain tendency to luxury, which her son inherited.

[1] *Historiettes*, vii. 177.

[2] I will not here discuss the question whether Armande Béjart was a sister or a daughter of Madeleine. This is not the place for an exhaustive biography of Molière. I myself think that there is no evidence against the supposition, which is founded on official documents, that Molière's wife was the sister of Madeleine, and my opinion is supported by good authorities, among others, L. Moland and G. Larroumet. I cannot deny, however, that equally distinguished biographers of Molière adhere to the other opinion. The dispute will scarcely be settled, unless a certificate of the birth of Armande is found some day.

The Poquelin family lived in the Rue Saint Honoré, (fig. 10) close to the Pont Neuf, and here Jean, or Jean Baptiste, as he was afterwards called, was born in January 1622.[1] As eldest son—he was the firstborn of six children of his father's first marriage—he was destined to follow his father's profession and to inherit his business.   He became an apprentice in the upholsterer's shop, was taught reading, writing and arithmetic, and not much more.

His mother, whose delicate health was inherited by her children, died young, when little Jean Baptiste was only eleven years old.   And though the court upholsterer soon took to himself a second wife, the children of his first marriage were, no doubt, allowed, to a great extent, to take care of themselves, for his second wife was quite deficient in the domestic sense of order, for which the first Mme. Poquelin had been distinguished; she died, moreover, after three years' marriage.

The quarter in which the Poquelins lived and had their business was one of the liveliest in Paris.   The Pont Neuf, in particular, was distinguished by a remarkable and variegated life.   There the great quacks set up their shops and from their platforms attracted the public by dramatic displays, in order to advertise their miraculous ointments.   No doubt, little Jean Baptiste stood many times on the bridge listening to the grotesque jokes of the Italian mountebank, Christoforo Cantugi, also called the Orvietan (fig 11), or watching all the tricks played by his French colleague Bary, to make people buy his un-

[1] The certificate of his baptism is dated January 15th ; he may have been born on the same day or the day before, for in those days children were christened very soon after their birth.

9

10

11

9—Madeleine Béjart.　　　　**10**—The house where Molière was born.

11—Booth of the "Orvietan."

rivalled antidotes. At the same time he imbibed the
feverish passion for the theatre, of which no antidote—be
it ever so bitter—could cure him afterwards.

His theatrical inclinations seem to have revealed themselves early, and to have met with some encouragement
from his grandfather, who also loved the theatre and often
took the boy with him to the play.[1]   He certainly cannot have considered it any degradation for an upholsterer's
son to become an actor.   Perhaps it was owing to this
" unreasonable " grandfather that Jean Baptiste became
the poet and actor we know by the name of Molière, and
not the respectable court upholsterer Poquelin that his
father would have liked him to become.

At any rate he is said to have helped his grandson,
of whom he was very fond, to obtain permission to leave
his father's business and attend a grammar school.   At
the age of fourteen Jean Baptiste was placed in the
College of Clermont, an enormous school managed by
Jesuits and numbering about two thousand pupils ; and
as this learned educational establishment was that most
in fashion, he there associated with many young men
belonging to the best society, and formed connections
which became useful to him in later life.

In five years he had finished his studies, and (in
1641) he left the school with the reputation of being " a
very good humanist and even greater philosopher."
Among his school-fellows he had been specially attached
to two original whimsical poets, Chapelle and Cyrano de
Bergerac.

So it was with a solid basis of scholarship and educa-

[1] Grimarest : *La Vie de M. de Molière*, 1705, pp. 6, 7.

tion that young Poquelin started on his career in the
world.   He then passed his examination as a lawyer,
which in those days was probably more of a formality
and a question of money than the result of long study,
and with this step the scholastic part of his career
ended.

His theatrical inclinations drew him away from
regular paths.   In him the Italian Comedians *dell' arte*
found an enthusiastic admirer, and his special ideal was
the burlesque actor, Tiberio Fiorilli (Scaramuccia) who,
it is said, even became his teacher and instructed him in
the technique of the Italian stage.   The title-page of the
notorious libellous pamphlet *Elomire hypocondre*, which
we shall afterwards have an opportunity of mentioning
more in detail, gives a ludicrous picture of Molière taking
a lesson of Scaramuccia, who, whip in hand, is forcing
him to mimic all his grimaces (fig. 13).

Nothing could quench the ardour of young Molière.
His father made him try the effect of change of air, and
sent him as his own substitute to Languedoc, where his
services as court upholsterer and *valet de chambre
tapissier* were required.   But Jean Baptiste returned
more unmanageable than ever.   Then after making
acquaintance with the Béjart family, who were as
passionately fond of the stage as himself, he joined them
in founding the dramatic company called *Les Enfants de
Famille*, which shortly after obtained the position of a real
professional troupe.   And thenceforth Jean Baptiste
never left the stage till death tore the bond asunder.

At last after a tedious time of waiting, while the workmen were converting the old tennis-court close to the

13—Molière taking a lesson.

Tour de Nesle (fig. 14) into a play-house—an interval spent by Molière in a short excursion to Rouen, which resulted in the engagement of a new actress, Catherine Bourgeois—the little company was able to open its " Illustrious Theatre " on New Year's day 1644.

The actors, of course, were on tenter-hooks. Would Paris be conquered ? that was the question. Young Poquelin with his ardent nature — by the bye, on this solemn occasion he had thrown off his commonplace name of Poquelin and adopted the more sonorous " M. de Molière "—must have trembled with excitement.

The Parisians also, it seems, had come with great expectations and interest in the young company. Alas! their anticipations were disappointed, and their interest died away.

We possess but very scanty information about this first attempt of Molière in his dramatic career. And even the best accounts hail from a very suspicious source. Much later, when Molière stood at the zenith of his fame, and consequently had plenty of antagonists and enviers, an otherwise unknown author (possibly a physician) published a libellous pamphlet in dramatic form against him, entitled *Elomire hypocondre ou les Médecins vengés* (1670). But though this play abounds in the meanest slander, which fully justified Molière in asking and obtaining its suppression by legal authority, it contains information about facts which the historian cannot pass by with the contempt otherwise due to the ignoble spirit of the work. We read, for instance, a description of the struggle for existence in Paris carried on by the " Illustrious Theatre," which is found nowhere else, but which has an air of probability.

Elomire (*i.e.*, Molière) gives a brief outline of his life, and says of the first steps in his theatrical career : " I was now without a means of livelihood (having given up the bar), and I was meditating how I might best serve my country with the talents I possessed, but I could think of nothing but the Drama, for which I felt I had a marvellous genius; so I resolved to do something in this profession, the like of which had never been seen in a whole century : that is to say, in short, the unheard of, wonderful things with which I am now delighting people's eyes and ears. . . . Therefore, when I had made up my mind to follow this career, I looked round for other actors, who like myself might be able to gain distinction in this important work. But as I happened to be hissed by experts, and as I could not succeed in forming a select company, I was obliged to engage a band of wretches, the best - looking of whom stammered, were one-eyed, or lame. In the way of ladies, I should have preferred the most beautiful on earth, but meeting with refusals from dark and fair alike, I fell back on the red, and she satisfied me in spite of the smell of perspiration, which I remedied with alum-powder. . . . Well, after my company had thus been formed, I placed myself at the head of it; and, if I remember right, we began on a holiday [it was New Year's Day], for never has the pit echoed with so many ' Oh! ohs !' at the most unsuitable places. But the following days were neither Sundays nor holidays, and there was no money in our pockets to hurt our hips, for except duns, relatives of the company, or an occasional waterman, no living creature appeared in our theatre, for which reason, as you know, we packed up our bundles."

In spite of the malicious tone, we cannot help thinking that the facts are stated pretty correctly. In the first place, the troupe was no doubt anything but select. It consisted of young persons without experience, whose enthusiasm had to make up for their artistic deficiency. Young Molière himself may still have been vacillating. Very likely he yielded too much to his inclination for tragedy, a tendency which never quite left him, but which in maturer years he had the strength to keep under. In the serious style fortune always forsook him, even when he had gained practice and experience; how much more must he have suffered from a merciless public during the first part of his career! Even several years later, in the provinces, on one occasion, when playing a tragic part, he had to leave the stage because the spectators persisted in pelting him with roasted apples which they had bought at the entrance.

Equally it cannot be denied that one of the best members of the company was a stammerer. It was Joseph Béjart (fig. 15) who was afflicted with this defect, unquestionably a great misfortune in an actor, and one which, in the serious plays that were mostly acted by the troupe, must have produced a somewhat misleading effect. Otherwise, Joseph Béjart was by no means a "wretch," but an educated and most respectable man. He was much liked by the company, to whom he was useful in

different ways—for one thing by publishing a large work
on heraldry, which reflected honour upon his companions
in the eyes of the nobility.   He remained a member of
Molière's company till his death in 1659.

The malicious libeller speaks of another member as
one-eyed and limping; and it must be confessed that
both these epithets applied to the younger brother, who
squinted and limped.   In trying to prevent two of his
friends from fighting, he had hurt his foot; the wound was
badly dressed, and he remained lame for life.   In 1644,
however, he was only thirteen years old, and not yet a
member of the company.   Afterwards he became a great
favourite with the Parisians, and his lameness, far from
hindering his success—he mainly played the comic valets
—was copied by those who followed him.   Molière, on
whom no good opportunity was lost, in his *L'Avare* (the
Miser) has immortalised his brother-in-law and his lameness, by making Harpagon say of La Flèche: "It does
annoy me to see that lame dog here!"   As long as
Louis Béjart played La Flèche, these words called forth
loud applause from the pit, thus showing the popular
comedian that his misfortune made no difference in
their delight at seeing him.

As to the women alluded to by the libeller, the red-
haired lady whom he qualifies by a most unsavoury
epithet, is Madeleine Béjart.   But the dark and the fair
ladies, who are said to have refused the offers of Molière,
are Mlle. de Brie and Mlle. du Parc, who did not
belong to the company till later.

In spite of these little chronological inaccuracies, the
statement that the Illustrious Theatre had but poor

success in Paris is correct in the main. Probably they did not understand what the public wanted. Young Molière had several friends among the authors of the modern style, which was tragedy. The company even engaged as member an actor, Nicolas Desfontaines, who was also a fertile writer of tragedies, and he now provided the new stage with a number of works from his pen, among them *Saint - Alexis ou L'illustre Olympie*, *L'illustre Comédien ou Le Martyre de Saint Genest*, and *Perside ou La Suite d'Ibrahim Bassa*. Magnon and Tristan l'Hermitte, moreover, and other solemn writers, whose names are now as forgotten as their works, supplied the company with their productions. All these "illustrious" works, however, were probably too much for the Parisians, especially since they had only to go to the Hôtel de Bourgogne to see the master-pieces of Corneille performed with an art, which to the taste of those times was the model of perfection.

Molière himself does not seem as yet to have thought of wielding his pen, but as an actor he probably revelled in the solemn tragic style, though he was never able to grasp it. No doubt, he was then already the leader and financial guarantee of the company, a position of trust which brought him more annoyance than advantage.

Only a year after its opening the theatre at the Tour de Nesle had to be closed. But, as we read in *Elomire hypocondre*, "as the failure was attributed solely to the place," they made a fresh start in another quarter of Paris—in the tennis-court of the "Black Cross"—with new courage, but with the old ill-luck. Things came to such a pass that we find Molière in a debtor's prison as surety for his theatre.   After a few days, however, he was released on bail; but still the unhappy young actors were living under a constant threat of bankruptcy.   The company gradually dissolved.   The first to leave it were Nicolas Bonenfant and Georges Pinel; shortly afterwards their example was followed by Desfontaines, Catherine Desurlis, Madeleine Malingre, and Denis Beys, the original manager.   But Molière and the Béjart family did not give up the fight just yet.   A third place was tried—the "White Cross" tennis-court—in vain!   Paris was more obstinate than a mule, and refused to be persuaded that their art was worth seeing.

Then at last the struggle must be considered hopeless; and as none of our enthusiasts thought for a moment of giving up their art, no resource was left but to turn their backs on the ungrateful capital, and try their luck with the more responsive and less exacting public of the provinces.   For some years Molière, in company with the Béjart family, had fought to win a name; now he had to pack up his poor belongings, his few scenes, and the costumes which had not been pawned, and go out into the world, as unknown as before, though wiser by the kind of experiences which enlighten, but do not enrich.   The struggle was to go on for twelve years longer until, after traversing France in all directions, he could return to Paris and bring it to his feet.

Twelve years, indeed, of hard fighting, but not—we may suppose—of the sour and bitter toil which hardens the heart and paralyses thought.   A free and merry battle with the ups and downs of fortune, where defeat was

14

15   16

14—The Moat near the Tour de Nesle.

15—Joseph Béjart.   16—Gros René.

borne with good humour, and the good days were enjoyed *en grand seigneur*, as a natural compensation. A wandering existence, full of obscure adventures, which the historian of the theatre and the biographer of Molière try in vain to unravel; a life full of work and excitement, but pervaded also by an atmosphere of love and feminine intrigues, which we suspect without being able to define. In short, an existence which ripened in Molière the manliness which, combined with his profound knowledge of human nature and his disillusioned humour, renders him so great in our eyes.

IV

Molière's Wanderings—New Adversities and Trials—Fortune smiles—
First Comedies of Molière, and Sojourn of the Company in the South
of France—Actresses of the Troupe, and Molière's relations with them.

THE nucleus of the little company which in 1646 started on its adventurous tour with Molière—a youth of twenty-four—was, of course, the Béjart family, among the members of which Madeleine was charged with the great tragic female parts and the soubrettes, Geneviève, who on the stage was called Mlle. Hervé (her mother's maiden name), with the second female lovers, and Catherine Bourgeois, probably, with the other female parts. At this time the company does not seem to have included other actresses.

On the male staff Denis Beys had been replaced by another man of theatrical experience, the former provincial manager, Charles Dufresne, who for some time

had lent his name to the company, while practically
Molière continued to be its leader, and soon after undertook the full responsibility of management. Dufresne,
of whom we know very little more than that he was the
son of a Court painter, played tragic parts of the second
rank and fathers in comedy. The heroes, properly
so called, were represented by Molière himself, and
the lovers were performed by Joseph Béjart, who had
made a not entirely successful attempt to be cured of his
stammering.

The company had acquired an excellent addition in
the comic actor René Berthelot, called Duparc. His
cheerful temperament and corpulent body [1] naturally
qualified him for the post of jester in the company, and
for several years "Gros René" was the standing buffoon
in the comedies of Molière (fig. 16).

Louis Béjart, who was still very young, had also
joined the ranks, and, as already mentioned, he undertook the second comic valets. He went by the name of
l'Eguisé, "The Sharp," on account of his shrewd tongue.

Besides these the company included a few members
of secondary importance, so that they numbered about
ten altogether, no more—the usual size of a provincial
troupe.

Though much more than might have been expected
has come to light during the last few years concerning
the provincial wanderings of Molière and his companions,
especially data fixing the principal places at which they
set up for a time, we are as uncertain as ever about our

---

[1] [Je] "suis homme fort rond de toutes les manières," Molière makes
him say of himself in *Le Dépit Amoureux*, i. 1.

most essential concerns : their private life, their répertoire, and their style of acting. This, however, seems
certain—that, to begin with, things went as miserably as
in Paris. The magistrates and the clergy in the provincial towns looked askance at these strolling jugglers,
who carried off the citizens' money, and they put all
imaginable obstacles in their way. Frequently, when
attracted to some place by hearing of a festival, which
might afford opportunities of gaining money, they were
stopped by the brief and brusque announcement of the
magistrate, that a council must be summoned to consider
whether a licence to act could be granted. Sometimes
they obtained such a licence, but on condition that the
proceeds of the first—probably the best—day of performance should go to a convent or poorhouse.

In the towns they acted in the tennis-court or the
town hall; but when the curiosity of the townspeople
was satisfied, the company did not disdain to visit the
villages, where a stage was erected in a large barn, and
tragedies were performed to the accompaniment of
lowing cattle and braying donkeys. We can imagine,
also, large country seats opening their gates to Molière
and his waggons (Comp. fig. 17), and their halls
resounding with the sonorous Alexandrines of the great
Corneille and of the less distinguished Magnon, followed
by a merry little improvised farce, interlarded with spicy
jokes adapted to the rustic taste.

If Molière and his actors had had the whole field to
themselves, very likely matters would have gone more
smoothly from the beginning, but this was far from being
the case. A number of companies traversed the country

in all directions,[1] and these were by no means humble
bands beneath competition.   Enthusiasm for the theatre
ran high in those times, and many a student, many a
young poet, many a nobleman even, preferring to culti-
vate the free and rising art of the actor to leading a life
of regular and time-honoured work, joined the strolling
" troupes."

If many of the French actors in those times bear
grand names, with the tempting little particle of nobility
attached to them, most of them—Molière's among the
number—are fictitious ; still, not a few were really entitled
to bear arms, and the fact that the dramatic profession
included many noblemen perhaps explains, to a certain
extent, why others who had no right to it adopted the
little handle to their name.

Gradually, however, the little company succeeded in
fighting its way to an honoured position, and overcame
the worst financial difficulties.

As long as they remained in the West of France
their struggles were severe enough.   In Nantes there
was strong competition to overcome from the puppet
shows of the Venetian Segalla, which, at first, were much
more appreciated by the public than Molière and his
plays.   But when they arrived in the southern climes,
with their clear sky and merry population, fortune at
last began to smile on the sorely tried children of Thalia.
Molière himself had now begun writing for the stage,
and his tragic inclinations seem to have vanished.   His
first plays, some of which have been preserved, are mere

---

[1] Chappuzeau in his time (*circ.* 1674) reckons fifteen ; but "the number
is unlimited," he adds. *Le Théâtre François*, Brussels, 1867, p. 109.

farces, partly imitations of the Italian *Commedia dell' arte*, such as *Le Médecin Volant* (The Flying Physician), from *Il Medico volante*, by Scaramuccia, and partly farcical plays of an unadulterated Gallic stamp, such as *La Jalousie de Barbouillé* (The Jealousy of Barbouillé), a forerunner of *George Dandin*, which most resembles the old mediæval farces.

Molière's love and admiration for the Italian comedy were always great. We have seen how he received his first real dramatic instruction from the famous Scaramuccia, Tiberio Fiorilli ; his first productions as a poet were also quite unquestionably influenced by Italian taste, and his first real comedy, *L'Etourdi* (The Blunderer), was a free imitation of *l'Inavertito*, by Nicolo Barbieri.[1]

It was probably the first performance of this merry piece of intrigue which turned the scale in the fate of the company. It took place in March 1653[2], in the city of Lyons, and became an enormous success, so much so, that even respectable elderly officers in the town fought duels about the right to occupy seats in the theatre.[3]

Henceforth all was sunshine for Molière and his companions. Lyons became their headquarters, but other southern towns, such as Pézénas, Montpellier, Avignon, and others, were visited successfully, and the Molière-Béjart company was soon considered to be

---

[1] Comp. vol. ii., *Middle Ages and Renaissance*, p. 289.

[2] In La Grange's Register we read 1655, but several other circumstances and statements speak decidedly in favour of the earlier date, and it is this latter year which La Grange mentions as the right one in his biographical Introduction to the edition of Molière of 1682.

[3] Comp. Loiseleur, *Les Points obscurs de la vie de Molière*, pp. 162 f.

unquestionably the best of all provincial troupes, "both as to good actors and fine clothes," as we read in a contemporary report.

A considerable part of the final victory gained by the brave little troupe may perhaps have been due to the concord which had been its distinctive mark in contrast with most other travelling companies. "Provincial troupes," Chappuzeau remarks,[1] "have so little solidity, that as soon as one is formed it thinks of dissolving." Molière and the four Béjarts formed the solid nucleus of this company, so that it always preserved its original character, even if some members were replaced by others. The intercourse of the party, in later times also, more resembled that of a large family than of a chance association of actors.

Though we must be very careful not to believe all the love stories which the pamphleteers of the time relate, especially with regard to noted actresses, we can scarcely doubt that Molière was the lover of Madeleine Béjart. But we may assume that the relations between them—at least at this period—were based more on mutual interests and friendly sympathy than on any passionate inclination. It is certain, at any rate, that both parties showed a remarkable tolerance. Their characters supplemented each other admirably, particularly as theatrical leaders. She, the elder, was practical, provident, accurate, orderly, and of even temperament ; he was of an ardent, idealistic turn of mind, bold, lively, and full of ideas. We can only wonder that a dramatic company with two such leaders, who, it must be re-

[1] *Le Théâtre François*, p. 81.

17

18

19

17—A Company visiting a country seat.

18—Mademoiselle de Brie.   19—Mademoiselle du Parc.

membered, were also exceptionally talented, had to fight
so long to secure a position.

Now when the little company, who had stood so
faithfully by each other all the years of trials and
struggle, at last met with success and general recogni-
tion, they could afford to increase their undeniably small
staff of actors. And when good fortune comes to a theatre,
there are always plenty of aspirants who wish to share it.

When Molière was in Lyons there was also a company there, under the leadership of a man named Mitalla.
His staff included two very fine and charming, but also
very different actresses, both of whom Molière succeeded
in attaching to his company.   One of them was the
gentle, graceful Mlle. de Brie, née Catherine Leclerc du
Rozet (fig. 18), the other the proud and magnificent
Marquise [1] Thérèse de Gorla, soon after married as
Mlle. du Parc (fig. 19); and both these women
became of great importance to Molière—in his plays
as well as in his life. Mlle. de Brie was already
married when Molière engaged her. Her husband,
Edme Villequin, Sieur de Brie, was a coarse, brutal
fellow—the rôles allotted to him by Molière were the
fighters, such as Silvestre in *Les Fourberies de Scapin*
and the fencing-master in *Le Bourgeois Gentilhomme*—
but as a husband he was very lenient indeed. As an
actor he could at most be called a "utility-man," and it
is evidently as an unavoidable appendix that he entered
into the bargain, when his wife was engaged. He was
what our modern [Danish] managers would call the

[1] "Marquise" was Mlle. du Parc's first name, not her title nor her sur-
name, as many have supposed. Marquise, or Marquèse, is a Christian name
of frequent occurrence among old Gascon families.

"bone" which has to be bought, if we want the meat that is attached to it.   Molière did not like him.

All the more did he value the wife.   In a little libellous pamphlet,[1] which long after the death of Molière was published against Mlle. Molière, we read how this man, with his strong, amorous tendencies, first fell in love with Mlle. du Parc, "but their feelings did not agree on this point, and this woman, who was justified in aspiring to a more distinguished conquest, treated Molière with so much contempt that he was obliged to direct his attentions to Mlle. de Brie, who received him more favourably ; and her power over him became so strong, that, feeling unable to part with her, he found means to attach her to his company, together with Mlle. du Parc.   The Béjart was much annoyed at his *liaison*, but on finding that there was no help for it, she had common sense enough to seek consolation, preserving all the time the influence over Molière which she had once acquired, and forcing him to conceal the relations which were established between him and Mlle. de Brie.   They went on for some years living on these terms of understanding."[2]

The story told in the pamphlet in all its unsentimental brevity bears the stamp of truth ; at any rate, history has accepted it as authentic.   Mlle. de Brie stands before us as the comforter of Molière, the woman who loves with resignation, to whom he, the passionate, restless, nervous man, turns for consolation when the others have torn his heart asunder.   When Mlle. du Parc

[1] *La fameuse Comédienne ou Histoire de la Guérin au paravant femme et veuve de Molière. A Francfort*, 1688.   The rare little book has been several times reprinted.   The edition used here is that of Jules Bonnassies, 1870.

[2] *Op. cit.*, pp. 7 f.

has turned him off, when his wife has brought ridicule on
him and fooled him, the gentle, affectionate Mlle. de Brie
is always ready to heal his wounds and calm his mind.

Madeleine Béjart was the practical, clever, unsentimental, but cheerful and good-looking woman of business; Catherine de Brie the tender, gentle, languishing
woman, the delightful performer of Molière's captivating
female characters,[1] and finally Mlle. du Parc, the beautiful, radiant, but unapproachable coquette, who captivated
the senses, but left the heart cold.

Marquise Thérèse de Gorla, daughter of a well-
known quack-doctor of Lyons, became attached to the
company of Molière by falling in love with the fat comic
actor Duparc, alias Gros René. She must have possessed
a remarkable power of attraction, if her charm was not
due merely to her beauty and her reserve, for no less
than five of the great men of the century had sighed at
her feet; first of all Molière, then both the brothers
Corneille, the great Pierre, whom she proudly rejected
on account of his white hair, and who for this reason
addressed a scathing poem to her,[2] and the less eminent

[1] Mlle. de Brie afterwards performed all the first female lovers in
Molière's plays. She was Eliante in *Le Misanthrope*, Mariane in *Tartufe*
and *L'Avare*, and Armande in *Les Femmes savantes*. She created Agnes
in *L'Ecole des Femmes*, and won such favour in this part that, when at last
she gave it up and was to be replaced by a younger actress, the audience
was so ardent in its request to see her in it, that she had to be sent for;
whereupon she came, and amid great enthusiasm acted the part in her
ordinary clothes.

[2] It ends in the following self-satisfied and somewhat acrimonious lines :—

> Chez cette race nouvelle,
> Où j'aurai quelque crédit
> Vous ne passerez pour belle
> Qu' autant que je l'aurai dit.

(Among that coming race with whom I shall be of some credit you will only
pass for handsome just so much as I shall have declared you to be.)

Thomas ; then Lafontaine, and at last Racine, the only one who is supposed not to have sighed quite in vain. That this proud, beautiful and coquettish woman gave her heart to fat René, while so many great men of genius courted her favour, is one more proof that genius does not suffice to win a woman.

As an actress she became of great value to the company, though scarcely as much so as Mlle. de Brie. Besides her dramatic talent, which was evidently in the tragic line, she was a clever and original dancer. "She made some peculiar caprioles," an old chronicler tells us,[1] "for as her skirt was split down both sides, her legs and part of her thighs could be seen, with silk stockings, fastened at the top to short drawers." So in addition to her other qualities Mlle. du Parc had the merit of being the inventor of the ballet-skirt.

In addition to these two ladies the company acquired a third, who deserves to be mentioned, because her name is known in a twofold way in the history of the theatre. Marie Ragueneau was the daughter of the well-known Parisian pastry-cook and poet immortalised by Edmond Rostand in his play *Cyrano de Bergerac*, and afterwards wife of La Grange, the friend and companion of Molière, whom later we shall have an opportunity of mentioning more in detail. She joined the company as maid to Mlle. de Brie. Though she herself afterwards became an actress, she never distinguished herself in that capacity. Her father, the pastry-cook, was also of

[1] *Lettres sur la vie de Molière et des comédiens de son temps*, in the *Mercure de France* of May and June 1740. These letters are ascribed to Mlle. Poisson, daughter-in-law of the famous Crispin.

the party, and was employed by the troupe as super and candle-snuffer.

With a considerably reinforced company—it included more members than are enumerated here—Molière was able to compete with all the other companies, and, indeed, we soon find him eclipsing them and winning a name as the first man of the theatrical world in the provinces.

He met with another piece of good luck in the coincidence that his old school-fellow, the Prince of Conti, was just then residing in Languedoc, acting as governor of that province, in which one of his estates was situated. The Prince, who, by the bye, afterwards became devout and a hater of the theatre, at this moment took a warm interest in the stage ; and by an even more fortunate chance, his secretary, Sarrazin, fell in love with the bewitching Mlle. du Parc. By these means they succeeded in ousting all their competitors. Molière's company received a " pension " as the Prince of Conti's own players, and continued to bear this name as long as they acted in the provinces.

Henceforth we hear no more of poverty and want, of miserable performances in barns and stables, and of the struggle for daily bread. Wherever they acted there was a crowded audience, and even though the magistrates still interfered with the prices of admission, thereby greatly diminishing the ordinary proceeds of the performances, the patronage of the Prince of Conti helped to obtain very considerable subsidies from the exchequer, which was in his hands. We find the company receiving the large extra subsidies of 5000 and 6000 *livres* (corresponding to five times as much nowadays) for its services.

The actors lived in wealth and luxury and wore magnificent clothes. The table of the Molière-Béjart household was hospitably open to friends and acquaintances, and the poor were not forgotten—but a short while ago they had known poverty themselves.

One of the queer originals of the time, the strolling singer and musician Charles d'Assoucy, who met the company in 1655, and who, as an old acquaintance of Molière's, enjoyed his hospitality, gives us, in his *Aventures*, a very vivid picture of the life of the company during its period of comfort, a picture, too, which shows the invariable kindness of heart and the generous mind of Molière.

D'Assoucy wandered about France, lute in hand, and always accompanied by two pages with whom he sang his merry songs. He was dominated by one great passion, gambling, which constantly threw him into great distress, but he never learned wisdom from his troubles. He tells us how he met Molière and the Béjarts in Lyons, and in their society forgot all his grievances, among others that one of his pages had left him. He embarked in a Rhone boat with the company to go to Avignon, as he had been told that a singer with an excellent voice was to be found in that town ; and on his arrival there, with forty *pistoles* in his pocket, the remainder of his fortune, "inasmuch as a gambler cannot live without cards, even as a sailor cannot do without tobacco, the first thing I did was to go to the 'academy'" (*i.e.* the gambling-house).

There, of course, he lost all he possessed to some Jews, and had gradually to pledge most of his clothes, so that at last he left the "academy" as naked as Adam in Paradise. " But," this genuine Bohemian continues, " as a man is never poor so long as he has friends, and as I am esteemed by Molière and on friendly terms with all the Béjarts, I felt, in spite of the devil, fate, and the whole Hebrew people, richer and more contented than ever. For these liberal folk were not satisfied with helping me as a friend ; they wanted to treat me as a relative. As they were summoned to come to the Chamber of Deputies, they took me with them to Pézénas, and I cannot say how amiably I was treated by the whole family. They say that the best brother tires of giving to his brother after a month, but they were more liberal than all the brothers in the world, for they never tired of having me at their table for a whole winter." [1]

The enthusiasm of d'Assoucy breaks out into poetry when he describes the excellent table of this house. " Never was a beggar thus fattened," he exclaims in delight.

And his words conjure up before our eyes the picture of Madeleine Béjart, strong and well built, with her bright, intelligent face, presiding over the sumptuous table, where seven or eight courses were the usual fare ; Molière, with his large brown eyes under the dark bushy brows and a humorous smile about his full, sensitive mouth, watching the greedy,

[1] *Aventures de Charles Coipeau d'Assoucy*, i. 309, quoted by Loiseleur, *op. cit.*, pp. 194 f.

loquacious poet of the highroads, who is having an argument with the sharp-tongued Louis Béjart, while the quiet elder brother sits by and enjoys himself in silence. But after the meal musical instruments are brought out, the sparkling, ruby - coloured muscat is placed on the table, and merry songs and stories go on, till Madeleine's authoritative voice gives the signal to break up, and everyone goes about his business. Molière retires to work at a new five-act play in verse, Joseph Béjart puts the last touch to his work on heraldry,[1] Madeleine goes to her accounts, while d'Assoucy makes an effort to tear himself away from the sweet muscat wine.

For this easy - going life by no means made the leaders of the company forget their work. As early as 1656 Molière had finished *Le Dépit amoureux* ; it was performed at Béziers towards the end of the year, and no doubt won as great favour with the public as *L'Étourdi* ; it is known, at least, that this second of Molière's regular comedies produced a great effect and long maintained its place in the répertoire in Paris. From an artistic point of view, the new piece marked a great advance in its author. His first play had been a fairly slavish imitation of his Italian model ; *Le Dépit amoureux* shows a considerable emancipation. The graceful love-scenes, in particular, and the charming personality of Lucile are entirely his own, and may perhaps have been inspired by the whirl of love-intrigues, in which he himself seems to have been involved.

[1] *Recueil des titres, qualités, blazons et armes des Seigneurs Barons des Estats Généraux de la Province de Languedoc tenus à Pézénas*, 1654 (Lyons, 1655).

At the same time Madeleine Béjart was as watchful for the material well-being of the company as was Molière for its artistic honour, and we see the energetic woman claiming, with unbending perseverance, the payment of the promissory notes, which the accountants of the Chamber of Deputies were quite willing to issue but not very eager to redeem.

During all this time the thought of Paris probably stood before Molière's mind as the final goal of his long Odyssey. He had not let the capital entirely out of his sight. It was the custom for provincial troupes to spend Lent in Paris, as at that time there was not much playgoing in the provinces. Lessons were then taken of the great masters in the capital; the stage managers engaged fresh actors, and the actors who could find employment in Paris, after their apprenticeship in the provinces, remained there.[1]

We know of at least one such visit of Molière to Paris (in 1651). While he was far down in the south with his company, it may have been difficult enough for him to pay visits to the capital. Now, however, he is gradually approaching the great focus. In 1658 we find him leaving Lyons with his company, going first to Grenoble, then to Rouen, the town of the brothers Corneille, where he acted in the tennis-court of "The Two Moors," and by that time he had evidently quite made up his mind to attempt Paris. As early as July of the same year Madeleine Béjart hired a tennis-court there for eighteen months; Molière made frequent journeys to the capital; he was introduced to the young King Louis

[1] Chappuzeau: *op. cit.* pp. 109 f.

XIV. and to the Queen mother; in short, everything was prepared for the great and daring stroke.

V

Return to Paris—Molière acts before Louis XIV.—The first signal success is obtained with *Les Précieuses ridicules*—Prosperity of the Petit Bourbon Theatre—Additional Members—M. de La Grange, Molière's right hand.

AT last the decisive day arrived. The company of Molière—probably through the patronage of the Prince of Conti—was ordered to play before the King and Court on October 24th, 1658. The performance was to take place in the " Salle des Gardes " of the old Louvre,[1] and the programme chosen by Molière consisted of *Nicomède*, a tragedy by Corneille, and a little farce of his own composition, *Le Médecin amoureux*, which is no longer extant. The appearance of the new actors seems to have roused some expectation in the theatrical world, for the actors of the Hôtel de Bourgogne were present in a body, which, of course, was an additional stimulus for the newcomers to exert themselves to the utmost. The tragedy had a tolerable success, which was especially due to the beautiful and talented actresses.

After this first part of the entertainment, Molière appeared alone on the stage, and in one of the little harangues for which he was celebrated in the provinces, and which he himself took pleasure in making,[2] he

---

[1] Now the *Salle des Cariatides* in the Section of Antiquities.

[2] " He liked addressing the audience, and never neglected an opportunity of doing so.   He even went so far that when any servant at the theatre died, he profited by the opportunity to make a speech on the next day of performance."   Grimarest : *La Vie de M. de Molière*, Amsterdam, 1705.

modestly thanked his Majesty for the kindness with
which he had been pleased to excuse the shortcomings
of his company and himself, who had, not without
trembling, ventured to present themselves before such
an exalted assembly; "and," he continued, "their great
desire to have the honour of entertaining the greatest
King on earth had made them forget that his Majesty
had in his service most excellent models, of whom they
themselves were but faint imitators. But since the King
had been good enough to put up with their rustic
manners, he humbly begged of his Majesty to allow him
to present one of his little 'divertissements,' by which
he had gained some reputation, and with which he
had been in the habit of entertaining the public in the
provinces."

The tone of this speech appears nowadays too humble,
and not quite suitable for a man like Molière. But it
must be borne in mind, in the first place, that the King
could hardly be addressed in any other tone; and
secondly, that Molière was still far from being the
Molière whom we admire. He was a modest provincial
manager, the author of half a score of light farces and of
two comedies, which were entirely unknown in Paris.
His veneration for his celebrated colleagues of the
Hôtel de Bourgogne may have been genuine enough
at the time. Soon, it is true, he was to change his
tune.

On this occasion, at any rate, Molière's modesty probably had its effect. If the tragedy had been received
with kindly respect, the farce, in which Molière played
the principal part, quite took the public by storm. Louis

XIV., who, at any rate, in his youth, possessed a strong sense of humour, evidently saw at once that Molière was a man after his own heart.   After this trial performance he allowed the company to settle in Paris, and even gave it a stage in the old theatrical hall of the Petit Bourbon,[1] for the use of which it was to pay 1500 livres a year to the *Commedia dell' arte* company, who had a previous right to act there.   The latter had the theatre on Tuesdays and Sundays, the former on Mondays, Wednesdays, Thursdays and Saturdays.   The Duke of Orleans, brother of the King, allowed the new actors to use his name, and the company assumed the title of the *Troupe de Monsieur.*[2] At the same time he allowed an annual pension of 300 livres to each of its members.   In mentioning this last favour, however, La Grange, the faithful recorder of all the financial vicissitudes of the company, adds the following laconic statement: "*Nota*, the 300 livres were never paid."

However, in spite of this little forgetfulness on the part of the distinguished Duke, whose pockets were always empty, Molière and his company had obtained more than they had dared to hope or to expect. Installed, so to speak, in the Royal Palace itself together with the popular Italians, noticed by the Monarch, patronised by his brother—the only thing that now remained to be desired was the favour of the public, and for this they had not long to wait.

On the 2nd of November in the same year the

---

[1] Comp. above, p. 30 and fig. 8.

[2] *Monsieur* (with a capital M) was the official title of the eldest of the King's brothers.

company[1] for the first time appeared before a large Parisian audience, and Molière was wise enough to introduce himself with one of his own plays: *L'Etourdi*, which was a novelty in Paris, and gained immediate success.

He then ventured forth with a number of tragedies by Corneille, but was violently hissed in *Rodogune* and in *La Mort de Pompée*.[2] The roasted apples with which he had been pelted in the provinces, began to be his lot again in Paris, but they never succeeded in driving him from tragedy. He speedily made up for his failure by his second comedy, *Le Dépit amoureux*, and after all, his first theatrical year in Paris ended with a good balance.

The new company was already becoming fashionable. A contemporary, but somewhat younger author, de Visé, gives a description of their theatre in its first year, which, for the very reason that he is unfavourably disposed towards Molière, gives us a much more vivid impression of it than the commonplace outbursts of admiration, with which later biographers fatigue the investigator. He writes: "As he was a sensible man and knew what was

---

[1] After their arrival in Paris their number—perhaps for financial reasons —was somewhat limited, and consisted of only ten persons in all, viz.:—

Actors—	*Actresses*—
Molière.	Madeleine Béjart.
Du Fresne.	Mlle. du Parc.
Du Parc.	Mlle. de Brie.
De Brie.	Mlle. Hervé.
Joseph Béjart.	
Louis Béjart.	
Croisac, *gagiste* (*i.e.*, not a shareholder in the company).	

[2] It is in this last play that he was painted by his friend Mignard (comp. fig. 32).

required to secure success, he did not open his theatre till he had paid several visits and gained a number of well-wishers. He was judged incapable of acting a serious play, but the respect which he was beginning to inspire caused him to be tolerated.

"After having for some time performed old pieces,[1] and gained a fairly firm footing in Paris, he played his *L'Etourdi* and *Le Dépit amoureux*, which won favour quite as much through the interest he began to inspire in the general public as through the approval of those whom he had invited to come and see them.

"After the success of these two plays his theatre gradually filled with people of rank, not so much owing to the amusement which they found there (for only old plays were performed), as because they had got into the habit of going there, and because those who were fond of society, as well as those who liked showing themselves off, found ample opportunity of satisfying their inclination. In short, people went there from habit, without intending to listen to the play, even without knowing what was acted."[2]

This was written in 1663, and the few lines quoted above seem to bring us into the time itself. There is this danger connected with the study of the great

[1] This is not correct. He began at once with *L'Etourdi* ; unless, indeed de Visé alludes to the court performance.

[2] *Nouvelles nouvelles*, 3e partie, p. 217.—This book, which contains sharp though cautious attacks on Molière and Corneille, is ascribed to Jean Donneau de Visé, the adroit founder of *Le Mercure galant*. Victor Fournel, in his great compilation, *Les Contemporains de Molière*, has attempted to lay the authorship of the *Nouvelles nouvelles*, as well as that of *Zélinde*—a play antagonistic to Molière—to the charge of the actor de Villiers ; but later investigators disagree with him, and the responsibility for the malicious attacks on Molière continues to rest with de Visé.

men who lived before our excellent daily press was established, that we see too little of the seamy side of their work. They are too invariably seen with a halo of glory round their heads, and we persist in wondering that their contemporaries could not discover it before it actually existed.

However, with this part of the seventeenth century we have come well into the time of literary cliques and theatrical intrigues, and anyone who takes the trouble to go deeply into the sharp skirmishes which took place between the parties, obtains a much more trustworthy impression of the men of the time than one who contents himself with reading the often somewhat embellished reports of the biographers.

De Visé belonged to a party hostile to Molière, but his description is not without truth. There can be no doubt whatever that Molière had to bow low and humbly before advancing so far that he could establish his theatre in Paris, and most probably the upper classes went to the Petit Bourbon because it had become fashionable to go there. It is equally correct to say that only old plays were acted there. Even *L'Etourdi* and *Le Dépit amoureux* were several years old, though in Paris they passed for new.

But de Visé is wrong in his subsequent judgment of the talent and courage of Molière. On the whole, Molière's contemporary colleagues among dramatic authors could not possibly understand what the qualities were that created his extraordinary reputation. His humour and wonderfully inventive genius, his boldness in hitting at the fashionable weaknesses of his time, his deep know-

ledge of the human heart, and his ease of composition
were in their eyes nothing but hunting after effect, and
angling after the favour of the public. And at this
period, no doubt, to the literary cliques he stood in the
light of an impudent little actor, who tried all means to
attract general attention to himself.

It seems as if, to begin with, no dramatic author
meant to write for him, or as if none *dared*, for fear of
losing favour with the two rival theatres, the Hôtel de
Bourgogne and the Marais,[1] for during the whole of the
first year we do not find a single new play performed at
the Petit Bourbon.

So Molière had to undertake the writing of his new
plays himself, which was probably not the worst thing
that could have happened, for his own time or for
posterity. With the acutest perception of what was ripe
for collapse, and with a boldness quite extraordinary in
so new a man, he composed the little play, which by one
stroke was to make him the hero of the day, and his
theatre the best filled in Paris. This play was *Les
Précieuses ridicules.*

It is not the object of the present work to describe
the literary importance of this or any other of Molière's
plays. This task devolves on the editor and biographer
of Molière. We only dwell on events which belong to
theatrical history. Besides, everybody knows that the
little farce ridiculed the literary movement which had
originated in the Hôtel de Rambouillet, and extended
over the country, with the object of improving and

---

[1] Something to the same effect we read also in the brothers Parfaict,
Histoire du Théâtre François, viii. 327.

20—Title of the original edition of Molière.
(Molière as Mascarille and Sganarelle.)

purging the French language, but which, with its extreme affectation of refinement, threatened to convert the clear French language into the most confused and absurd tongue in the world. It is quite possible that Molière had borrowed his idea from the Italians, who had acted a similar play.[1] But what gave importance to his play was not the subject, but the wonderful humour and inventive power with which the style of the Précieuses was parodied, the mastery of language and the wit, which, of course, the Italian play did not possess, and which, to this day, make us enjoy this little literary satire on a school which has long been extinct, almost as vividly as those who saw it at the time when it was written.[2]

The best description of the effect of the play is given by one of the "precious" poets himself. The generous and respected linguist and poet Ménage, who belonged completely to the over-refined school, says, in speaking of the first performance, " I went to the first performance of the *Précieuses ridicules*, by Molière. Mlle. de Rambouillet[3] was there, as well as Mme. de Grignan,[4] the whole 'Hôtel de Rambouillet,' M. Chapelain,[5] and several others of my acquaintance. The play was acted to the

[1] This, at all events, is asserted by de Visé in the *Nouvelles nouvelles* ; and the *Dictionnaire des Théâtres* of de Léris (Paris, 1763), mentions a play by the Abbé de Pure, *Les Précieuses*, which is said to have been performed *circ.* 1659.

[2] Mascarille, we know, is one of the crowning parts of Coquelin aîné, with which he has made the tour of, so to speak, the whole civilised world.

[3] Julie d'Angennes, daughter of the Marquise de Rambouillet, Catherine de Vivonne, the originator of the "precious" fashion.

[4] The beautiful but cold daughter of Mme. de Sévigné.

[5] One of the staff of the Hôtel de Rambouillet, an unimportant author who acquired Herostratic fame by his attacks on Corneille, and by his bad heroic poem, *La Pucelle*.

general applause, and for my own part I was so pleased
with it, that I at once saw the effect it would produce.
In leaving the theatre I shook hands with M. Chapelain,
and said to him, 'Monsieur, you and I have approved of
all the follies which have been ridiculed here with so
much delicacy and common sense.   But, believe me, as
St Rémi said to Clovis: We must burn what we have
worshipped, and worship what we have burned.' So it
was done, and after this first performance we abandoned
that nonsensical and affected style." [1]

The immense sensation created by this little play,
which constituted only a third part of the evening's
performance, is best shown by the following figures.
On the first evening—Nov. 18th, 1659—the proceeds
were 533 liv., but on the second they increased to 1400
liv., a very considerable amount for those days.

It was then that the new company arrived for the
first time at being mentioned by Loret, the only dramatic
chronicler of the time; in his *Muse historique* of Dec.
6th, 1659, he briefly states the event, though without
adding the name of Molière.   He speaks of the play as
insignificant, but so amusing that people of all classes
rush to see it, and says that no other piece, not even those
of du Ryer, Corneille, Boisrobert, Quinault, and many
others, has had such a run.   "As to myself," he adds,
" I paid my 30 *sous*, but on hearing their fine witticisms,
I had more than 10 *pistoles*' worth of laughter."

That the company itself was aware of the success

---

[1] *Menagiana II.* 22, *éd.* 1729.—Of course neither Ménage nor the others
were thus cured of the "precious" style at one blow ; and Molière satirised
it again in *Les Femmes savantes*, where the comic pedant, Vadius, is a
caricature of Ménage himself.

Molière had procured for them is shown by the present of 500 livres which they made him after the second performance.

From the cast of *Les Précieuses ridicules*, by the bye, we learn that the company had undergone some alterations. The two lovers here are called La Grange and du Croisy, but these two names indicate two new actors, not the names of persons in the play. Moreover, one of the valets is named Jodelet, and was no other than the well-known comic actor whom we have mentioned above,[1] and who for several years had been acting now at the Hôtel de Bourgogne and now at the Marais.

There had probably been some discord in the company, for, shortly after their arrival in Paris, M. and Mme. du Parc—the first heroine and the first comic actor next to Molière—gave up their posts and went to the Marais. Dufresne, Molière's former fellow manager, definitely retired.

At the same time Molière engaged Jodelet and his brother l'Espy from the Marais theatre. Both, however, were somewhat advanced in age. Jodelet, whose nasal utterance and ludicrous face had afforded so much amusement to the Parisians, was evidently no longer at his best. Perhaps he was also out of health. At all events he died the following year. Not long after their arrival in Paris, the company suffered a loss and a real sorrow in the death of Joseph Béjart. That he was indeed valued by his companions may be seen from the fact that the theatre remained closed for a week after his burial.

[1] Comp. pp. 15 and 29.

The "first lovers," which had been performed by
Joseph Béjart, now fell to the share of a young man who
had just been engaged, and who was to become of the
greatest importance to the company. His name was
Charles Varlet de la Grange (fig. 21). Born in 1640 at
Amiens, he was scarcely twenty years old when, after playing for some time in the provinces, he came to Molière.
He was like clay in the hands of his master of thirty-seven,
who trained him to be a lover according to his own ideas
of perfection, not the empty-headed, blandly-smiling,
insipid doll, which had been the fashion hitherto, but the
"character" lover, who is not always the same, but differs
according to circumstances, now representing the youthful,
trustful, open-hearted bourgeois (Horace, in *L'Ecole des
Femmes*), now the lively, impudent dandy (Clitandre in
George Dandin), or the kind-hearted, honest, sensible
youth (Valère in *Tartufe*), or, finally, the unscrupulous,
perverted, and cold-hearted Don Juan. He became the
prototype of such lovers as the nineteenth century
possessed in Bressant and Delaunay. Of medium height,
elegant and well made, with marked features and a
small, sarcastic mouth, fluent of tongue, and graceful of
movement—such was La Grange, and such was henceforth the model *jeune premier* of the French theatre,
equally far removed from the tall, sentimental, rather
slow and angular, English type, from our own (Danish),
ever-smiling, curly-headed wooer, and from the square
and burly lover who is the ideal of a German audience.

La Grange became the performer of all Molière's
lovers, besides, of course, acting many and various parts
in other plays. By his refinement, his pleasant manners,

and his eloquence, he rose to great importance in the company by degrees as he gained promotion. Molière charged him with the very important function of "Orator," of which we shall have more to say on a later occasion, and after the death of Molière it was he who became the mainstay of the company.

A man of most methodical mind, from the moment when he joined the company he kept the minutest accounts, and put down in his account-book every event which occurred at the theatre. In this way he unintentionally became the recorder of his company, since his *Régistre*, as he terms it, has fortunately been preserved. With its detailed accounts and miscellaneous remarks about a variety of things, it affords the historian of the theatre much curious and important information, which otherwise he would have missed. The present company of the Théâtre français, who possessed this work in MS., and were thoroughly aware of its importance to theatrical history and to biographers of Molière, had it published in 1876 in an exceedingly fine edition, accompanied by notes and explanations from the hand of Edouard Thierry, the principal keeper of the theatrical archives.

La Grange afterwards married Marie Ragueneau, the pastry-cook's daughter, who had formerly accompanied the troupe as maid to Mlle. de Brie, or rather, as a kind of pupil, who in return for the instruction given her waited upon the elder actress. She was without talent for the stage, and seems to have been an ugly, coquettish little woman, with a marked inclination to economy. Perhaps it was the latter quality which attracted La

Grange, for if he sometimes appeared as a careless spend-thrift on the boards, this was certainly not his nature in real life. However, the two seem to have spent their lives peacefully together, without being harassed by con-flicting love affairs, which were otherwise of common occurrence in the theatrical world.

Posterity owes a debt of gratitude to La Grange for having published, with Vinot,[1] the first complete and trustworthy edition of Molière, which appeared after the great author's death (fig. 20).

The second new man whose name ·e meet with in the cast of *Les Précieuses ridicules* was Du Croisy. He too became one of the strongest pillars of the company, though he did not gain the same importance as La Grange, either as actor or as man of business. Philibert Gassot du Croisy was about thirty when he joined the Petit Bourbon Theatre. A young nobleman—he was one of the actors who had a right to the particle of nobility[2]—he had been driven by his theatrical inclinations into a wandering life, and he had even been the manager of a company. Now he sought a harbour with Molière, who employed him in many comic parts, both of the finer and of the coarser sort. He was the original Oronte in *Le Misanthrope*, Mer-cury in *Amphitryon*, M. de Sotenville in *George Dandin*, Géronte in *Les Fourberies de Scapin*, and Vadius in *Les Femmes savantes*. His most important creation, however, was Tartufe, especially important

---

[1] *Oeuvres de Molière* [by Vinot and La Grange], Paris, 1682, 8 vols. 12mo.

[2] This was not the case with La Grange. He called himself Sieur de la Grange, but his real name was Varlet. La Grange was the family name of his mother.

because it gives us an idea of the manner in which Molière himself wished this much-discussed character of his to be represented.

Du Croisy was a handsome man, but very fat, and comic parts were his proper branch. Now, at the Théâtre français, as elsewhere, Tartufe is played by the juvenile lead or the serious character-actor. We know that Coquelin aîné, as long as he belonged to the Théâtre français, was never allowed to carry out his conception of this character. If Molière chose Du Croisy, the fat, good-looking man, whose comedy was combined with a certain inborn refinement, to represent his Tartufe, the reason was that he had formed a certain idea of the character, which he wanted to be distinctly individualised, not to be generalised as the typical hypocrite with haggard cheeks and shifty eyes, whom we are accustomed to see.[1]

It is remarkable that while, after his Tartufe, Molière had so much to suffer from the fury of the religious fanatics that they even refused to allow him to be buried in consecrated ground, Du Croisy, the

---

[1] It would be well, on the whole, to give up the tendency to generalisation in dramatic art, by which Tartufe is made to represent the Roman Church and its tyranny ; Shylock, martyrised Judaism ; and Hamlet, restless, irresolute melancholy. This kind of interpretation may be permissible in literary criticism, but dramatic art can only express the general by means of the individual. In the eyes of those, therefore, who do not wish scenic representations to be merely declamatory and moralised guides to literature, but a vivid and artistic picture of human character, it is a good thing that a few modern actors have begun to break with the nineteenth century sentimental and philosophic generalisation, in order to restore the classic figures to the less lofty but more human representation of character which were usual during the lifetime of the poets who created them.

actor of Tartufe, lived in peace and friendship with his parish priest, who even took his death so much to heart that he had not the strength to throw earth on his coffin, but asked a colleague to do it for him.

The wife of Du Croisy was also engaged as a member of the company, but her position was as inferior as that of Mme. La Grange. Molière did not like her. The only thing we know about her is the little part which she played under her own name in *L'Impromptu de Versailles*. There Molière says to her, in explaining their parts to the actors : "You represent one of those people who are meekly charitable to all the world, yet who always leave a little passing sting with their tongues, and would be sorry to hear their neighbours well spoken of. I believe you will not acquit yourself badly in the part."

With these new additions, and with M. and Mlle. du Parc — who, after a year's absence, returned from the Marais to Molière — the company may be said on the whole to have been well equipped in most branches. The exception was tragedy, which was somewhat poorly provided for, as there was no tragic hero besides Molière himself, and he was not at all popular in that genre.

However, after *Les Précieuses ridicules*, the company was sure of general attention, and Paris possessed one more permanent theatre.

21

22

23

21—La Grange.   **22**—Costume *à la Romaine*.   **23**—Turkish costume.

THOUGH the name of Molière has been closely associated with that of Louis XIV. through anecdotes true
and fictitious, and though it is generally thought, and
not without reason, that he owed his position in Paris
to the favour of the " Roi - Soleil," it must not be
supposed that the company under his leadership was
financially the most favoured ; far from it.

At the period we have now reached—about the year
1660—Paris possessed four established companies. First,
the Italians ; second, the company of Molière—these two
acting in the Petit Bourbon ; third, the Royal company
in the Hôtel de Bourgogne ; and fourth, the Marais company. Of these the Italians were the most favoured,
as they received a royal pension of 15,000 francs ;
next came the Royal company with 12,000 ; the
Marais troupe probably received something, at any rate
they styled themselves " supported by His Majesty " ;
while Molière's troupe was absolutely without any subvention.

Not till several years later — from August 1665
onwards—did the King, in a moment of especial delight
with Molière, grant the company an annual pension of
6000 francs, and this sum was not increased during the

life-time of Molière. Its official support therefore only amounted to half that of the Hôtel de Bourgogne.

Apart from the royal subsidies, the material and administrative conditions of the theatres were very much alike, and it is interesting to know them, because they form the basis of the almost unique position of the Théâtre français of the present day, where fraternal self-government is still the ruling system.

Old Chappuzeau, whose little book on the French theatre, which appeared a few years after the death of Molière, is one of the chief sources of information with regard to the administrative condition of the companies, makes the following very appropriate remark : "No people on earth appreciate monarchy more than actors, profit more by it, or are more enthusiastic for its glory, but within their own circle they hate it ; they will have no particular master, and would be frightened by the shadow of one. However, their system of government is not quite democratic either ; it has an aristocratic element in it."

This must be understood to mean that, while in all matters relating to their art the actors were obliged—and apparently were quite willing—to submit to the supremacy of a few distinguished men of their profession, in practical matters of business they were co-ordinate and managed their affairs in common and by vote. Not that all French or Parisian actors formed one large professional alliance ; each company was a little republic by itself.

This is particularly emphasised by Chappuzeau. "Of the acting companies," he says, "neither the settled

ones which do not leave Paris nor the travelling companies which go to the provinces and are called *troupes
de campagne*, unite at all in any large federation. Each
company forms a "band" by itself and has its special
interests, and they have not succeeded in joining together
in close alliance. Though their manners and customs
are alike, and the same laws are observed by all, they
have no Amphictyonic or common Council like the seven
cities of Greece; in short, they are not confederate
states, nor are they very favourably inclined towards
each other. I have promised not to flatter, but to state
the facts as they are. But I find the same order of things
prevailing in all the states of the world, in all towns, and
all families, so we cannot be surprised that it also prevails among actors."[1]

The little socialistic state formed by such a company
was based on very simple principles; all actors properly
so called were shareholders in the common enterprise;
the functionaries alone received fixed salaries. The
oldest contract known of such a society is dated
December 17th, 1644.[2] The rules are very simple, and
the principal stipulation is, that after deduction of all
expenses connected with the performance, the surplus
shall be divided into certain shares. It is forbidden,
under penalty, to miss a performance.

The shares were equal in so far as the society always
started with a fixed number of them, which could not be
increased; but each partner had not a full share. The
youngest and least efficient, for instance, received a

---

[1] *Le Théâtre François, III., chap. xviii.* (Brussels, 1867, pp. 86. f.).
[2] It was discovered by Eudore Soulié, see his *Recherches sur Molière.*

fourth part of a share, the medium class half a share. and only the real exponents of the répertoire had a whole share each.[1]

The contracts of the Hôtel de Bourgogne which have been preserved, are a little more complicated, though the principles of division are the same there as in all other companies of the time. But the Hôtel de Bourgogne had a pension fund besides, which according to certain rules payed annuities to the retired members of the company.

Very unlike the idea we frequently conceive of the histrionic artists of former times, as a flock of easy-going Bohemians, the actors of the time of Molière, far more than those of our own day, were anxious to provide means of subsistence for their old age.

"Among the features of their policy," Chappuzeau remarks, "this deserves notice : they do not suffer any members of their state to be poor, and they prevent anyone of their profession from being exposed to want. When old age or infirmity compels an actor to retire, it is the duty of his successor to pay him a decent pension as long as he lives ; so that, when a clever man obtains a footing on the Parisian stage, he may count on a good annual income of three or four thousand livres, as long as he continues to work, and on a sum suffi-cient to live upon when he retires—a very praiseworthy custom, which formerly prevailed in the Royal company only, but which the new company recently established by the King [viz. the combined troupes of Molière

---

[1] Exactly the same arrangement prevails nowadays among the *sociétaires* of the Théâtre français, though the division of the shares is somewhat more intricate.

and the Marais] will adopt as a sound basis for its continuance."[1]

At the Hôtel de Bourgogne it was customary also, on the death of an actor or an actress, for the company to make a present of a hundred *pistoles* to the nearest relative, by which they "afforded him [or her] a more powerful consolation than by the finest compliments."

Owing to consistent adherence to this principle of division the salaries of all the actors of a company were almost equal, for at least in Molière's time there were only a few who did not rise to a full share. As we have seen, a company of actors in those days was not very numerous, so all members had to do a great deal of work.

Of course the amount of each share varied according to the annual receipts. In Molière's company during the years 1660-73 (up to his death) the average value of the shares was 3600 livres,[2] a very decent sum considering the high value of money in those days ; and if we remember that it was the ordinary salary of all competent actors. Nowadays this would correspond in value to about £650.

After the death of Molière the shares of his company diminished to an average amount of 2659 livres until, after 1680, when there was only one theatre, and performances took place every day (except in Easter week, on the great festivals, and during court-mourning, etc.), they rose very considerably, up to the year 1688, with an annual average of 5993 livres.

[1] *Théâtre François, III., ch. xii., pp.* 80. *f.*
[2] This and the following calculations are based on the figures given in the *Régistre* of La Grange.

Years followed in which the shares became very small—during the War of Succession and the Regency; however, we lack accurate accounts from this period. Afterwards they rose again, and in the last years before the great Revolution reached the amount of 30,000 livres, which corresponds in value to about double the amount in modern money.[1]

The item of revenue which we still call *feu*, and which in our theatre (the Royal Danish) is a percentage on the proceeds of a performance, while in France and elsewhere it is a fixed premium, consisted in those times of a sum destined to cover the cost of light and fuel in winter. It was introduced on September 28th, 1682. Each time an actor played he received five sols[2] for fuel in his dressing-room and two *sols* 6 d. for light. In 1700 the *feu* had risen to twenty *sous*, in 1760 to two *livres*.

Though even to modern eyes these sums must appear fairly considerable, the actors seldom became rich; "they were contented to live honestly," says the ever polite Chappuzeau.

There was one item of expenditure which cut very deep into the salary, that of costumes. This expense devolved on the actors themselves, and the claims on their purses on this score were very heavy. For the costumes *à la Romaine*—which were used in tragedies on Greek or Roman subjects, and bore but a slight resemblance to the real Roman dress (fig. 22)—nothing but genuine, very fine gold and silver was used, as the

[1] In all cases I have calculated the money of Molière's time at five times its present value.

[2] *sol* = *sou* = $\frac{1}{20}$ *livre* or *franc*; d = *denier* = $\frac{1}{12}$ *sou*.

sham metal soon deteriorated, and was easily detected by the spectators sitting close to the actors. Such a costume *à la Romaine* or *à la Grecque*—no distinction was made between the two styles—might easily be worth about 1500 livres (£300) or more. There were actors whose wardrobe expenses amounted to more than 10,000 livres (£2000), though no great variety of dress was required, the principal three items being, the modern, the Roman and the Turkish dresses (fig. 23).

But in private life as well as on the stage it was a matter of honour, to some extent even of necessity, for actors and actresses to be expensively dressed. They had frequently to appear at Court, and they associated much with persons of distinction; so they were obliged "to follow the fashions and incur fresh expenses for ordinary dresses, which prevented them from investing large sums on interest."[1] Sometimes even they invented new fashions, which were soon adopted by the public. Thus, for instance, Riccoboni[2] tells us that the so-called *Andrienne*[3] and several other garments had originated on the stage.

The payment of the shares took place in the simplest manner. When the play was over, the audience had gone and the actors had changed their dress, the accounts were made up. All the shareholders had a right to be present at this distribution of the proceeds. But three

[1] Chappuzeau, III., xxviii., pp. 92 f.

[2] *Réflexions historiques.*

[3] This named after *L'Andrienne*, a play by Baron, after the *Andria* of Terence. The *Andrienne* was an open garment with a long broad pleat proceeding from the neck and descending down the back, sometimes ending in a train.

of them were in duty bound to be on the spot and discharge the accounts.   These three were : the Treasurer,
the Secretary, and the Controller.   They were chosen
from among the members of the troupe, and their offices
were honorary—not paid.   The cashiers brought the
money, it was counted, the expenses of the day deducted,
and the remainder divided into shares, of which each
member received his due.   The common accounts for
large sums were paid every month, and the rent of the
theatre regularly every quarter.[1]

This simple mode of division, which has also been
described by Corneille in his play *L'Illusion comique*, was
maintained for a very long time ; we do not know for
certain when it was discontinued.   The regulations of
March 1720 show that the shares were still paid daily.[2]

The paid functionaries—*gagistes*, as they were called
—received their wages, some by the day, week, or
month, and some, no doubt, by the quarter, or the year.
All functionaries at the theatres were called " officers,"
those who received payment were *Bas-Officiers*, those
who did not, were called *Hauts-Officiers*.

To the latter class belonged, among others, the three
officers above mentioned : the Treasurer, the Secretary
and the Controller.   The Treasurer was in charge of the
reserve fund of the company, and all the money that was
laid aside to pay author's fees, the cost of new " machines "
(scenery, etc.), rent, repairs, etc., sometimes also for the
payment of debts.   " The public is not rich," Chappuzeau
observes, " but there are rich individuals who, when

[1] Chappuzeau, III., ch. xxix., pp. 95 f.
[2] Jules Bonnassies : *La Comédie Française, histoire administrative*,
(1658-1757), 1874, p. 306

necessary, advance money, which is loyally paid back."
Each month the Treasurer rendered accounts to his
companions.

The Secretary kept the account-book and received
money and accounts from the cashier.   He kept a register,
besides, of the members who joined the company and
the terms of their engagement.   As was natural, the
offices of treasurer and secretary were frequently united
in one person.   Thus La Grange for a long time occupied
these two posts of trust.

The Controller revised the accounts and examined the
cash-box, which were in charge of the two other functionaries.   The following remark of Chappuzeau's testifies to
the confidence which the members of the company placed
in these officers whom they themselves had elected :
" The Marais company possessed two keys which opened
different locks [in the safe], and they were kept by two
different members of the troupe, in order to avoid the
slightest misuse ; but this is no longer done in either
of the two companies,[1] and so great is the good faith
which prevails among the actors, that their accounts are
never out by a single *sou*."[2]

A very important office at the theatre was that of
the Orator.   Those times did not possess all the means
of announcement which are at the service of our modern
theatres, such as advertisements, notices, puffs in the
daily press, etc. ; they had to be content with calling
attention to the forthcoming play by play-bills and by
the recommendation that could be given from the stage

[1] At the period when Chappuzeau writes (1674) there were only two
French troupes in Paris, the Royal and the united Molière-Marais troupe.

[2] Chappuzeau, III., ch. li., p. 117.

itself.   The Orator was entrusted with both these charges.
He had to draw up the play-bill (fig. 24), which did not
mean stating the title of the play, and the names of the
author, the characters and their performers, but giving
a short and tempting eulogy of the play, sometimes even
an outline of its most important events, as was already
customary in England at the time of Shakespeare.[1]   On
the other hand it was considered unnecessary to an-
nounce the names of the characters in the play, and even
more so to mention those of the actors.   At the utmost
the name of the author was given, and not even this was
done till some decades on in the seventeenth century.
Formerly the actors contented themselves with announcing in print that their author had written a play
with such and such a title.   The custom of printing the
names of the actors is of a much later date, scarcely
more than a hundred years old.

The second task of the Orator was much more difficult
and important than that of writing the play-bill.   After
the close of the performance he appeared alone before
the audience, and in a brief, cleverly worded speech
recommended the play which was to be acted on the
next day of performance.   This was by no means a
short and sweet affair; such an announcement required
much tact and presence of mind, for the appearance of
the Orator was always looked forward to with great
eagerness, and often became a little after-play, in which
the spectators shared as improvised fellow-actors.

What the office chiefly required was an actor who first
and foremost was sure of his popularity, and possesssed

[1] Comp. vol iii. *The Shakespearean Period in England*, pp. 105 f.

LES COMEDIENS DV ROY
ENTRETENVS PAR SA MAIESTÉ

COMME les diuertiſſemens enjouez ſont de ſaiſon, nous croyons vous bien
régaller en vous promettant pour demain Mardy iiij iour de Fevrier, la plai-
ſante COMEDIE du IODELET MAISTRE, de Monſieur SCARON:
Auec vne DANSE de SCARAMOVCHE, qui ne peut manquer de vous
plaire beaucoup.

A Vendredy ſans faute les AMOVRS du CAPITAN MATAMORE, ou
l'ILLVSION COMIQVE, de Monſieur de CORNEILLE l'aiſné.

En attendant les ſuperbes Machines de la CONQVESTE de la TOISON d'OR

Ceſt à l'Hoſtel du Marais, vieille rue du Temple, à deux heures

24

25

24—Play-bill of the Marais Theatre.

25—Molière as " Orator " in the costume of Sganarelle.

some power over his public. It was always therefore one of the most prominent members of the company who was chosen for this post.

At the Hôtel de Bourgogne the first Orator was the much admired Bellerose, afterwards the excellent actor Floridor. "When they appeared to make their announcement, the whole audience listened in deep silence, and their 'compliment,' which was short and well turned, was received with as much pleasure as the preceding play. Each day they invented a new 'trait' which kept their hearers awake and testified to the fertility of their wit."[1] Floridor was succeeded by Hauteroche, a less distinguished actor, but a refined and capable author.

As a matter of course, Mondory was the first Orator of the Marais theatre ; after the outbreak of his illness the office was undertaken, first by d'Orgemont and afterwards by Floridor, as long as he remained at this theatre. And when Floridor went to the Hôtel de Bourgogne, Laroque became the trusted man of the Marais company, and occupied this position for as much as twenty-seven years. "And we can say without offending anybody," observes the ever prudent Chappuzeau, " that he has supported the Marais theatre to the last by his discreet behaviour and by his valour, for he has given evidence of both in difficult times, when the troupe was running great risks."

Laroque or Regnault Petit-Jean, as his real name was, did not obtain his position through his talent, for as an actor he was only of moderate capacity ; he was one of those men who are better qualified for helping others

---

[1] Chappuzeau, p. 133.

than for creating anything themselves.   But he was good-looking, he had a fluent tongue, and above all, he was very courageous, and this latter quality was quite indispensable, especially at the Marais, where noise and disturbance were the order of the day. When the mischievous pages and impudent lackeys had penetrated among the audience without paying their fees, when the door-keeper was lying wounded or perhaps killed in the entrance hall, when the pit echoed with the wild shouts of savage and tipsy musketeers, Laroque was the man to restore order, both with gentle words and, if necessary, with the sword.   And time after time he helped the company out of the most unpleasant scrapes by his perfect fearlessness. " He inspired the would-be *bravos* with fear and the real ones with respect," are Chappuzeau's words on him.

We meet with a very different type of Orator in Molière.   If the representative of the Hôtel de Bourgogne was correct and elegant, the Orator of the Marais bold and coarse, Molière was above all witty. In private life he was mostly a silent observer, but he was fond of addressing the audience, and—we may be sure—was never at a loss what to say.   When, after the performance, he appeared alone on the stage, his flat cap in hand, and an arch smile on his lips, as we see him in one of his few authentic portraits, (fig. 25), prepared to make his " compliment " to the audience, the pit was wild with delight, and the wits whetted their tongues to try if they could not for once drive this devil of an actor into a corner.   Then the war of wits began, the sallies flew hither and thither like battledore and shuttle-cock between the stage and the audience.

Molière's repartees fell like flashes of lightning on those who were foolhardy enough to challenge him, and the laugh always remained on his side.

At last, however, this extra performance became too much for Molière; the hour became later and later, the audience would not leave the theatre, and perhaps sometimes overstepped the proper bounds in trying his patience. Under November 14th, 1664,[1] La Grange's account-book has the laconic statement: " I have begun announcing for M. de Molière." As Orator, La Grange of course differed very much from Molière. Refined, elegant, correct, he possessed authority enough to keep the excited minds under restraint, but we do not hear that he was particularly witty or fertile in ideas. He seems, however, to have been much appreciated in his office, for he retained it as long as he remained on the stage, even after his troupe had united first with the Marais and later with the Hôtel de Bourgogne.

He had many violent storms to brave, for the house of Molière too was exposed to riots, such as in our days would seem incredible, but which give a good insight into the close, if not always cordial, relations existing between the two powers on either side of the footlights.

Until, at the instigation of Molière, the King interfered with a peremptory interdict, it was very common to see people who were in some way connected with the Court—especially officers—and therefore considered themselves justified in forcing their way into the pit

---

[1] Chappuzeau states that La Grange undertook this function six years before the death of Molière, in 1667. Either he must be mistaken or the discrepancy in dates must indicate that during the first years he now and then officiated for his chief.

without paying their fees, fly into a rage when they were denied admission. Armed crowds would come to their assistance, kill the door-keeper who tried to prevent their intrusion, and attempt to force their way through the pit to the stage in order to take revenge on the actors. It was on such an occasion as this that young Louis Béjart, made up as the old man he was to represent in the play, suddenly made his appearance, fell on his knees and exclaimed in a trembling voice : " Oh, gentlemen, spare at least an old trembling man who is now seventy-five and has but a few days longer to live." This time, for once, the whole riot ended in laughter, and the struggle ceased for a while.[1]

But the ticket question remained a burning one, and there were always people who wanted to sneak in or to force themselves in without paying. In the report of a lawsuit in 1662 we read that both companies, the Italians represented by their chief members, Tiberio Fiorilli[2] and Ottavio Constantini,[3] and the French by Molière and Du Croisy, complain of a band of seven or eight lackeys who had tried to force an entrance, and when stopped by the doorkeeper[4] had abused him, and finally drawn their

[1] That, at least, is how Lemazurier tells the story in his *Galerie des Acteurs français* (Paris, 1810). The anecdote appears to be somewhat embellished, and is not confirmed by contemporary documents. This, however, does not apply to the stories that follow, which are taken from different collections of documents found in archives, and published by E. Campardon (*Documents inédits*, etc., *Nouvelles pièces*, etc., *Les Comédiens du Roi*, etc.) in order to throw light on the theatrical conditions of the time.

[2] The famous Scaramouche. Comp. vol. ii., *Middle Ages and Renaissance*, pp. 289 ff.

[3] Father of the celebrated Mezzetino, Angelo Constantini. Comp. *op. cit.*, p. 300 ff.

[4] The door-keeper of Molière's theatre was called Saint-Germain. We do not hesitate to say that his was the most dangerous function in the

swords, so that he had been obliged to seek refuge in a neighbouring house ; but even there the lackeys had shot after him.

On another occasion we read of some pages who, being bent on mischief, flung a large tobacco pipe on to the stage while Molière was acting in his *L'Amour médecin*.[1] They beat other spectators in the pit, and when the Procureur du Roi appeared on the stage and commanded : " Pages, be so kind as to stop, and lay down your sticks ! " they refused to obey. One young man, in particular, in a black velvet coat, a sword at his side, and a white feather on his hat, was very abusive ; when a respectable gentleman, one of the spectators on the stage, said to him : " You forget whom you are talking to ; respect your judge ! " he replied impudently, " What the d—— do we care about judges ? We have no judges." A great disturbance followed, which ended in the pages taking possession of the pit.

We can understand that it was not very easy to act under such conditions. Sometimes, indeed, the noise became so overwhelming that the performance had to be stopped, but, of course, this entailed a considerable loss to the actors, so they did not like to do it.

It happened once at a performance in 1691 that some drunken officers caused so outrageous a scandal that La Grange had to interfere. The police reports[2] give a

troupe, and no small sum had to be spent in plaster for the wounds he received in the discharge of his duties. Not long before the event mentioned above it seems that he had been in even worse plight ; for we read as an item in the accounts of La Grange (March 20th, 1661) : " Given to Saint-Germain for his wounds, 55 livres."

[1] Campardon, *Documents inédits*, pp. 35 ff.
[2] Published by Campardon, *Comédiens du Roi*, pp. 290-297.

very characteristic picture of the coarse attacks of the
audience to which the actors were sometimes exposed,
and of the passions which might be kindled by the mere
question of free admission.

One afternoon when *La Devineresse*, by Thomas
Corneille,[1] was being performed, a party of five officers
arrived at the theatre, all in high spirits, and one of
them, Captain de Sallo, in a very tipsy state. He was
going to enter without a ticket, and when stopped by the
door-keeper said that his brother had taken a ticket for
him. When the man asked him to wait till his brother
came, as by the King's order he could admit nobody
without a ticket, he pushed him aside and entered the
pit, where in a loud voice he said to the audience :
"*Mordieu !* those rascals want money of me, and I won't
give them any."

In the entr'acte all five officers went to Procope, the
seller of lemonade, to have something to drink. What
they drank was probably not lemonade, for when they
came back and the door-keeper repeated his request for
the ticket, dé Sallo became furious. He seized the
ticket-seller and pulled off his wig, then drew his sword
and gave the door-keeper so dangerous a stab in the side
that he had to be carried away to be bandaged. After
this feat he wanted to divert himself with the play, and
entered the pit, but there he made such a noise that the
performance had to be stopped, and M. La Grange came
forward to ask if the play was to go on or not. The
audience said, yes, and the actors continued. But the

---

[1] And by de Visé. *La devineresse ou madame Jobin* was performed for the
first time on November 19th, 1679. The subject was taken from the history
of the notorious poisoner, Voisin.

play was scarcely resumed, when the officer, who evidently did not find the performance amusing, took some of the footlights and threw them at the heads of the actors, after which he drew his sword and tried to climb up on the stage. La Grange came forward again and attempted to reason with the officers. The audience for the second time desired the play to be resumed, and the act began once more. But as soon as the players appeared the captain roared, " Be off, you d—— rascals ! And you, you ——, take yourself away ! I have got pistols here, and I will smash your head for you !"

All the actors then left the stage except La Grange, who informed the audience that they might have their money returned. At that moment De Sallo—drunk and furious—jumped up on the stage with his brother and another companion and swore that the play should be acted at once, or he would spit all the actors against the wall with his sword. He then extinguished all the footlights, tried to cut the ropes which held the chandeliers, destroyed the scenery and swore that he would burn the whole house. The three actors, Poisson, Sévigny and Rozélis came forward and tried to convince him that it was quite enough for him to have wounded their functionary and violated the King's order by his conduct. To this he replied that he cared not a pin for the King's orders. But, as we read in the report, " when the above-mentioned man in the red coat, who addressed him as brother, heard this, he said to him : 'This is not right, the King's orders must be respected.'" These words, however, did not produce much effect on his brother, for he started to rush off at once to the tiring-rooms and abuse the actors; but this time he and his companions were caught and shut up, and afterwards they were put in prison.

In the meantime the audience had stormed the ticket-office and stripped it of everything of any value. The remainder was spoiled.

Clearly, it was not only the Orator who had to suffer at the hands of the audience ; the subordinate function-aries were even more exposed to their attacks.

Though we do not as yet meet with the astonish-ing number of functionaries which nowadays every French theatre with any self-respect employs in its service, it was customary, even in the days of Molière, to be supplied with a considerable number of *bas-officiers*.

There was the Porter, part of whose business it was to go all over the building after the performance in order to prevent fire ; the Ticket-seller, who, besides his proper functions, was responsible for all false or injured coin which happened to be found in the cash-boxes, and therefore must know all about the weight and value of money ; the Controllers and the Door-keepers, on whose difficult tasks the above descriptions have thrown light, and who were generally picked men of a bold and resolute stamp. The Hôtel de Bourgogne had the privilege of selecting soldiers from among the guards for these offices. The theatrical painter, *décorateur* as he was called, had the business of decorat-ing the stage and the auditorium, and in conjunction with the Machinist, of producing all the scenery and *machines* used in the then fashionable plays of illusion. His business, strangely enough, also included the task of "removing from between the wings certain little fellows, who crowd there and besides annoying the actors at their entrances and exits, look very ill on the stage and are an eyesore to the spectators."[1]

Finally the *décorateur* had to provide two Candle-snuffers to snuff the candles of the footlights and the chandeliers between the acts. In return he had a right to appropriate the bits of candle that were left over.

Then the theatre had its Box-openers, its permanently engaged Tallow-chandler, Printer and Bill-sticker, the last of which had the charge of punctually and accurately sticking up the play-bills at all street-corners and other places indicated beforehand. The bills of the Hôtel de Bourgogne were red, those of Molière's theatre green.

The official now called the *Régisseur* in those days went by the name of *premier garçon de théâtre*; he had to superintend all the properties and keep account of them, to supervise the supers or *assistants* used in the different plays, and to see that "all who appear before the public are decently dressed and wear proper shoes and stockings."[2] He also performed small parts, rang the bell when the play was to begin, and warned the actors when it was their turn to enter. Under his orders there were four stage-servants, half "machinists," half call-boys.

An important functionary, then as now, was the Prompter, or, as he was called in those days, the *Copiste*. His original task had been to copy plays and write out parts, a task which even nowadays is at many

[1] Chappuzeau III., ch. lii. (p. 121).
[2] Regulation of June 9th, 1758. Comp. Bonnassies : *Comédie Française Histoire administrative*, p. 350.

theatres the business of the prompter. The natural
consequence was that he became a kind of archive-
keeper, as all the manuscripts and parts of the company
were entrusted to his care. Of his duties as prompter
Chappuzeau says : " It is part of his office to stand with
the book at one of the wings, while the play is going on,
and constantly to keep his eyes on it, so as to help any
actor whose memory fails him, which in technical language is called *souffler*. Therefore he must be careful
and able to distinguish when the actor stops on purpose,
and makes a necessary pause, during which he must not
speak to him, as it would disturb instead of relieving
him. On those occasions I have heard actors tell the
over-officious prompter to be quiet, either because they
did not need his help, or on purpose to show that they
could trust their memory, though it might indeed sometimes forsake them. He therefore who prompts must
do it in a voice which, as far as possible, can be heard on
the stage without reaching the pit, in order to avoid
calling forth the laughter of certain spectators, who
laugh at everything, and who burst out into mirth at
passages in the play where others would not even
smile."

The memory of the actors seems to have been well
trained ; at all events they had so much practice in
improvisation that even in poetry they had no great
difficulty in substituting one line for another, rather
than expose themselves to the unpleasantness of being
too audibly helped by the prompter, which always rouses
ither mirth or displeasure in the audience. That
licrous mistakes, such as the actors speaking the

stage-directions instead of the speeches of the play—
a favourite means of effect in parody—also occurred in
those days, is clear from a passage in a piece by Cyrano
de Bergerac[1] : *The Pedant deceived*, in which a play is
acted within a play.   The lines run as follows :—

> *Granger.* " Come here, Paquier.   Have you told my
> father that in spite of his order, I have
> resolved to go on with it ? "
> *Paquier.* Prompt me, Corbineli.
> *Corbineli.* (*whispering*) " No, sir, I forgot."
> *Paq.* " No sir, I forgot."
> *Gran.* "Oh you rascal, your blood shall give me
> revenge for your perfidy" (*draws his sword*)
> *Cor.* Now run away quickly, for fear he will strike
> you.
> *Paq.* Is that in my part ?
> *Cor.* Yes.
> *Paq.* " Now run away quickly for fear he will strike
> you."

Chappuzeau asserts that he has observed that women
have a better memory than men.   This, very likely, is
the case nowadays.   He adds :   " I think they are too
modest to wish me to say that the r judgment is equally
superior."   In that respect, no doubt, matters have
changed.

[1] Cyrano de Bergerac : *Le Pédant joué* (1654), Act V. Sc. 10.

VII

AT this phase of theatrical development the structure
of the theatre in its main features presented no essential
difference from the modern play-house. The stage and
the auditorium were situated in the same relation to
each other; the boxes of the balcony and upper storeys
ran round the auditorium in an oval curve; the sloping
floors of the stage and the pit inclined towards each
other, and so forth. But as to the distribution of seats
some very peculiar customs prevailed, which to our
eyes would give the inside of a seventeenth century
theatre a very strange appearance.

From the very beginning of the century it had been
the custom in the Shakespearean theatre for young
noblemen, or any one who would pay for it, to have
small seats placed on the stage.[1] This bad custom was
not introduced in France till some decades later, but
then it was carried so far as to become a great impedi-
ment to the development of dramatic art, and fatal, we
may say, to all dramatic literature.

Much was done to put a stop to the ever increasing
influx of smartly dressed, ill-behaved dandies, who
flooded the stage to such an extent that the actors had

[1] Comp. vol. iii. *The Shakespearean Period in England*, p. 120.

26

27

26—Petit Maître on the stage.

27—Interior of the Théâtre Français in 1726.

scarcely room to move or to make their entrances and exits ; but all in vain. The demand for seats on the stage was so great, and the actors' power of resistance to the distinguished clients and their jingling *louis* so small, that for more than a century the French theatre presented this extraordinary spectacle ; and it required the energy of a Voltaire, combined with the liberality of a noble "theatrophile," to effect the purging of the stage.

From our knowledge of Molière's character we might easily have concluded how much these pushing, crowding intruders annoyed him, even if he had not with his usual frankness spoken his mind about them from the stage itself. At the beginning of *Les Fâcheux* (the Bores) Eraste, a character which he played himself, describes the manner in which such an insolent *petit-maître* sometimes behaved (fig. 26).

He tells us how one day after dinner he had gone to the play to be cheered up. " I was on the stage, quite prepared to listen to the piece, which I had heard many praise ; the actors had begun ; everyone was silent ; when a blustering fellow, with big knee-ruffles, who looked a regular *broc*, came rudely in. ' Hulloa ! ho ! bring me a chair directly,' he cried out, surprising the whole audience by his pronounced manners, and interrupting the play at its finest part. ' Good Heavens,' said I, ' will Frenchmen, who are so often sneered at, never act like sensible men? Must we show off our worst faults on the public stage, and thus confirm, by a senseless conduct, what our neighbours everywhere say of us ? ' While I shrugged my shoulders the actors tried to go on with their parts, but he made a fresh disturbance as he seated himself, for he strode across the stage with big strides, although he might have been quite comfortable near the wings, planted his chair right in front, and with his broad back turned insolently to the audience, hid the actors from three-fourths of the pit. A murmur arose which would have made anyone else ashamed but he did not take any notice of it. There he sat, as firm as a rock, and would have remained unmoved, if as my ill-luck would have it, he had not caught sight of me.

" ' Ah, Marquis,' he said to me, seating himself near me. ' How are you? Let me embrace you.' The blood rushed to my face at once, so ashamed was I to be seen with such a lout; I only knew him slightly, but it was easy to see he was one of those fellows who make out they know you on the slightest cause, whose salutations you must endure, and who take upon themselves to address you familiarly.

" He immediately asked a hundred frivolous questions in a louder voice than any of the actors used. Everyone cursed him, and hoping to check him, I told him I wanted to listen to the play. ' You have not seen it before, Marquis? Ah! God bless me, it is a very comical play, and I am not a fool at this sort of thing. I know by what rules a perfect work is fashioned; Corneille used to read me all he wrote.'

" Thereupon he gave me a summary of the play, scene by scene, telling me what was coming next, and even going as far as to recite aloud to me some lines he knew by heart, before the actors. I tried in vain to restrain him. He followed up his advantage, and rose to leave long before the end. Men of fashion you know, who give themselves airs, never think of staying to hear the finish."

All the spectators on the stage may not have been so troublesome as this, but certainly there was a constant humming and whispering among the variegated, chattering swarm of *petits-maîtres*, who filled up the space between the wings, passing in and out with their bespangled flunkeys at their heels, flirting with the actresses, tapping the actors familiarly on the shoulders, and making a show of themselves and their glittering finery, instead of paying attention to the play. Sometimes even they were drunk. One evening when a play by the actor d'Ancourt was being performed, the Marquis de Sablé came in tipsy, and took his seat on the stage. D'Ancourt himself just happened to be singing the following lines of his play :—

En parterre il boutra nos blés.
Nos prés, nos champs seront sablés.

(He will turn our corn-fields into his garden, and our meadows and fields will be sanded.)

In his hazy state de Sablé thought his name was being ridiculed from the stage, and with the dignity of a drunken man he went up to the actor and gave him a beating. Circumstances were such that d'Ancourt had to pocket the insult without murmur.[1]

---

[1] We even hear that Molière had to put up with a no less grave affront from the Count de la Feuillade, Duke of Rouannais. This foolish courtier was generally supposed to be the original of the idiotic Marquis in the *Critique de L'Ecole des Femmes*, who keeps repeating as his sole argument against Molière's play : " *Tarte à la crème ! tarte à la crème !* " When a last he discovered that he had been ridiculed, being incapable of inventing

Conditions somewhat improved when the spectators on the stage were locked up behind a fixed balustrade with benches placed inside, and became still better when the entrance was no longer through the green-room, but from the balcony. These improvements, however, were not introduced till the eighteenth century, and the last-mentioned very late in that century.

In a print by Coypel of 1726 (fig. 27), though the curtain is down, the new seats on the stage are seen pretty distinctly, and the plan (fig. 28) which dates from 1752, shows clearly what part of the stage the spectators had usurped.

We see, for one thing, that the elaborate system of scenery had gradually disappeared, leaving nothing but a back cloth and at most a few wings to indicate the place where the scene was laid.

It might happen occasionally, even in Molière's time or a little later, that the scenery of certain plays required the whole stage, so that no spectators could be admitted. Thus it was, for instance, in *Circé* (1675), the great spectacular play by Thomas Corneille. But these cases were exceptions, which never occurred when plays of real value were performed, like those of the great

any clever means of revenge, he went up to Molière one day when he met him in a gallery at Versailles, with outstretched arms as if to embrace him (as was the fashion of the time) ; and when Molière, mistaking his intention, made a bow, the Duke seized his head and rubbed it against the buttons of his coat, repeating furiously : " *Tarte à la crême, tarte à la crême !* " It is very painful to us to see the great and noble-minded poet in the humiliating plight of being forced to suffer so gross an insult from this idiot of a noble-man. But it must be confessed that the spirit of the time makes the anecdote seem quite credible. It is told for the first time in the biographical introduction to the Amsterdam edition of the works of Molière (1725), and the biographer asserts that he had the story from an eye-witness. It is now repeated in all biographies.

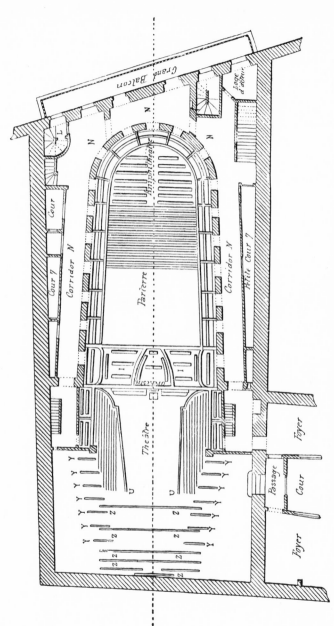

28—Plan of the Théâtre Français in 1752, with seats for spectators on the stage.

Corneille, the tragedies of Racine, or the finest of Molière's comedies. These were acted in the midst of a noisy crowd of the chattering monkeys, on whom Molière revenged himself by ridiculing them to their very faces.

The actors might even congratulate themselves if the spectators were not more disorderly, as happened once, when a rich man with a taste for practical jokes took it into his head to place himself on the Pont Neuf where he distributed tickets for the stage to all the hunchbacks he could get hold of. When the curtain rose in the evening, and the audience discovered the eccentric assembly of deformed individuals on the stage, the impression produced certainly did not promote the success of the tragedy.

Quite apart from jokes of this kind and the excesses described above, this absurd custom naturally affected theatrical literature. If the French classical tragedy developed into a series of conversations and long speeches, sublime, passionate, spirited, but never characterised by a distinct *milieu* and always taking place in some indefinite spot, if we seldom *see* an effective event and only hear the description of it, may not the blame of all this talk without action be laid, to a certain extent, on these spectators on the stage, who disturbed all illusion, who not only prevented the public from seeing, but the authors also from writing plays with vivid dramatic action and picturesque situations? Certainly the times were not romantic, and the notion of local colour was not as yet in existence, but we may be allowed to suppose that, if the stage had been free,

the imagination of the poet might have had a wider
scope for its flight than it could have in the cage, of
which the little barons and marquises now formed
the gilt bars.

The picture by Coypel mentioned above is in-
structive also in other points of information concerning
theatrical arrangements of the time.   It shows, for
instance, the characteristic " standing " pit (a pit without
seats).   The floor which nowadays contains the best
and most expensive seats in the theatres was in those
times the most popular and the cheapest part of the
auditorium ; the ordinary admission fee was only fifteen
sous.   As there were no seats, of course no ladies went
there.   Indeed, even long after the " standing " pit had
been converted into the elegant *fauteuils d'orchestre*
or stalls, female spectators were excluded from the floor,
and so recently as twenty years ago no lady was seen
in the seats in the *orchestre* of the Théâtre Français.

The pit extended right up to the stage, as the
orchestra was not placed where it is now, but occupied
a box at the back of the theatre, where, according to
Chappuzeau, " they could make more noise than from
any other place that could have been found for them."
He adds that it would be also a good thing for them
" to know the last lines of the act by heart, so as to
enable them to begin the symphony at once without
waiting for the cry : ' Play ! ' which is often heard." [1]

Later the musicians were placed in front of the
stage, but only in a small central enclosure, on each
side of which seats were placed for spectators who did

[1] Chappuzeau, III., chap. lii. (p. 119).

not wish to stand (comp. fig. 28). These seats in the orchestra gradually increased in number and encroached upon the pit, which was finally reduced to the back part of the floor. This was the origin of the modern French arrangement, an elegant and expensive *Orchestre* and a very cheap, unnumbered *Parterre*.

In order to avoid the scandals we have described, of people from the pit climbing up on to the stage, a railing was put up in front, as shown in the print by Coypel.

The pit was occupied by a set of people who differed very much from the audience on the stage, and the two parties were constantly at war ; a play might be hissed by the one and madly applauded by the other, and these demonstrations were always accompanied by more or less insulting remarks aimed at the opposite camp. Thus, for instance, at the first performance of *L'Ecole des Femmes*, the philosopher Plapisson, who was sitting on the stage, shrugged his shoulders disdainfully each time the pit burst out laughing, and said angrily : " Laugh away, stupid pit, laugh away ! "

The boxes were mostly occupied by ladies, and indeed, a *femme du bel air* could go nowhere else. A box contained eight seats, but the ample dresses of the ladies—especially when *paniers*, as they called, came into fashion—took up so much space that it was impossible to make room for so many. So it became the fashion for people of distinction to engage a whole box,[1] where the ladies were spared the incon-

---

[1] The ordinary price of a box was 24 *livres*, but the prices were frequently doubled when the play was particularly attractive. The boxes in the upper tiers were much cheaper. In 1699, when a poor-tax of $16\frac{1}{4}$ per cent. was laid on the theatres, the prices were increased 20 per cent.

venience of being overcrowded, and were accompanied only by some gentlemen in attendance.

The pit, however, was the ruling power in the theatre and decided the fate of the play and the actors—a troublesome and sometimes ill-behaved flock, but always independent in its opinions, and though living under absolute monarchical rule, a hundred times more unbiassed in its judgment and more impatient of restraint than the democratic public of our own day, which is cowed by the Press, the police and its own snobbishness. It is a good thing to remember, that Molière was essentially supported by his faithful pit, whereas the wiseacres of literature thought nothing of him.[1] This right judgment at first hand atones for many sins.

The pit was not a comfortable place ; but something was done for the convenience of the spectators. There was a little bar nicely lighted by small chandeliers, and sparkling with cut glass and expensive china jars. Here a smart and smiling barmaid sold lemonade and sweets : raspberry-syrup, lemonade and cider in summer, and in winter beverages "to warm the stomach," such as Spanish wines, *sciontades*, *rivesaltes* and all kinds of drinks. There were also dried fruits, lemons, oranges and the roasted apples [2] which became fatal to Molière in his tragic parts.

At the back of the house were two large stoves, which

[1] The only man of literary distinction contemporary with Molière, who—even at an early date—understood his greatness, was Boileau, but his judgment alone, sagacious and bold for his day as it might be, was not sufficient to create the success of Molière. A play must find response the public, or it is doomed to die.

[2] "Are there apples enough in Normandy for *tarte à la crème*?" asks the Marquis in *La Critique de L'Ecole des Femmes* (sc. 7).

diffused some warmth in winter. The spectators on the stage went to the actors' green-room, where bright wood fires were burning in the large fireplaces. These rooms, therefore were called *les foyers* (the hearths), a name which has since become the international term for the places where the actors and the spectators respectively retire during the intervals.[1]

As we have repeatedly mentioned, performances did not take place every day, only three or four times a week. Not till the close of the century, when Paris possessed only one French theatre, were plays acted every night, or rather afternoon, for what we call evening performances were unknown.

At the beginning of the seventeenth century, as in the Middle Ages, it was still customary to play in the day-time, but the hours became gradually later. A police regulation of 1609 orders the Hôtel de Bourgogne to open its doors at one o'clock and begin the play punctually at two. Officially this order was still in force in the time of Molière, but it was far from being carried out, in spite of the play-bills, on which " 2 o'clock punctually " continued to be printed.

A little scene in the amusing play *Le Poète Basque* (the Basque Poet), by R. Poisson, the well-known player of Crispin (fig. 29), gives us a clear glimpse into the real state of things. A country nobleman has come from Gascony to Paris and wants to see a play. We see him mounting the stage, and the following conversation takes place between him and the actors:—

---

[1] In England the retiring room of the audience is called " the lobby," that of the actors "the green-room."

The Baron : " How is this ? not a single soul here
    yet ? "

M. de Hauteroche : [1] " He is afraid of being late,
    Who is it, I wonder ? "

Mlle Poisson : [2] " It is a 'provincial' who is coming
    to take his seat."

The Baron : " Hullo ! whatever does this mean ?   It
    is as cold as ice and past two o'clock !   Why
    don't they bestir themselves more ? "

M. de Hauteroche : " But, Sir, we don't begin till four
    o'clock."

The Baron : " Then what you print is only rubbish ! I
    read on your play-bill : two o'clock punctually—
    What liars you are !   For your sake I have left
    merry women, wine, cards and jollity, and now
    I find myself here like a hermit alone in the
    desert.   A nice thing indeed !   Why don't you
    keep to what is said on the play-bill ? "

Mlle Poisson : " Oh, that play-bill has long told the
    same tale, but we don't begin any earlier for that."

They did not even begin at four, if we are to believe the
same play, in which later Mlle Brécourt [3] comes rushing
in to the other actors and says : " Now, gentlemen, you
must begin ! What does this mean ?   All the *passe-volants* [4]

[1] *Orateur* of the Hôtel de Bourgogne.   Comp. above, p. 89.

[2] Wife of Raymond Poisson, *alias* Victoire Guérin.   She played *con-
fidentes* in tragedy and second female lovers in comedy.

[3] Etienne des Urlis, actress at the Hôtel de Bourgogne, married to the
well-known actor Brécourt ——, who had been for some years with Molière
but left him in 1664.

[4] *Les passe-volants*, a name given to the sham soldiers who filled up the
ranks at reviews ; hence to the "paper" audience, who made people believe
that the house was full and the performance about to begin.

are going away. This isn't fair on them ; it is nearly five o'clock."

By and by five o'clock became the usual hour for beginning, and remained so for many years.

The preparations for "staging" a play, the negotiations with the author, the acceptance of it and the rehearsals, were much the same as nowadays, but we notice that authors and actors lived in much more intimate and brotherly relations with each other in those times.

The acceptance of a play at the theatres of the present day is almost invariably the manager's business, and the actors have as little to do with it as the workers in a factory with the acquisition of new machines ; as a rule they know nothing whatever about it before they are summoned to rehearse it.

It was not so in the time of Molière. When an author wished to have a play accepted, he went to the theatre on a day when performances were going on, and told the actors that he had written a play and would like to read it to them. A day and hour were appointed, and all the actors assembled on the stage or elsewhere to hear the new play. Though the ladies had a right to be present at these readings, and though in many cases they might probably have been able to give as good an opinion as the men, it was customary for them to absent themselves, out of modesty, leaving it to the men alone to judge of the acceptability of the play in question.

Then the author began reading, and when, after finishing the first act, he took a rest, the actors discussed what they had heard and pointed out what they thought might be altered, which scenes appeared too long, what effects might be too strong, or which speeches too tedious, etc., questions which were discussed more fully when the author had finished reading and was able to join in the consultation.   Some little change might be agreed upon, and when the play was accepted, the party would adjourn to a wine-shop and ratify the bargain by a drink.

Of course it also happened sometimes that a play was rejected, though probably less frequently than nowadays, in proportion to the number of plays offered.   An author of some note might nearly always be sure of having his plays performed, which is far from being the case now at theatres dependent on the State or the Court and managed in an official rather than an artistic spirit, which frequently seem to consider it as their principal task to turn off importunate dramatic authors.

If the author was not yet known, he used to go to work in a roundabout way.   He applied to an actor, " the one whom he considered the most intelligent and most competent to judge," [1] for his advice as to whether he had better read the play to the company or not.   By this means—as the author was almost compelled to follow the actor's advice—rising playwrights were spared some official rebuffs, and the company a good deal of trouble.

The pecuniary conditions varied very much according to the names of the authors.   Whereas now, if our memory serves us right, most European theatres of any importance—except the English theatres—have a fixed tariff of payment, which holds good for all plays, in those

[1] Chappuzeau, II., ch. ix. (p. 54).

times it was only the poets of repute who were liberally paid, frequently even without regard to the success of their work. The beginner, on the contrary, had to be contented with very little or nothing, as he was considered an apprentice, who ought to be glad if his works enjoyed the honour of being performed at all. The author was either paid a certain sum down, after which the manuscript belonged to the company,[1] or—which was most frequently the case—as long as the run of the play lasted, he entered as shareholder into the troupe, as a rule with two shares, though of course only on the days when his play was acted.

In this way the remuneration of authors might amount to considerable sums. A fair average taking for an evening was about one hundred *livres* (£20), and we understand that Molière, who at times possessed as much as five shares in his theatre, could be registered as possessing an annual income of more than £3600, besides the money he received from his publisher and from the King and the sums he gained by private performances in the great Parisian houses, the amount of which it is impossible to ascertain.

Then, as now, it was important for the author to choose the right season for the appearance of his play. As a general rule the winter was reserved for heroic plays, while the summer was chosen for comic performances. But the period from All Saint's day (1st Nov.) to Easter, during which the whole Court resided in the Louvre or at St Germain, was considered the best time of

---

[1] According to the ideas of the time a play once printed was public property.

the whole year.   A great author did not willingly choose any other time for his "first night."

The distribution of parts was no doubt a ticklish affair under this republican *régime*.   Even Chappuzeau, our principal source of information on the internal affairs of the theatre, who sees everything through rose-coloured spectacles and represents all actors as angels of justice and reason, acknowledges that in this question " frequently little difficulties arise, as everybody of course has a good opinion of himself or herself, and thinks that a leading part will give him or her a firmer footing in the esteem of the audience."

It will possibly cause less astonishment than it should if we state that it was the ladies who caused most of these " little difficulties."   " As there is not one of them who would not like to be thought endowed with perpetual youth, they are not very eager to play the Sisygambis parts.[1] If the author creates mothers, they must not be past the prime of life, and he must take care not to give them sons who convict them of being past forty.   To tell the truth, both in the theatre and in all other places, there is diffi-culty in ruling women, and not so much in ruling men."

With the parts of comic old women the actresses would have nothing whatever to do, and the actors created a special branch for themselves in these so-called " nurse-parts " (*rôles de nourrice*).

Thus the Hôtel de Bourgogne had its Alizon and its dame Gigogne, and Molière had André Hubert, for whom he is said to have written his *Comtesse d'Escarbagnas*,

[1] So called after Sisygambis, the old mother of Darius Codomannus, who figured as a character in several historical plays of the time, *e.g.*, in Alexandre Hardy's *Mort de Daire* [Death of Darius].

and who was also the first performer of Mme. Pernelle,
Mme. de Sotenville, Mme. Jourdain, etc. After the
retirement of Hubert, Beauval undertook his rôles.
These actors of female parts were masked and spoke in
a falsetto voice; but after their death, the taste of the
time had changed so much, that actresses were obliged
to undertake such characters, and the very talented
Mme. Champvallon was the first who at the beginning
of the eighteenth century won fame in these comic
female characters.

The rehearsals, it seems, were conducted very
deliberately. When the actors were hard pressed, however, and when it was absolutely necessary to have a play
ready by a certain day, things could be achieved at
almost incredible speed. Molière himself tells us that
his three act comedy in verse, *Les Fâcheux*, which had
been ordered by Fouquet, the minister of finance, a man
of vast wealth but very little honesty, for a magnificent
festival in honour of Louis XIV. and his Court,[1] was
"conceived, written, read and performed in the course of a
fortnight."[2] But he begins by saying that "never had a
theatrical enterprise been more precipitate."[3]

[1] The principal object of this festival was to win back the favour of the
King. This hope, however, was disappointed. On August 20th, 1661, *Les
Fâcheux* was performed with a prologue by the philosopher Pellisson, the
confidant of Fouquet. On Sept. 5th both Fouquet and Pellisson were
arrested. But the play, feeble as it is, held its ground and gave great
pleasure to the gracious monarch.

[2] *Avertissement* to *Les Fâcheux*.

[3] Indeed, at the performance, he apologised adroitly enough for this
haste. As soon as the curtain had risen, he appeared in his everyday dress,
and turning to the King, with an expression of confusion on his face,
stammered his excuses for coming alone. But he had neither time nor
actors and was unable to procure His Majesty the amusement he seemed to
expect. At the same moment twenty natural fountains began to play, a

Under ordinary circumstances the actors took their own time. When they felt sure of their parts the first rehearsal was held; it was, as nowadays, merely a preliminary instruction and general arrangement; the last rehearsal—what we call the dress-rehearsal—was exactly like the public performance. The author generally conducted the rehearsals of his own plays, and explained his intentions to the actor, corrected him "if he overstepped nature in voice or gesture, if he showed more or less warmth than was required for the passions he was to express."[1]

The actors also helped each other at the rehearsals, only, of course, in so far as the clever and intelligent gave their advice to those who had less talent or experience; and there seems to have been such good fellowship among them, that one actor accepted useful advice from another without feeling wounded in his professional dignity.

In Molière's theatre the conditions were exceptional. Not only because Molière was an author as well as an actor; this was the case with many others;[2] but his superior talent, so to speak, predestined him to take the lead, and the actors involuntarily submitted to his

large shell opened, and out of it issued Madeleine Béjart as a charming though somewhat elderly naïad, in which character she recited Pellisson's "heroic" prologue.

[1] Chappuzeau, II., ch. xvii. (p. 62).

[2] At the Hôtel de Bourgogne there was a whole series of more or less fertile authors, such as Montfleury, author of the tragedy *Hasdrubal* (the many other plays bearing the name of Montfleury as author, are by the actor's son); de Villiers, who among other plays wrote some polemical comedies against Molière; Raymond Poisson, an amusing writer of farces. Hauteroche, who wrote Crispin-rôles for his comrade Poisson (*Crispin médecin, Crispin musicien*); Champmeslé, Brécourt, etc.

powers, and allowed him to rule them—in professional questions—just as he liked.

He was hot-tempered and excitable and had a sharp tongue and not too much patience; but in spite of this he was much liked by his subordinates. To some extent his company might be called the ideal association of actors; a staff voluntarily submitting to a chief selected by the members from among themselves, who, being an actor and ruling his colleagues by means of his superior talent, is, by extraordinary good fortune, a great playwright as well, whose comedies provide the troupe with excellent parts and plenty of money for the treasury. How different from the syndicates or despotisms, which in our days threaten to convert distinguished European stages into large—and stupid—wholesale emporiums of theatrical boredom!

Molière has left us a little memorandum of his work as stage-manager in one of the short, almost improvised plays which he poured out lavishly at the feet of his spectators and in the face of his adversaries. In the *Impromptu de Versailles* he represents himself at work with the actors, preparing the performance of a play for a court-entertainment at Versailles, and it is the rehearsal itself with its interruptions and with Molière's observations to each of the actors, which forms the subject of the play.

This little episode, most wittily written, forms a link in the great controversy between Molière and the Hôtel de Bourgogne, which we shall afterwards have an opportunity of studying. It is only of interest here in so far as it shows Molière at his daily work.

First we hear him scolding and swearing to call the actors together. " Now, ladies and gentlemen, you are slow indeed! it looks as though you were trifling with me. Are you never coming? Plague take them!" He goes on raging for a while, till his fit of temper culminates in the classical exclamation : " Ah! what an awkward team of animals comedians are to drive!"

Next, the troupe, which has assembled meanwhile, unanimously complains at having to learn new parts in so short a time. To Molière's arguments Madeleine Béjart replies: " You are not to be pitied ; as you have written the play, you need not be afraid of tripping." He answers eagerly : " And have I nothing to fear but a slip of memory? Do you call it nothing to be anxious about the success which rests entirely upon me? Do you think it a light matter to provide something amusing for such an audience as this? to undertake to make people laugh whom one has to respect, and who only laugh when they feel inclined? What author would not tremble when put to such an ordeal? Should it not rather be my place to give anything in the world to get out of it ?"

At last, after easing his mind in this way, he begins explaining the play to the actors, and finally characterises each part to its performer.

For instance, he says to du Croisy, " You play a poet's part, and you ought to be fully taken up with your impersonation. Indicate the pedantic air he preserves throughout his intercourse with the fashionable world, his sententious tone of voice and precise pronunciation of every syllable; and do not miss a single letter of the most correct spelling."

For all their brevity these hints are excellent and quite sufficient for an actor to form a clear idea of the author's conception.

To Brécourt[1] he says: "You must act a good courtier, as you did in the *Critique de L'Ecole des Femmes*, that is to say, you must assume a calm manner, a natural tone of voice, and gesticulate as little as possible."

Thus he explains to each the character he or she has to interpret,[2] and when this is done, the real rehearsal begins.

Molière describes to them the scene, which takes place in the King's antechamber, where two marquises[3] meet. Molière himself acts one of them, La Grange the other.

"You must be careful," Molière instructs his younger

---

[1] Guillaume Marcoureau de Brécourt joined Molière's troupe in 1662 at the same time as La Thorillière. They came from the Marais theatre. But Brécourt, who was of a very restless disposition, left the company as early as 1664.

[2] It is on this occasion that he says to La Grange; "To you I have nothing to say," which little sentence is constantly repeated in all biographies of Molière, and is quoted as a proof of the esteem in which he held the mature art of La Grange. But some pages further on in the play we discover that at that moment Molière had nothing to say to him because he had prepared the part with him previously. At the rehearsal proper he corrects him at once and sharply.

[3] It is in this same piece that Molière says in reply to his wife's complaint, "Marquises again!" "Yes, marquises again. What the deuce else would you have me hit upon for a character acceptable to the audience? A marquis nowadays is the funny man of a play; just as in all the old comedies there was always a clownish valet to make the audience laugh, so in all our plays now, there must always be a ridiculous marquis to amuse the company." It is clear that Molière did not spare even his best paying clients

colleague, "to remember what I told you, that you are
to come in, there, with what is called a well-bred air,
combing your wig, and humming a tune, la, la, la, la, la,
la, get out of the way, everybody, for two marquises
must have plenty of room : they are not people who are
content with a small space ; (to La Grange) come,
go on."

La Grange : "Good-day, Marquis."

Molière : "Good Heavens! that is not how a marquis
talks.   You must talk louder than that ; most
of these gentlemen affect a particular manner
of speaking, to distinguish themselves from the
rabble : 'Good-day, Marquis.'   Now begin
again."

When Brécourt who, as we know, acted the
sensible courtier, begins his speech, Molière at once
interrupts him : "Here is the other talking like a
marquis! Did I not tell you that your part was one
in which you should talk naturally ? "

Brécourt : "You are right."

Molière : "Come then!—'Chevalier—'"

Thus we must imagine Molière at the rehearsals :
constantly active, working with each performer, correcting a wrong accent, explaining each character and each
nuance, suffering when he meets with stupidity, false
interpretation, and above all unnaturalness, but delighted
at the point of perfection to which genuine talent can
be brought.

False declamation, which glides smoothly into the
ear of the ordinary hearer, was even physically a torture
to him.   One day, during the performance of *Tartufe,*

the actor, Champmeslé[1] called, wishing to speak to Molière. They were sitting in his tiring-room, which was close to the stage. In the midst of their conversation Molière suddenly exclaimed: "Oh, you dog, you hangman!" Champmeslé, thinking he had gone out of his mind, stared at him in great bewilderment, Molière, noticing his astonishment, excused himself and said: "Don't be frightened at my temper. I heard one of the actors recite four lines of my play most miserably and with a false accent, and I cannot hear my children ill-treated in this way without suffering the torments of hell.[2]

This delicate ear for accentuation, which is the surest indication of the born actor, made him work out a kind of graphic system to be used by the young pupils whom he trained. Young Baron, who gained such great distinction as an actor, is said to have acquired his unerring, natural delivery by the systematic instruction of Molière, and by following this system of notation.[3]

His instruction seems to have gone very much into detail and to have been most scrupulous; this now and then irritated the actors, especially those who most needed correction, and called forth objections. But Molière was always equal to the occasion, and parried their interference with a sharp and witty reply.

[1] Charles Chevillet, sieur de Champmeslé (b. 1642—d. 1701)—a tolerably clever actor and author, whose name, however, is best known through his wife, the excellent interpreter of Racine's characters, Mlle Champmeslé, *née* Marie Desmares—was originally a provincial actor. From 1660-70, during which time *Tartufe* appeared, he was at the Marais. Afterwards he went to the Hôtel de Bourgogne, but left it again in 1679, to return to the Marais, which was then united with the Molière company.

[2] Grimarest: *Vie de Molière*, Amsterdam, 1705, pp. 128 f.

[3] Loiseleur: *Points obscurs*, p. 331.

During the preparation of *Le Malade imaginaire* he is said to have been particularly difficult to please at one of the rehearsals. In this play the part of the maid-servant Toinette was played by the irritable and unmanageable Mlle Beauval,[1] and her husband, who was very slow of perception, had the part of the idiotic pedant Thomas Diafoirus. Mlle Beauval had several times given curt replies, when Molière corrected her. At last she exclaimed, " You torment us all, but you don't say a word to my husband." " I shouldn't think of it," Molière replied, " it would spoil his acting, nature has guided him better for this part than I can do."

Taken altogether, the little scraps of information which we can gather here and there give us a distinct impression that the preliminary work on the stage— which the public does not see, and of which, therefore, it can know very little—was carried out with great care at all theatres, and that Molière's company possessed a really superior artistic power, which impressed a stamp of unity on its productions, and which, in the judgment of real experts, raised it above all the rest.

And indeed, it was his theatre which afterwards

---

[1] Jeanne Olivier Bourguignon, who married Jean Pitel, sieur de Beauval, was born about 1649 and joined Molière's company in 1670. She remained there till his death in 1673, after which she went to the Hôtel de Bourgogne. She was a large, coarse, exceedingly ignorant woman, but not without talent. In spite of her difficult temperament Molière seemed to appreciate her. She played *soubrettes*, and her delivery suffered from involuntary fits of laughter, which probably suggested to Molière, on whom nothing was lost, the idea of writing the part of the laughing Zerbinette in *Les Fourberies de Scapin* on purpose for her. Her husband was most insignificant, but very honest. Thomas Diafoirus became his best part. He also, as we said above, acted comic old women.

absorbed the two others and became the Théâtre Français properly so-called.

VIII

Beginning of Hostilities between the Company of Molière and the Royal Actors—Leading Actors of the Hôtel de Bourgogne—Montfleury and his Art—Poisson, the Comic Actor, and his Crispin—Floridor and the Actresses of the Hôtel.

MOLIÈRE'S *Les Précieuses ridicules* achieved so great a success, that the importance of the company was at once established, and the public was so intensely amused at his Mascarille that he was assured of its favour.

In this play, however, there was one little speech which, though apparently innocent, contained a sharp sting, and which was the first open outbreak of a very obstinate and bitter controversy.

In his conversation with the two *"précieuses ridicules"* Mascarille on one occasion boasts of having written a play, upon which one of the stilted damsels asks him : " To what company will you give it ? " Mascarille replies : " What a question ! To His Majesty's servants, they alone are capable of doing justice to plays ; the rest are ignorant persons who recite their parts just as they talk, and do not know how to make the verses tell, or to pause at a fine passage ; how can people know the fine passages if the actor does not emphasise them, and thereby indicate that a burst of applause is expected ? " [1]

This sarcastic tone is very far removed from the modesty with which on his first appearance Molière

---

[1] *Précieuses ridicules*, sc. ix.

called himself and his comrades " feeble imitators " of the excellent originals of the Hôtel de Bourgogne.

What had happened ? Merely this, we suppose ; that on closer examination Molière had come to the conclusion that the excellent Royal originals, whose fame was far spread in France, were not quite so good as their reputation, and that, at any rate, he could not sympathise with their style of acting. Some bitterness at finding that authors, probably arguing like Mascarille, always passed his door and knocked at that of his rival, may have mingled with these feelings, and the result was the little masked attack in Mascarille's speech, which in Molière's own witty mouth no doubt had the sharp edge which struck home where it was aimed.

The old Hôtel was still ruled by Montfleury, whose proper name was Zacharie Jacob. He was now (in 1659) somewhat advanced in age—he was born at the close of the sixteenth or the beginning of the seventeenth century, and his bulk had so increased that on the stage his enormous stomach had to be held up by iron hoops.

It was not his age, however, which rendered him old-fashioned, or placed him in opposition to Molière. They were antipodes in their art, and the difference between them was the same which at all times is a burning question in mimetic art between unnatural inflation and sober truth, a struggle in which the public does not always, and the dramatic authors very seldom, take the side of truth. Nor can we say that, from the artistic point of view, Molière gained the victory in this struggle. Montfleury continued to enjoy high appreciation as an actor, and probably there were only three voices, those of Molière, Cyrano de Bergerac and Boileau, that brought discord into the chorus of homage in which all the other literary men of distinction joined to honour him.

And indeed, we cannot suppose Montfleury to have been an insignificant actor. His powerful voice and colossal size in themselves gave him a commanding appearance, nor did he lack education and mental culture. He wrote several tragedies, one of which, *The Death of Hasdrubal*[1] has been preserved ; he was equally popular as a comic and as a tragic actor, which was quite exceptional at this period, and he acted the heroes in the best plays of Corneille and Racine to the satisfaction of the authors, and with a power that carried the spectators away and made them forget the exaggeration of his acting.

Montfleury, like Mondory, seems to have fallen a victim to his own violence. After a performance of Racine's *Andromaque*, in which he had called forth great enthusiasm as Orestes—he was an old man then (in 1667) —he fell ill and died a few days after.

Guéret, one of the authors of the day (in his *Le Parnasse réformé*) makes him narrate his own death in a characteristic manner: Montfleury, who had rolled himself to the foot of the mountain, said in a voice calculated to make all Parnassus shake : " I think you are talking of comedy here." Whereupon, having discovered Tristan, he turned towards him and continued : " Ah, it's very fine indeed that you should object so much to amusement on the stage. Perhaps you want them to

[1] *La Mort d'Asdrubal*, Paris, 1647, 4to.

play nothing but *Mariamne*, so that every week a
Mondory may die for your benefit.   I wish no tragedies
had ever been written, then I might still have been able
to appear on the stage of the Hôtel! . . . If anyone
wants to know what has killed me, don't let him ask if it
is fever, pleurisy, or gout, but tell him it was *Andromaque*.
We are great fools to take so closely to our hearts
the passions which have only hung at the point of the
poet's pens.   It would be much better to be always
playing the fool and amusing the citizens by
bursting with laughter than bursting with pride
and wit to please the authors.   But what annoys
me most of all is that *Andromaque* is becoming more
famous on account of my death, and that in future there
will not be a poet who does not want to make an actor
burst once in his life."

If Montfleury was anything but insignificant as an
actor—his massive appearance and powerful delivery
alone would forbid the use of such an expression about
him—his personal character was cowardly and mean.
Of his timidity we have given an example in a former
chapter;[1] his baseness of mind reveals itself in his
controversy with Molière, which we shall have an
opportunity of mentioning on a later page.

Of the old staff who played in the boisterous style of
Montfleury, one actor still remained, Beauchâteau, whom
we have already mentioned.   His real name—he was
of noble birth—was François Châtelet.[2]   His powers of

---

[1] Comp. above, pp. 26 f.

[2] Scudéry in his *Comédie des Comédiens*, ii. 1, sneers at the fancy of actors
or adopting fine names.   " Messrs de Bellerose, de Belleville, Beauchâteau,
Belleroche, Beaulieu, Beaupré, Bellefleur, Belle-Epine, Beau-Séjour, Beau-

attraction were probably somewhat on the decline; still he remained popular till his death, which occurred in 1665; he had then worked thirty-two years at the Hôtel de Bourgogne.

De Villiers also continued to be one of the leading actors of the Hôtel de Bourgogne, both in tragedy, where he was an adherent of the bombastic school, and in comedy, where he played the merry valet, Philippin. The latter character, however, was gradually overshadowed by another typical valet, Crispin, who became immensely popular and maintained his place on the French stage till far on in the nineteenth century. This character is inseparably connected with a family of actors who through three generations gained celebrity on the French stage, and whose ancestor, Raymond Poisson, was just now in his full glory at the Hôtel de Bourgogne.

We generally find Raymond Poisson mentioned as the inventor of the Crispin character. This, however, literally speaking, he was not. In 1654, when Poisson was a young man,[1] and had recently been engaged at the Hôtel de Bourgogne, a play by Scarron entitled *The Scholar of Salamanca*, was acted at the Marais, and in this play we meet for the first time with the character which was to gain such popularity afterwards in the hands of Poisson, though,

Soleil, Belle-Ombre; in short, they alone possess all the beauties of nature." This custom prevailed far on into the eighteenth century, when among the celebrities of the Théâtre français we meet such names as Beaubourg, Bellecourt, Bellemont, etc.

[1] He was born in Paris in 1633. His father was a poor mathematician who lived in an attic close to the Palais de Justice. The young man first studied medicine, and for some time cultivated surgery, which was held in small esteem in those days. But following his theatrical inclination, he went into the provinces as an actor, whence he became engaged at the "Hôtel" about 1652.

as we see, he could not have originated it.   In this play
Scarron makes one of his personages, Don Felix,
introduce the new valet in these words :—

> *Don Felix :* " Now I will show you his ludicrous
>   messenger, a very rare animal, half pedant,
>   half rascal.—Hallo, Crispin ! "
> *Crispin :* " *Adsum.* "
> *Don Felix :* " Can't you speak like a Christian, you
>   fool ? "
> *Crispin :* " *Non possum.* "
> *Don Felix :* " I will take a stick and beat you !
>   Because that rascal knows three words of Latin,
>   he thinks he may be allowed to bother us with
>   it.   Now then, what is my good-for-nothing of
>   a son doing ? "
> *Crispin :* " *Male facit.* "
> *Don Felix :* " Again ! I will strangle you, you ass of
>   a pedant ! "
> *Crispin :* " Very well, sir, very well ! I won't say
>   another word. "

Towards the end of the scene we get a piece of
information about Crispin's dress, which harmonises with
his later traditional costume.   Don Felix says : " How
is that, you fool ?   Do you wear long boots like a light
horseman ?   How did you come here ? "   Crispin replies :
" By the post, sir, in a carriage. " [1]
The characters in Scarron's play are all Spanish, and
Crispin, as we know him from Edelinck's Portrait of

---

[1] Scarron : *L'Escolier de Salamanque ou Les Généreux Ennemis, tragi-comédie,* i. 3.

R. Poisson (fig. 29), also appears in Spanish costume : black, tight-fitting coat, white ruff, a sword, broad leather belt, and finally the famous long boots, which, as some older historians of the theatre assert, R. Poisson adopted because his legs were thin and not well made, but which, according to later authorities, it was customary for servants to wear in bad weather. Both opinions are mistaken ; as we see from the quotation from Scarron's play, Poisson adopted the long boots as an already known peculiarity of the Crispin costume. Its origin is unknown ; possibly it was introduced from Spain.[1]

R. Poisson was a fairly big, square-built man with a roguish, expressive face, in which his large mouth and splendid teeth were prominent features. In several contemporary plays we find allusions to this mouth, as, for instance, in *La Femme juge et partie* (*Woman as Judge and Respondent*) by Montfleury the younger, in which Poisson has to say about himself: "As to my face, without being too harsh, there is something grand about it."—"Oh yes," his interlocutor says, "it is the mouth."

Poisson was quite a "comic" of the old school, still

[1] The tradition of the long boots is still kept up. Samson, the excellent French actor of the middle of the nineteenth century, wrote a play on the three generations of Poissons, which here (in Copenhagen) was acted under the title of *The Three Crispins*. One of the actors seeing my print of Raymond Poisson by Edelinck, exclaimed : "Ah, there are the long boots ! I remember, when playing *The Three Crispins*, my old teacher objecting to my costume because I did not wear the long boots. I asked if they were really necessary and what they meant. 'I don't know, my boy,' he replied, 'but they belong to the part. You cannot play Crispin without the long boots.'—So I put them on." Much of the secret history of theatrical tradition is hidden in these boots.

retaining a flavour of the court-fool, acting off the stage as well as on it, and always trading on his humour with the great men who did him the honour to laugh at his jokes and allowed him to share in their drinking-bouts and orgies or gave him an old coat in return.

His poems—of which he left a considerable number, which are prefixed to the complete edition of his comedies—are nearly all versified petitions for money to the King, the Ministers of State or other influential people. But he induces them to swallow his undignified importunities by presenting them in a coating of never-failing humour. As a specimen we may mention a petition to Louis XIV., in which he implores the King's help to pay a pension which he is under an obligation to supply to the widow of the actor Bellerose. Most un-sentimentally, Poisson asserts that Mlle Bellerose had got a cold in her head the day he signed the contract to pay her a pension of a thousand francs. She looked so miserable, that he thought she could not live a week, or he would never have done it. But she conspired with her cold, and now she never dies, but each quarter sends for her money, thus obliging him, at least once every three months, to wish her at the devil.

Louis XIV., who on the whole made much of great comic actors—we may recall his predilection for Scaramouche, Dominique[1] and Molière—was also a great friend of Poisson's. It is said to have been the King who procured him the engagement at the Hôtel de Bourgogne, and on the occasion just explained he actually granted him a deduction of 400 fr. of the pension

---

[1] Comp. vol. ii., *Middle Ages and Renaissance*, pp. 296, 297.

to Mlle Bellerose,[1] a favour for which Poisson expresses his gratitude in a short poem ending with the desire that his family may be visited by all misfortunes, and that Mlle Bellerose may enjoy twenty years of health, if he neglects one single day of his life to pray for His Majesty.

The best critics[2] did not place Poisson so high, either as actor or as author, as the King and the general public did. However, we can still enjoy reading his plays; they are redeemed from insignificance by their merry humour and pleasant naturalness, qualities which also seem to have been his strong points as an actor.

Raymond Poisson retired from the stage in 1685 and died in 1690, but his Crispin was undertaken at once by his son Paul, who adopted all the attributes of the part; the costume, the boots and the peculiar jabbering delivery (*bredouillement*), which had characterised the elder Poisson. From the son the part was handed on to the grandson, François Arnould, who adopted the whole traditional costume, and the popularity of the old character does not seem to have diminished, for after the last Poisson Crispin, the celebrated Préville (d. 1800) undertook the part with the same success.

Few families have contributed so large a contingent to the theatre as the Poissons. Besides the father, the

---

[1] Comp. Campardon : *Les Comédiens du Roi*, p. 226 f, where we find a quotation of the royal letter of July 28th, 1670, which fixes the pension of Mme. Bellerose at 600 fr. instead of 1000. So, if it is said by the brothers Parfaict (vii., p. 348), that Poisson's petition procured him a pension of 400 fr., this statement is not quite correct.

[2] Thus when Louis XIV. a few days after Poisson's death, observed that it was a great loss to the theatre, and that he had been an excellent actor, Boileau is said to have answered : " Yes, to play Don Japhet ; he only distinguished himself in Scarron's wretched plays."

son and the grandson, a brother of François Arnould appeared both as actor and author,[1] a sister as a writer of tragedies ;[2] a brother of Paul Poisson was an actor in the French company of the King of Poland, and Raymond's wife and those of his son and grandson were all actresses, though not of high rank, at the Théâtre Français.[3]

If the Hôtel de Bourgogne possessed a genuine and popular comic actor in its Crispin, in Floridor it acquired a really refined and distinguished tragedian, an actor who seems to have been the very opposite of Montfleury, but who upheld the absolute superiority in tragedy of the Hôtel de Bourgogne with much more right and dignity than the empty-minded leader of the fashionable school we have already mentioned.

Contemporary opinions of Floridor differ so little, that we modern historians of the theatre are scarcely able to form an idea of him ; we read nothing but eulogies, without a single adverse criticism which, by pointing out some defect, might afford some hold for characterisation.

In private life he seems to have been equally blameless, a quality which naturally was more appreciated by his contemporaries than by later biographers.   His real

[1] Philippe Poisson was an extraordinary man, inasmuch as, in spite of his popularity as an actor, he had an invincible dislike for the theatre, which caused him, while still young, to retire from it twice, and the second time, finally.   The reverse is much more frequently the case.

[2] Madeleine Poisson, married to a Spanish nobleman, Don Gabriel de Gomez.

[3] The most noted of them was the wife of Paul Poisson, a daughter of Du Croisy, the player of Tartufe.   Her notoriety is not due to her acting, for she was said to have been entirely without talent for the stage, but to her articles on Molière and the actors of his time, which she wrote when very old (she was born in 1658), as contributions to the *Mercure de France* of 1738.

name was Josias de Soulas, sieur de Prine-Fosse ; his nobility was genuine, and was distinctly confirmed by a royal rescript of 1668, a proof that the histrionic profession did not entail the loss of nobility. Originally an officer, he soon left the army for the stage, where he assumed the name of Floridor.

In Paris he worked first for some years at the Marais ; but in 1643, when the affected Bellerose retired from the Hôtel de Bourgogne, Floridor was engaged at that theatre, and undertook the parts both of first lover and Orator.

There he gained an unequalled and unanimous popularity which never waned throughout his career. De Visé—a critic by no means lacking in acuteness— writes of his Massinisse in P. Corneille's *Sophonisbe* : " After the superfluous rôle of Erixe, let us see if Massinisse, who is more necessary to the play, is a gain to it. Yes ; though this is not due to the author, but to the actor who represents him, M. de Floridor, who bears himself with such ease, and plays with so much taste that sensible people never tire of saying that he acts like a gentleman. He really gives the idea of being what he acts, in all the parts he plays. All the spectators would like to look at him constantly, and his bearing, his gesticulation and his movements are so natural, that even without speaking he inspires general admiration. To condense much praise into one word, we only need mention his name, which in itself contains the essence of all the panegyrics that might be pronounced upon him. I can say this boldly without fear of rousing jealousy in those who are of the same profession ; he has

long been above inspiring jealousy, and all have confessed long ago that he is the greatest actor in the
world, and at the same time one of the most courteous
and very pleasant to deal with." [1]

Even Molière in the heat of battle lowers his sword
to Floridor; he is the only one among the leading tragic
actors of the Hôtel to escape his sneers.

Besides the refined and elegant Floridor, a genuine
type of a seventeenth century tragic lover, we have the
tall and bony Hauteroche, a man of about the same age,
who acted the inevitable confidant.   He was probably
a bad actor, but he was a clever dramatic author, whose
plays — *Crispin Médecin* and others — maintained their
place in the *répertoire* of the Théâtre français till far on
in the nineteenth century.

As to the female members of the staff, the Hôtel
de Bourgogne, at this time, seems to have been rather
poorly equipped.   The actors we have mentioned were
all married, and their wives were all in the theatre, but
none of them occupied a leading position.   The most
frequently employed was probably the sweetly sentimental Mlle Beauchâteau (*alias* Madeleine Dubouget).
But the only leading lady of the Hôtel was Mlle des
Oeillets, who played the heroines in the tragedies of
Corneille and Racine, which were the strong point of
the theatre.

Very little, however, is known about this actress,
though she must have possessed a peculiar talent.   It
was not her outward appearance that beguiled the
spectator, for her ugliness was almost proverbial.   A

---

[1] Donneau de Visé in the *Mercure de France*.

remark of hers has survived to prove that she possessed an unusual power of self-criticism and appreciation of a younger rival. When Mlle des Oeillets was old, the afterwards very famous Mlle Champmeslé appeared in one of her parts. Though in very bad health—she died the same year (1670)—the celebrated *tragédienne* wanted to see the young actress make her début in this part. Not a word did she speak during the whole performance; as she left the theatre she said merely this : " Des Oeillets is no more."

In a letter to a friend, her fellow-actor Poisson writes in speaking of her death : " This is a great loss ; Mlle des Oeillets was a marvel on the stage. Though neither young nor good-looking she was one of its chief adornments."

And he adds the following lines :—

> Et justement on dira d'elle
> Qu'elle n'était pas belle au jour
> Comme elle était à la chandelle :
> Mais sans avoir donné d'amour,
> Ni sans être jeune et belle,
> Elle charmait toute la cour.

(It will be said of her with justice that she was not handsome in daylight as she was by candle-light : but without inspiring love and without being young or handsome, she charmed the whole court.)

IX

The Great Theatrical Controversy between Molière and the Hôtel de
Bourgogne—The Molière Company moves to the Palais Royal—
Don Garcie de Navarre and its Failure—*L'Ecole des Maris*
and *Les Fâcheux*—*L'Ecole des Femmes*, its Extraordinary Success
and the Consequences—Polemics from the Stage—Boursault and
Molière.

THE jealousy which Molière's success had aroused
among the "great" and "unique" Royal actors—as
they called themselves—was very soon to break out
openly.   Barely two years had passed since Molière's
company had become stationary at the Petit Bourbon
theatre, and they had only just had time to acquire
a firm footing in the public favour,[1] when a blow fell
which might easily have been fatal to them.

A man named Ratabon was superintendent of the
royal buildings, which included the Petit Bourbon
theatre as belonging to the Louvre.   One day—on the
11th October 1660—in the middle of the season,
Ratabon set to work, without the slightest notice, to
pull down the theatre, the use of which had been granted
by the King to Molière and the Italians.   To the
stupefied actors' demand for an explanation, he replied that the demolition of the building had long ago
been decided upon, and that now Perrault, the architect,
had requested that it should be carried out, to make
room for the new colonnade of the Louvre.   So far,

---

[1] After *Les Précieuses ridicules* Molière obtained an almost equally great
success with his fourth play : *Sganarelle ou Le Cocu imaginaire*.   It was
performed thirty-four times at the Petit Bourbon in May 1660 and the
following two months, besides nine times at the command of Louis XIV.

he was perfectly right; only there was no call for such haste in this brutal ejection of Molière and his companions, for the new buildings were not begun till five years later, and the general opinion was that the want of consideration shown by the superintendent had been inspired by the chink of certain "arguments" from the Hôtel de Bourgogne.

Molière, therefore, found himself suddenly and unexpectedly in the street. It is clear, however, that the King was really fond of the merry author and actor, for he had scarcely complained of the injustice done to him, when, in compensation, the King made him a present of the magnificent old theatre of Richelieu, which the Cardinal had bequeathed to the King together with the whole palace. Its name was now the Palais Royal, and it continued to be so called after becoming a theatre.

The worst of this arrangement was that the theatre of Richelieu, having been out of use for about twenty years, was in a bad state of decay. "Three beams of the roof were rotten . . . and half of the auditorium had no ceiling and was falling into ruins," says La Grange in his Register.[1]   But this drawback also was remedied by the King, and he profited by the opportunity to reprimand his superintendent, giving him peremptory orders to have the Palais Royal theatre repaired at once.   At the same time he allowed the actors to remove the boxes and all the other fittings of the Petit Bourbon.   They did not, however, get the "machines," as the Signor Vigarani, who had been recently called

[1] *Régistre de La Grange*, pp. 25 f.

to Paris from Italy as "decorator," reserved them for himself under the pretext that he wished to use them for court performances in the Tuileries, whereas in reality he burned them one and all, being jealous of his deceased predecessor and countryman, the highly distinguished Torelli, whose ingenious inventions in the way of theatrical "machines" he wanted to destroy, so as to annihilate even his memory.[1]

The rebuilding of the Palais Royal took about three months—three months of the good winter season, and we can understand that the two companies of the Hôtel and the Marais profited by the opportunity to lay snares to tempt the actors away from the rival company, in order to put an end to its existence.   But it must be recorded, to the honour of Molière's comrades, that not one of them forsook him at this critical moment, when the other theatres were holding out assured positions as bait.

"The whole 'Troupe de Monsieur' stood together," says La Grange in his notes ; "all the actors were fond of their chief, M. de Molière, who besides his talent and extraordinary ability, possessed an honesty and a charm of manner which compelled them all to declare that they would try their fortune together with him, and that they would never leave him, whatever proposals were made them, and whatever advantages they might be offered elsewhere."

It is as beautiful as it is rare to see such a spirit of solidarity and such submission to superior powers, as shines in these lines.   Perfect concord is always rare among actors, but especially so when times are bad ;

[1] *Régistre de La Grange*, pp. 25 f.

and as we can scarcely suppose humanity to have been much better then than now, it testifies to a unique power in Molière of winning the confidence and affection of those about him.

This confidence was never for a moment disappointed. While the rebuilding of the new theatre was in progress, the company earned the money needed to pay the workmen by playing in many private houses and at Court. And at the beginning of the following year, on January 20th, 1661, they were able to open the Palais Royal theatre with *Le Dépit amoureux* and *Le Cocu imaginaire.*

At first, however, there was no great rush to the new place. The intrigues of jealous enemies may have done some harm ; it must be confessed also that Molière was not happy in the new play he brought out there. Once more—for the last time—he had yielded to his inclination for the heroic drama and written *Don Garcie de Navarre*, in which he himself appeared as the Spanish Prince who suffers the torments of jealousy.

The play was a complete failure—it is the only work of Molière's which had no success at all ;—it was only acted seven times, and on the last occasion the proceeds were seventy francs. And Molière as performer of the principal part reaped as little approval as the heroic comedy itself.

It is not easy to reconstruct a deceased actor's manner of acting, and we know little of Molière's attempts as a tragedian, except that they were failures.

This, however, we do know, that the tragic style of the Hôtel de Bourgogne—the leading style and the only

one in favour—prescribed a kind of chanting declamation.[1]
This school, the absurdities of which held their ground for
a long time and constantly reappear, though at the present
day they have no really noteworthy advocate or apologist,
was naturally distasteful to Molière. To his unaffected
mind naturalness was the principal point in art, and he
could not understand that in the serious drama the actor
had to go against nature if he wished to feel or to inspire
enthusiasm. For this reason he tried to introduce into
tragedy a delivery as natural as that which he employed
successfully in comedy; but he probably lacked the
histrionic power which might convince others of the
correctness of his own method. For in art neither
principles nor naturalness alone are sufficient. In serious
representation especially, physical means and tragic
temperament are indispensable, if naturalness is to be
converted into sublime art. And here, no doubt, lay
Molière's shortcoming.

At all events, as far as we know, he did not find a
single adherent in his attempts at reform, and after the
last failure he gave up experimenting with the "heroic"
style. He did not even print *Don Garcie*, but used some
of its scenes for his *Misanthrope*,[2] the unromantic subject
and more everyday characters of which were far more
suitable to his talent.

[1] The author of *Entretiens galants*, published by Barbin, 1681, distinctly
says so in speaking of the celebrated Mlle Champmeslé; "the recitation of
actors in tragedy is a *kind of song*, and you will acknowledge that la Champmeslé would not please you so much, if she had a less agreeable voice."

[2] Comp. *Don Garcie de Navarre*, ii. 5 and iv. 8 with *Le Misanthrope*, iv. 3.
In his *Amphitryon* also some verses of *Don Garcie* are reproduced. This
work was not printed till after Molière's death—in the complete edition of
1682.

To Molière's enemies his defeat as a tragedian became an inexhaustible source of gibes and sneers, which they never tired of pouring out in torrents on the head of their otherwise superior rival.

But hostilities had not yet broken out openly. The unfavourable impression he had made with his unsuccessful *Don Garcie* Molière quickly effaced by means of two other plays ; first with *L'Ecole des Maris*—a little masterpiece of natural and graceful comic power—and shortly afterwards with *Les Fâcheux*, a hastily written, but topical and amusing satire. These two real successes were very encouraging for the company and increased its popularity.

But this was nothing compared with the sensational, uproarious—we feel tempted to say, scandalous—success of *L'Ecole des Femmes* in the following year (December 26th, 1662). It is very difficult for us to understand how this play, the classical verses and ingenious situations of which we now enjoy with calm pleasure, but without the slightest excitement, at that time regularly turned Paris upside down and set sensible people raging against each other.

In his preface to the first edition of the play Molière writes : " At first many attacked this play, but the laugh remained on its side, and all the bad things said about it did not prevent it from becoming a success with which I have reason to be satisfied."

Such words are indeed quite insufficient to describe the uproar caused by this play—in our eyes so unexciting. To understand it, we must bear in mind that Molière was a regenerator of French comedy. In the highly literary and fashionable circles of the time tragedy was

considered the only acceptable form for dramatic authors
to choose.   Comedy was looked upon as a much lower
and much easier *genre*; and it must be confessed that
the majority of the comedies produced were of very
slight value; their characters were quite conventional,
and their action generally consisted of unreal farcical
situations.   Then Molière appeared and inspired this
hitherto unimportant *genre* of art with abundant reality,
with living, everyday characters, talking a vigorous,
natural and pithy language, which was quite new on the
stage, and very far removed from the inflated and
artificial brilliancy which was considered the acme of
perfection in dramatic style.

The general public was hardly able to understand
the nature of the new element introduced by Molière,
but it was amused and involuntarily attracted.   He
touched its old Gallic sound-board—which had never
fully responded to the over-ingenious and affected
style—and his ideas were not too high for the simple
intelligence of his hearers.

But the men of literature, both the exalted members
of the Academy—who never considered the greatest
poet of the century worthy of being admitted within their
circle [1]—and the less superior purveyors of literary food to
the theatres, who saw this newcomer, this arrogant up-
start and tasteless plagiary, as they considered him,
rising on so mighty a wave of popularity, conspired
together *en masse* and resolved to make a serious effort

[1] It was not till the year 1778 that the French Academy tried to repair
this wrong by unveiling a bust of Molière, on which as an apology and without exaggeration was inscribed the following motto : " His Honour lacked
nothing, but He was lacking to ours."

to defeat their dangerous enemy. It is said that even the great Corneille felt much annoyance at the extraordinary success of *L'Ecole des Femmes*.[1] At that date he was no longer young (fifty-six); his later tragedies were written in an artifical, bombastic style entirely foreign to that of Molière; and finally, he had for several years been strongly attached to the Hôtel de Bourgogne, which after the death of Mondory had been the principal home of his works.

If Pierre Corneille was really a member—or perhaps even in secret the originator—of the league which was now formed against Molière, the latter must be acknowledged to have revenged himself in an exquisitely noble way, for at a time when Corneille had become utterly unsuccessful, Molière attached him to his theatre and even paid him a very high remuneration for plays which had no attraction whatever for the public.

However this may have been, the Hôtel de Bourgogne was at any rate the workshop where all the intrigues against Molière were fabricated. It is very probable that this theatre had suffered considerably from the

[1] This accusation of jealousy comes, it is true, from a bitter enemy of Corneille's, the Abbé d'Aubignac, who at the same time ridicules him for adding *de*, the particle of nobility, to his name. He writes as follows : "What an idea of you, at your age, to improve your name and call yourself, M. de Corneille ! The author of *L'Ecole des Femmes*—pardon me for speaking of this play which exasperates you and which you have tried to crush by your intrigues ever since its first appearance on the boards—the author of this play, I say, makes one of his actors relate that a neighbour of his has surrounded a plot of meadow with a ditch, and then called himself M. de l'Isle, which they say is the name of your little brother."—4*ᵗᵐᵉ Dissertation concernant le Poème dramatique.* In another passage of the same dissertation the malicious Abbé returns to Corneille's jealousy of the comedy of Molière, which he calls the " trophies of Miltiades that keep Themistocles from sleeping."

interest which centred round the Palais Royal on
account of *L'Ecole des Femmes*. The proceeds of that
play were enormous for those times. *L'Ecole des Maris*
and *Les Fâcheux* had been considered very great successes, yet the daily proceeds of those plays—as we see
in La Grange's Register—were very far from equalling
those of *L'Ecole des Femmes*. The first twelve performances of *L'Ecole des Maris*, for instance, yielded an
average daily return of 810 francs, whereas the first
twelve times the play-bill announced *L'Ecole des Femmes*,
the average profits were 1173 francs. As in those days
the number of paying play-goers was not very large, it is
most probable that meanwhile the Hôtel de Bourgogne
stood empty.

Indeed, the great Royal Actors did not fail to accuse
Molière of luring people to his theatre by all kinds of
humbug and illegitimate means, in order that he and his
theatre might become the rage.

Theatrical criticism, properly so called, was in those
days written by two men, the good-natured chatterbox
Loret, who in his pamphlet, *Muse historique*, reported the
events of the day in abominable verses, and de Visé, a
polished writer of mediocre talent, whose apparent
impartiality and sober statement of facts concealed much
jealousy of great and highly-gifted minds.

Neither of these two, however, gave Molière any
particular reason to feel offended, though de Visé dealt
him some unpleasant blows like the following : "This
play produced quite novel effects. Everybody thought
it bad, and all rushed to see it. The ladies blamed it,
yet they went on going to it. It was successful without

pleasing, and it pleased many who did not think it good,"
etc., but he also adds high praise like the following :
" There are things in it as natural as if nature herself
had written them.   There are inimitable passages, and
so well expressed, that I cannot find words sufficiently
strong and graphic to give you an idea of them." [1]   At
the same time he accentuates a point which was evidently
of decisive importance for the success of *L'Ecole des
Femmes* ; that is, the manner in which it was acted.
It seems to have been performed with a precision
hitherto unknown, and with a perfection of *ensemble*
which was not generally seen.   " Never was a comedy
so well performed," he writes, " or with so much art.
Each actor knows how many steps he has to take, and
his every glance is counted."

It was this art of the *ensemble* which afterwards
became the pride of the French theatre, and which never
misses its effect on the spectators, even if they do not
possess sufficient critical sense to understand its value.

In the passages we have quoted from de Visé
Molière as poet and as stage-manager receives an appreciation which certainly could not offend him.   The
attacks on his new play did not come from critical pens,
but from verbal comments in the literary cliques, and
they must, like the slander of Don Basile, have risen into
a " powerful cannonade " since Molière was prompted to
retort from the stage itself.   He produced his own
Criticism of the School for Wives in the shape of a little
play which was acted about six months after the appear-

---

[1] *Nouvelles nouvelles*, Part III. (See Parfaict : *Histoire du Théâtre
français*, ix. 174 ff.).

ance of the former, and the two pieces were performed together (on June 1st, 1663) before an audience, which in spite of the summer season, was more crowded than ever.

" I have only just come from it," the Marquis says in the *Critique*.

" Indeed, Monsieur, and what did you think of it, may I ask ? " says Climène, the *précieuse*. *Marquis* : " It is perfectly silly." *Climène* : " Ah ! how delighted I am to hear you say so." *Marquis* : " It is the most wretched play imaginable. Deuce take it, I could hardly get a seat. I thought I should have been suffocated at the door. I was never so much trampled on in my life. Pray look, what a state my rolls and ribbons are in." Whereupon Elise observes : " That certainly speaks volumes against *The School for Wives*. You condemn it justly." *Marquis* : " I do not think there was ever a poorer play." [1]

It is the *Critique* that clearly reveals where the offences lay that had called forth the reproaches against Molière, and where his enemies were to be found. We see that first of all his old friends, the *précieuses,* were horribly scandalised at the coarseness of his language. They were utterly disgusted at Agnes's idea that children were born through the ear ; the " cream-tart " and the " soup " put them into a rage, but what revolted them most of all was the ominous " le." [2] This small and

---

[1] *Critique de L'Ecole des Femmes,* sc. iv.—The run indeed was so great that though *L'Ecole des Femmes* had been performed thirty-one times in the theatre, besides many times in private houses, it ran again for thirty-three consecutive performances when the *Critique* accompanied it ; and the first eight performances brought in an average result of 1400 francs.

[2] *Arnolphe :* "Did he not take anything else from you, Agnes ? (seeing her hesitate) Ah ! " *Agnes :* "Yes, he . . . *Arnolphe :* "What ?" *Agnes :*

apparently innocent word, which resolves itself in the
" ribbon," seems to have caused such a scandal, that
one of Molière's enemies alleged that people came
for the purpose of hearing that alone.

The marquises were not inventive enough to find
their own reasons for discontent, and could think of
nothing to say but " *tarte à la crème* " in a thousand
different ways. But the Marquis in the *Critique*, is
able to refer to the actors, to those, that is, of the other
theatres, for, he asserts, those who have seen the play,
have said the worst that can be thought of it. " Ah ! "
replies Dorante, who is the mouth-piece of Molière, " I
will not say another word ; you are right, Marquis.
Since the other actors speak ill of it, surely we ought to
believe them. They are all enlightened people, and
speak disinterestedly."

But the poets, his dear colleagues, were perhaps the
worst, and the tone in which he defends himself against
them reveals a repressed anger and disgust, which differ
somewhat from the disdainful humour with which he
laughs at the *précieuses* and the marquises. Thus, for
example, Dorante says, rather boldly, in the face of the

" Took " . . . *Arn.:* " Oh ! " *Agn.:* " The [" le "] *Arn.:* " What did you
say ? " *Agn.:* " I dare not ; you may be vexed with me." *Arn.:* " No ! '
Agn.: " Yes, you will ? " *Arn.:* " Good heavens, no ! " *Agn.:* " Swear
you won't ! " *Arn.:* " I swear it ! " *Agn.:* " He took my . . . you will be
angry ! " *Arn.:* " No." *Agn.:* " Yes." *Arn.:* " No, no, no, no ! The
deuce, why this mystery ? What did he take away from you ? " *Agn.:*
" He . . . *Arn.:* (*aside*) " I suffer the tortures of the damned." *Agn.:* " He
took from me the ribbon you gave me."

Uranie, the woman of sense in the *Critique*, defends this *double entente*
(and there is no denying that a *double entente* it is) as follows :—" She does
not utter one word indelicate in itself ; and if you choose to see anything
else underneath, the nastiness lies in your own mind, and not in hers ; for
she is only referring to a ribbon which was taken from her."

Court of the *grand monarque*: "The Court has some
ridiculous persons in it, I grant you, and, as you know, I am
the first to jeer at them.   But, upon my word, there are
plenty among professed wits ; and if we gibe at a few
marquises, I fancy there is much more ground for
ridiculing authors.   It would be fine fun to put their
learned affectations and absurd squeamishness upon the
stage, their vile habit of killing folks by their plays, their
greed after praise, their poverty of ideas, their traffic in
reputation, their offensive and defensive cliques, as well as
their wars of wit and their battles in prose and in verse."

His brother-poets repeat to him over and over again,
that tragedy is the highest and most difficult branch of
art, and that he sins against the sacred so-called
Aristotelian rules.   His scorn of these ridiculous reproaches goads him to advance some rather doubtful
theories.   On the sublimity and difficulty of tragedy he
speaks his mind with most refreshing sincerity : " I am
of opinion," he makes Dorante say, "that it is a great
deal easier to express deep feelings, to harangue Fortune
in verse, to rail at Destiny, and to reproach the Gods,
than to enter familiarly into the ridiculous situations of
life . . . When you draw heroes, you do as you like.
You have but to follow the riotous flight of your
imagination, which often drops truth to snatch at the
marvellous.   But when you depict men, it must be done
faithfully ; such portraits must resemble men and women,
they are useless unless the people of your age are
recognisable therein."

Nor does he much respect the sublime "rules" of
poetry.   In the *Critique* the poet Lysidas who thinks

L'Ecole des Femmes very bad, says : " Those versed in Aristotle and Horace see at once, madam, that this comedy sins against all the canons of art." To which Uranie replies : " I must confess that I am not familiar with those gentlemen ; I do not know anything about the canons of art." And a little later she continues : " I have noticed one thing in these gentlemen [the poets] : those who talk most of the canons and know more about them than others produce the comedies which no one thinks good." And Dorante now takes them seriously to task : " You are an amusing set with your canons, with which you confuse the ignorant and deafen us perpetually. To hear you talk it would seem that these canons of art were the greatest mysteries in the world ; and yet they are nothing but a few simple observations, made by commonsense upon that which may lessen the pleasure taken in these poems." And he adds the very dangerous maxim, which can only be excused by his irritation at the conceited pedantry which had provoked it : " I should much like to know whether the grand rule of all rules is not the art to please : if a play put on the stage does not attain that end, it has not followed a good course."

The swashing blow which Molière in his *Critique* directed against his enemies *en masse*, at once struck home in the right quarter.

Very shortly after the *Critique* there appeared a reply with the long-winded title : *Zélinde, or the real Critique of the School for Wives and the Critique of the Critique*, by de Visé, and subsequently a play at the Hôtel de Bourgogne entitled : *The Painter's Portrait*

or Counter-critique of the School for Wives, by the young
dramatic author Boursault.

There is not much difference between these two
attacks, the latter of which appears to have borrowed its
idea from the former.   De Visé seems to have seen a
satire on himself in the poet Lysidas—a figure so typical
that more than one author thought it aimed at himself—
and wrote his *Zélinde* in the form of a comedy, though it
was probably never performed in a regular theatre.
Ostensibly it was a purely critical attack, pointing out
with pedantic minuteness an endless number of faults
supposed to have been committed by Molière in *L'Ecole
des Femmes*, faults which for the most part centre round
the circumstance that Molière had laid the scene of his play
in the street, which undoubtedly causes several absurdities.

But underlying these complaints, which profess to be
impartial, we may discover a number of poisoned stings,
sharpened by de Visé's jealousy, which he is quite incapable of concealing.   He alludes to the insult which
Molière was said to have suffered at the hands of the
Duke de la Feuillade.[1]   He tries to excite the clergy
against him by insinuating that Arnolphe's law of matrimony is a profanation of the ten commandments ; the
courtiers, by wondering that they put up with being
ridiculed on the stage ; and the actors by asserting that
Molière no longer regards himself as their comrade, since
he has been acknowledged as an author.[2]

But the play, the scene of which is laid in a lace-shop

---

[1] Comp. p. 103 note.

[2] Alluding to the fact that at this period Molière had obtained a royal
pension of 1000 francs as a *bel esprit*, Louis XIV.'s delicate and decisive
way of making his voice heard in the controversy over *L'Ecole des Femmes*.

of the Rue St Denis, where different people meet and most tediously pour out their opinion about *L'Ecole des Femmes* and *La Critique de L'Ecole des Femmes*, is so long-winded and written with so little talent, that it can scarcely have produced much effect, even in reading. The only interesting part of it is a little description of Molière, who is supposed to be in the lace-shop, while the customers are in a room upstairs. They want him to come up to them, but the shopkeeper comes back and delivers the following speech : " Madam, I am very sorry, but I cannot satisfy you. After I entered the room Molière did not say a single word. I saw him leaning on the counter like a man dreaming. His eyes were riveted on two or three persons of distinction who were bargaining about some lace. He seemed to be paying attention to their talk, and by the expression of his eyes it seemed as if he were looking down to the bottom of their souls to discover what they did not say. I even think that he carried a little note-tablet with him, and hiding it under his mantle, secretly took notes of what they were saying." To this one of the customers replies : " Perhaps it was a pencil, and perhaps he was drawing their grimaces in order to present them naturally on the stage ? "

" If he has not drawn them on his tablet," the shop-keeper continues, " I am sure he has impressed them on his imagination. He is a dangerous person. There are people who never go out without their hands,[1] but it can be said of him, that he never goes out without his eyes and his ears." [2]

[1] A common saying about thieves in France.

[2] *Zélinde*, sc. 6 (reprinted in Schweitzer's *Molière-Museum*, I., vol. iii., pp. 40 f.).

The Painter's Portrait, unlike *Zélinde*, was written on purpose for the stage, probably indeed by order of the Hôtel de Bourgogne company. Edmé Boursault, its author, was a young[1] and aspiring dramatist, without education or name, but willing to serve the theatre which produced his plays, and—just like modern poets who are journalists as well—ready to attack the rivals of his patrons. Later he wrote plays, which were by no means without talent and had a great success,[2] but *The Painter's Portrait* reveals but few of his gifts. It is an extremely shallow imitation of Molière's *Critique*, but with an opposite intention, and the would-be witticisms are too silly for words. For instance: *L'Ecole des Femmes* ought to be called a tragedy, because the death of Agnes's cat occurs in it.

Boursault, who at that time was still unknown, indeed found his master, when he tried to make his way by enlisting against Molière.

Biographers of Molière are in the habit of pitying the great master and venting their scorn in scathing abuse of his antagonists for their low attacks on him. Their pity indeed is scarcely needed, and it must be admitted, judging from the literary remains of this theatrical controversy, that Molière himself, at the out-set at any rate, was by far the worst offender. De Visé is malicious, Boursault impertinent, but Molière flagellates his antagonists with whips of fire.

[1] De Visé was no older (they were both born in 1638), but, like many theatrical critics, he had adopted a tone of supreme authority, which even at the age of twenty-five made him appear a tedious old prig.

[2] For instance : *La Comédie sans titre, ou le Mercure galant,* a play in five acts, in verse, which remained in the *répertoire* for more than a hundred years.

Let us see how he treats Boursault in the *Impromptu
de Versailles*,[1] which was his prompt reply to *The
Painter's Portrait*.   He begins by insinuating that
Boursault is not the real author of the play, but that
all the actor-authors of the Hôtel de Bourgogne have
each added some strokes to the picture, without having
the courage to reveal their names, and that they have
purposely chosen an unimportant author to figure on
the play-bill.   When Mlle. de Brie suggests to him to
expose the little scribbler on the stage in return for his
impudence in writing against people who have done him
no harm, Molière replies: "How foolish you are!   M.
Boursault is a fine subject with which to divert the Court!
I should much like to know in what manner I could
set him forth to render him amusing, and whether, if
he were flouted on the stage, he would be lucky enough
to make people laugh.   It would be doing him too
much honour to take him off before an august assembly;
he could not desire anything better; and he attacks
me wantonly in order to inform me, in some way or
other, that he exists.   He is a man who has nothing to
lose, and the comedians have set him loose upon me
only to involve me in a silly quarrel, and by that artifice
to turn me away from other works I have to write.   Yet
you are all simple enough to fall into the trap, but,
nevertheless, I shall make a public declaration about
it.   I do not intend to make any reply to all their
criticisms and counter-criticisms.   Let them throw

---

[1] Comp. p. 117 f.   The *Impromptu de Versailles*, as its title shows, was
performed for the first time before the King at Versailles on October 18th,
1663, and in Paris on November 4th, with *Don Garcie*, the latter play being
revived with another actor in the title rôle.

all the abuse they can at my plays, I am perfectly willing.   Let them grab my plays after I have written them, turn them inside out like a cloak,[1] and put them on their stage, let them seek to profit by any amusing thing there may be therein, and by a little of my good fortune ; I agree : they are in need of it, and I shall be very happy to contribute to their subsistence, provided they are satisfied with what I can suitably grant them.   Courtesy, however, should have its limits : there are things which make neither the spectators laugh nor him of whom they are spoken.   I gladly yield to them my works, my figure, my gestures, my words, my tone of voice, and my method of delivery, to do with them and to say of them whatever they please, if they can extract any advantage therefrom. I do not object to any of these things, and I shall be delighted if the public is pleased thereby.   But if I yield them all this, they must have the goodness to leave me the rest, and not refer to such matters as those which I am told they fling about in their comedies. That is what I respectfully ask of the honourable gentleman who busies himself by writing for them, and that is all the answer they will have from me."

It is a treat to read such a well-turned attack, where the lashes fall from a firm and practised hand, and we seem to hear the applause called forth by such a speech from Molière, delivered with all the warmth of personal feeling on his own stage, applause from a sympathising audience, which was deeply interested in the battle

---

[1] Both *Zélinde* and *The Painter's Portrait* were, so to speak, old cloaks that had been turned, as they were written precisely in the form of Molière's own *Critique de L'Ecole des Femmes*.

between the two theatres and their authors. The attack, however, is not quite just. In his play Boursault has referred to no matter of a strictly personal nature; if the play was acted in the form in which we now have it in print.

Molière, nevertheless, did not limit his vengeance to this fierce attack. He knew and repeatedly stated in the *Impromptu de Versailles*, that " the great Comedians " were his principal enemies, and he found a very effective means of exposing them to public ridicule. Molière—as we have mentioned — possessed a unique talent for imitation. He had frequently amused his friends at their gay parties by mimicking the high-flown style [1] of his pretentious rivals ; and though he had but seldom an opportunity of going to their theatre,[2] he is said to have taken them off admirably.[3]

This talent was now utilised in the *Impromptu*, where he roused the laughter of the audience by exhibiting the affected tragic style of " the great actors," and his dangerous weapons were aimed in particular at the man who probably stood at the back of the whole controversy —the elder Montfleury.

A poet is supposed to come and ask if the company

[1] " Il a joué cela vingt fois au bout des tables,
  Et l'on sçait dans Paris que, faute d'un bon-mot,
  De cela chez les grands il payait son écot,"

says Alice in the *Impromptu de l'Hôtel de Condé*, sc. 6, in order to prove that the *Impromptu* of Molière was old and not improvised for the occasion.

[2] " As their days for acting are the same as ours [at that time Molière acted on Sundays, Tuesdays and Fridays] I have scarcely seen them more than three or four times since we came to Paris."—*Impromptu de Versailles*, sc. 1.

[3] This was acknowledged even by those who suffered by it. " It is quite true, he puffs and foams well, he can make his whole person swell, he has found means of dilating his face."—*Vengeance des Marquis*, sc. 2.

possesses any good tragic actors; for instance, who plays the kings (Montfleury's parts). A young man of pleasant appearance is introduced. "What?" says the poet, . . . "you are laughing at me? You want a King who is as big and as stout as four men put together; a King, i' faith, big-bellied as befits the part; a King of vast circumference who can fill a throne in proper fashion. Think of a King with a slim figure! There is one grave error to begin with."

He wishes to hear him recite some verses, and the actor recites in the most natural manner some verses by Corneille. But the poet at once interrupts him: "What! do you call that reciting? You are joking. You must say it with more emphasis. Listen to me!"

Molière next gives an exact counterfeit of the popular tragic hero, of whose manner we can form some slight idea by listening to Molière's explanations: "Do you see this attitude? Mark it well. Thus! Put the proper stress on the last line. That is what will attract applause and make people cheer (*faire le brouhaha*)."

And to the actor's objection that a King who is talking quite alone to his captain ought to speak a little more naturally, and not to roar like a spirit of hell, the poet replies: "You don't understand. Go and recite it your own way, and see if you will gain one single ' bravo.'"

When Montfleury has thus been dressed down, it is the turn of the two Beauchâteaus who acted the lovers' parts, of Hauteroche, the confidant, and of Villiers, the messenger of the tragedy.

Of the nature of these later parodies the play un-

29

L'ESCOLE DES FEMMES.

30

31

29—Raymond Poisson as Crispin.   **30**—Scene from *L'Ecole des Femmes*.

31—Armande Béjart, Molière's wife.

fortunately gives us no information, except a little remark about Mlle Beauchâteau's smiling face amidst the most heart-rending torments, a remark which has been quoted before.[1]

This method of attacking adversaries was almost as unusual in those days as it would be now, and though we may heartily wish that a style of art which is unnatural and detrimental to good taste should be thoroughly exposed to ridicule, we cannot wonder that those who received the blows did not look at matters from the same point of view, nor consider this mode of warfare permissible among educated people.   In particular Molière's sneers at Montfleury's fatness must necessarily have been in their eyes a violation of the rules of legitimate warfare.   This explains, if it does not excuse, the coarse attacks which were now directed against Molière.   But we must not entirely forget that they appear far more repulsive from a distant and literary standpoint, which only sees in them the low and mean assaults of insignificant and forgotten scribblers on a great and unique genius, than they did from a contemporary point of view, which knew them to be the hot-tempered repartees of rival actors to the burning blows of their adversary.

[1] Comp. p. 28.

X

THE *Impromptu*, as Molière had declared, remained his last " say " in the struggle.   While his adversaries now took up the fight in real earnest and overwhelmed him with the grossest insults, he henceforth adhered to strict silence, which was not even broken when the accusations against him became all but incriminating.

Just at this period a change occurred in Molière's private life, which was destined to render him vulnerable in a point, where he neither could nor would defend himself.

On February 20th, 1662 he had married Armande,[1] a very young sister of his old friend Madeleine Béjart, and this marriage was to become the most fatal event of his life.   It threw him into the painful and harassing companionship of a wife whom he loved, but who neither understood him nor was worthy of him, and that just at the time when he stood at the zenith of his life and talent, when he had gained the upper hand in the battle with his enemies, when he was rich and popular, when, in short, he was blessed with all the gifts that genius and fortune could bestow.

Armande, at the age of nineteen was a fascinating,

---

[1] Her full name was Armande Grésinde Claire Elisabeth Béjart, and she was born about 1643.   No certificates exist either of her birth or her baptism ; her exact age is therefore unknown, and there is no absolute certainty who her parents were.

nimble, and graceful young woman (fig. 31) ; no regular
beauty—her eyes were too small and her mouth too large
—but piquant and pretty ; not particularly clever, but
quick-witted and lively in her talk ; as swift as a bird and
as fanciful as a spoiled child, with the enticing and insinuating ways of a cat.   We can understand the man who
staked everything to win her favour, and pity him for losing
his equanimity and peace of mind in this game of passion.

Molière was forty when he married Armande Béjart,
aged nineteen, and he was generally considered to have
been the lover of the elder sister.   Nothing more was
needed to set tongues wagging in a city like Paris, which
in the "great century," even more than at the present
day, was the most fertile hot-bed for scandal.

Mlle. Molière, as she was called on the stage, was
not as yet well known to the public.   She had not acted
before her marriage, and a year and three months passed
after her wedding before she appeared on the stage and
at once took a share in her husband's theatrical struggle,
playing the part of the witty and ironical young girl
Elise in the *Critique de L'Ecole des Femmes* and afterwards a similar part under her own name in the
Impromptu—"*Mlle Molière, satirique spirituelle.*"—
as we read in the cast.   In course of time she became a
most excellent actress.   Born and bred on the stage,
with a great natural talent for brilliant and coquettish,
piquant, witty and satirical parts, but less for serious and
sentimental characters, instructed by such a teacher as
Molière, who according to de Visé "would have
been able to teach even a fagot acting," with an
appearance which was nowhere shown to greater

advantage than on the stage, a sparkling liveliness of manner and an unique taste for dressing in an original and effective style, she was bound to attain perfection in her own *genre*.

But we have reason to believe that friction arose very early between Molière and his wife, on account of the contrast between her coldly serene and lively temperament and his deep, warm and excitable nature. Otherwise it is scarcely probable that his enemies would have begun so soon after their honeymoon to come out with allusions of so gross a nature as those which became the nucleus of the attacks on Molière.

The mere fact that he had married the younger sister of his former mistress was considered almost a breach of propriety.   But matters assumed even a worse appearance, when it was asserted on many sides that Armande was not the sister, but the daughter of Madeleine Béjart.   The great disparity of their ages might justify this belief, and the out-and-out scandal-mongers positively maintained that Molière had married his own daughter.[1]

When Molière declares in his *Impromptu* that he

---

[1] It was a widely spread belief at the time, even among people who did not mean any harm by saying so, that Molière's wife was the daughter of Madeleine.   We read, for instance, in the *Correspondance entre Boileau-Despréaux et Brossette* (1858, p. 517) : " M. Despréaux told me that Molière had been in love with the actress Béjart, whose daughter he married." The more malicious libel *La Fameuse Comédienne* (ed. Bonnassies, p. 6) writes in as positive a tone : " She is a daughter of the late Mlle. Béjart, provincial actress, who favoured so many young men of Languedoc at the time when she was happily delivered of a daughter. . . . She has been supposed to be the daughter of Molière, though he afterwards became her husband.   However, the truth of this matter is not certain."   In *Elomire hypocondre*, which is the absolute acme of vulgarity, we read a remark which, if a little more disguised,

will reply no more to the attack of his enemies, and uses
in general such strong and scornful language about these
attacks, we feel bound to suppose that his matrimonial
affairs had been alluded to, either by casting aspersions
on his wife's birth or by enrolling him very shortly
after his marriage in the ranks of the deceived husbands
so much derided by himself.   In the printed versions of
the attacks quoted above we find no such allusions, but
it is not impossible that the actors may have added them
ex tempore, or that the authors may have been afraid to
publish them in print.

At all events there was no lack of them in the
subsequent attacks.

The method of warfare used by the Hôtel was such
as to justify Molière in accusing them of turning his old
clothes.   Just as *The Painter's Portrait* was an imitation
of the *Critique de l'Ecole des Femmes*, the subsequent
repartee, down to the very title, was an imitation of
L'Impromptu.   The new play was called *L'Impromptu
de l'Hôtel de Condé*,[1] and its author was a son of the
fat heroic actor Montfleury, who, as we know, had been
the principal butt of Molière's latest piece.   It was

is in even worse taste : It says in speaking of Arnolphe who is educating
Agnes for matrimony ; "Arnolphe began too late to form her ; he ought to
have done it before she was laid in the cradle, in the way it has been done
by somebody else." However, the fact that this opinion had spread far and
wide does not prove anything. From modern theatrical history we might
quote equally widespread rumours about questions of paternity, which have
been proved to be entirely fictitious. As a matter of fact, in the marriage
certificate she is put down as the daughter of Marie Hervé, widow of the
late Joseph Béjart, *écuyer, sieur de Belleville.*
    [1] Possibly because its first performance had taken place in the *salons*
of the Duke de Condé, just as Molière's little comedy had been played for the
first time before the King at Versailles.

not unnatural that the son should wish to avenge his father, but the cause for which he had to plead was a bad one, and his play therefore turned out to be nothing but an accumulation of gross insults, clothed in a form which he had borrowed from his adversary. For the rest, Antoine Montfleury was by no means without talent, and several of his plays, which are gay and well written, though not in good taste, were very successful at the time and remained long in the *répertoire : Woman as Judge and Respondent*, for instance, the success of which almost equalled that of *Tartufe*. As the son of his father, young Montfleury—in 1663 he was twenty-three years old—so to speak, belonged to the company, to which a few years later he became even more closely attached by his marriage with the daughter of the celebrated Floridor ; and very likely the fierce abuse with which the play was abundantly spiced, was dictated by the revengeful feelings of his father and the other actors ridiculed by Molière. At any rate the insults contained in it seem almost too numerous to have been invented by one man alone.

The scene is laid in front of a book-shop in the gallery of the Palais de Justice, where a large number of persons are assembled, evidently with the sole purpose of abusing Molière.   At the very beginning the audience is given to understand that Molière, who has scarcely been married a year, is already being deceived by his wife.   His cause is advocated by a ludicrous marquis, for as Molière himself had chosen such a character for his assailant, Montfleury thought best to employ a similar one as his defender.   The marquis comes to buy a book in the shop.   The shop-keeper asks what author he wants. "What author?" he exclaims, "how can you ask? Molière, of course, this modern writer of burlesques, this chastiser of morals, who without the slightest scruple draws a naïve portrait of every ridiculous character, this scourge of cuckolds, this fool of the time, this hero of farce who snaps at everybody, whose capacity for picturing morals is so remarkable, that he himself seems to be one of those whom he describes."

With such vulgarities and outbursts of ill-temper the piece teems from beginning to end. At the same time there is a touch of the bitter feeling of a martyr at seeing the deeply serious plays and grandiose declamation of the Hôtel de Bourgogne set aside by the public for the tomfooleries of a juggler, a farce-player, a clown. We should not waste our time over this stupid piece of work, were it not that it contains a malicious caricature of Molière as tragic actor, which, in ridiculing his faults, casts a ray of light on the kind of effect he produced on the stage.

In reply to Molière's caricature of the elder Montfleury in *Nicomède*, he is here brought before us as Cæsar in the *Death of Pompey* (by Corneille). "That man is admirable," the marquis says, "he is incomparable in all he does." "Yes," replies Alcidon sneeringly, "he recites with great art, as, for instance, in *Pompey*, where he acts Cæsar. Madam, have you noticed those heroes in the tapestry on the wall?" *The Marchioness*: "I have." *The Marquis*: "Oh, it is easy enough to scoff!" *Alcidon*: "He is just like one of them. He comes in with his nose turned up, his feet curving like brackets, one shoulder sticking forward; his wig, which follows the lead of his shoulder, is crowned with more laurel leaves than a Mayence ham ; his arms are akimbo, his head thrown back like a laden mule, his eyes in fine frenzy rolling, and in reciting his part, his speech is interrupted by a constant hiccough." [1] Whereupon he gives an example of his tragic style, caricaturing it just as Molière had caricatured Montfleury.

Molière evidently had a better opinion of his personation of Cæsar, for he had his portrait taken in this part by his friend Mignard (fig 32). But it is undeniable that in this very picture, which is one of the few absolutely authentic of the many hundred portraits of Molière, we may recognise some of the features ridiculed by Montfleury. We see the many laurel leaves, the arm akimbo, the head inclining backwards, etc. Of the hiccough which marred his delivery, mention is made also by other authorities, who bore him no ill-will.

Thus Grimarest, the chatty old biographer of Molière, speaks of " a hiccough (*tic de gorge*) which troubled him, and which rendered his acting unpleasant at first to those who did not know him." But he also says that when your eyes were once opened to his fine conception of character, and to the delicate manner in which he expressed an emotion, you forgot this peculiarity, and owned that he was an expert in the art of declamation. Grimarest thinks that Molière had got into the habit of these jerky interruptions of his speeches, because originally he had been inclined to allow his tongue to run with such speed that the words stumbled over each other.

[1] *L'Impromptu de l'Hôtel de Condé*, sc. 4.

32—Molière as Cæsar in *La Mort de Pompée*.

In making efforts to restrain himself, he had fallen a victim to this peculiar spasmodic contraction of the muscles. It does not seem quite impossible, moreover, that the disease of the lungs or heart, which put an only too speedy end to his life and may have been smouldering in him for several years before his death, produced asthmatic breathing in passionate scenes, which gave the impression of a kind of hiccough.   Otherwise Grimarest strongly commends his acting, especially for being very carefully studied, not "casual like the acting of those who, having no principles of declamation, are uncertain in their art."   But even he unhesitatingly classifies Molière as a comic actor, including, however, in this *genre* such parts as the Misanthrope and others which cannot be classed as "heroic" or tragic.   "He could not adapt himself to serious parts," Grimarest observes, whereas in comedy he was always successful, "though people of superfine taste accused him of being inclined to grimace."[1]

It seems as if Molière treated the railleries of the Hôtel de Bourgogne with supreme contempt.   Just like Socrates, when Aristophanes brought him on the boards in *The Clouds*, Moliere went to see the parody on himself,[2] choosing a place particularly exposed to view, a seat on the very stage.   His arrival there caused the greatest sensation, and he had scarcely sat down, when the audience broke out into a prolonged and deafening demonstration.

---

[1] *La vie de Mr de Molière*, Amsterdam, 1705, pp. 131 f.
[2] Probably not the last mentioned, but *The Painter's Portrait* by Boursault.

It is the next libellous work : *La vengeance de Marquis ou réponse à l'Impromptu de Versailles*, which describes this piquant situation : Molière sitting calmly as an unconcerned spectator in front of his bitterest enemies, who, to his face, deride his art and defame his private life. The new comedy, which is generally attributed to the actor de Villiers[1] but is probably the result of the co-operation of several persons —de Visé, no doubt, among the number—simply repeats all the familiar attacks on Molière, calls him a monkey, and accuses him of stealing his ideas from others and of repeating witticisms which have already, for many years, been used by the jugglers of the fairs. The merciless allusions to his wedded life are boiled up again under even less disguised forms. In his *Impromptu* on Boursault's plays Molière had put the following speech into the mouth of Brécourt : " I myself can answer for a dozen marquises, six précieuses, twenty coquettes and thirty cuckolds, who will not fail to clap their hands." And in the *Vengeance des Marquis*, Ariste says : " There were more cuckolds at *The Painter's Portrait* than he says. One day I counted up to thirty-one . . . thirty of them applauded violently, and the last did his utmost to laugh, but he did not feel very much inclined to do so." Of course Molière's style in tragedy is again held up to ridicule, and almost in the same words as in Montfleury's play : " Look at that hip, it is charming. He sometimes recites his speeches like this,

---

[1] He appeared in person in the play as Philippin, who in a ludicrous caricature of a marquis, acts the foolish closing scene and sings a little lampoon on Madeleine Béjart. As the naiad in *Les Fâcheux* (comp. p. 116), she is compared to an old fish.

crossing his arms and with a hiccough at the close of each line."

La Vengeance des Marquis was the last word of the Hôtel in this struggle, and indeed, it had said enough. But the hostilities continued and extended even to the third theatre, the Marais, which now took up arms. Its utterance, which was a kind of prologue to a play entitled *Les Amours de Calotin*, written by Chevalier, an actor of its company, is only interesting in so far as, by way of a change, it sides with Molière. On the whole it gives the impression that the Marais theatre occupied a considerably lower position than the other two. Chevalier seems to think that the whole controversy is only a sham fight got up to amuse the public and to make money.[1] This point of view may be natural enough in a company which had no share in the game. But it was not correct. It was a perfectly serious struggle, in which both parties struck their blows to the best of their ability and with the most sincere desire to hurt each other. This appears also from the impartial poem which formed the literary termination of the controversy, *La Guerre Comique, ou la Défense de L'Ecole des Femmes* by P. de Lacroix.

Here we see Momus, whose attention has been called to the fearful struggle on earth in which the actors are killing each other with bad verses, crying

---

[1] Ces messieurs n'ont dessein que de nous faire rire,
Et quand vous les voyez se faire à qui pis pis,
Ce n'est que pour avoir nostre demy louis.
　　　　　—Chevalier : *Les Amours de Calotin*, i. 3.

(These gentlemen's only object is to make us laugh, and when you see them tearing each other in pieces, it's only to get our half-louis.)

for help to Apollo: "Hallo! cast your eyes on Paris. Apollo, Apollo!" *Apollo*: "What the d—— do you mean by screaming like that?" *Momus*: "Apollo!" *Apollo*: "Well, what is the matter? Arrant fool! he goes on crying Apollo! What has he done? *Momus*: "Apollo!" *Apollo*: "Again, let him go to the d——, the ass! Confound the lunatic!" *Momus*: All is lost. Whatever are you doing? Are you in love? Are you making war? Are you asleep while poets and actors are fighting on earth like dogs? There is nothing but "Impromptus," "Critiques," "Portraits" of the satiric painter in the Palais Royal and in the "Hôtel." Have you ever seen the like of such confusion? They are devouring one another!"

After passing in review all the different standpoints and accusations in a series of "disputes," in which of course poets, actors and marquises are represented airing their usual grievances against Molière, de Lacroix, with sound common sense, at last makes Apollo settle the quarrel in favour of Molière, and orders all the others to bow in due respect to him and to his admirable *Ecole des Femmes*.

The war between the two companies struggling for and against Molière went on for more than a year. He himself maintained absolute silence from the moment he had vowed to do so. Yet in the eyes of all—perhaps even in those of his antagonists—the victory remained with him. Hitherto the battle had been fought, we may say, on both sides, with more or less clumsy weapons, yet all the time on a certain artistic field, which lent it an interest of its own. But this long and hard struggle,

which is no doubt unique in theatrical history, was to
have an epilogue, which leaves the rivals of Molière
entirely at the mercy of posterity and justifies its
severest sentence.

Probably in impotent rage at seeing his enemy, in
spite of all attacks, stand in unshaken favour with the
public and the Court, Montfleury, the elder, whom we must
constantly consider as the life and soul of the whole onslaught of the Hôtel de Bourgogne, had recourse to the
utterly unworthy expedient of sending the King a
complaint of Molière's marriage, asserting that young
Mme. Molière was a daughter of her husband's former
mistress, thus hinting that Molière had married his own
daughter.

Our knowledge of this contemptible trick comes
among other sources from the correspondence of Racine,
who writes, frigidly enough, in a letter of December 1663
to the Abbé Levasseur; "Montfleury has written a
complaint against Molière and sent it to the King. He
accuses him of having married the daughter of a woman
who had formerly been his mistress. But Montfleury
has found no willing ear at Court." [1]

It must be said to the great credit of Louis XIV. that
he rebuffed Montfleury in the most peremptory way, and
with exquisite tact expressed his sympathy with Molière
by standing god-parent two months later, together with
Madame (his sister-in-law), at the baptism of the firstborn son of Molière and his wife.

On the whole, it is worth pointing out that on this, as
on several other occasions, the King supported the great

---

[1] *Œuvres de J. Racine.* Paul Mesnard, vi. p. 506.

actor and writer in the most delicate and effective manner. It will be said, perhaps, that he only did his duty. But history has so constantly to record instances of the tactlessness, blunders and crimes committed by monarchs, that the cases in which they did just what we think it was their duty to do are worth remembering with gratitude.

XI

Popularity of the Theatre in Paris—The Troupe of Mademoiselle—The Little Actors of the Dauphin—The story of Raisin's Spinet—Baron as a child—Poetical Development of Molière—His Circle of Friends —Disloyalty of Racine.

MOLIÈRE had come off victorious in the great theatrical conflict. His fame as a poet was established, and his theatre had become more fashionable than ever. For the rest, the mutual relations of the three theatres remained the same.

The Hôtel continued to maintain the first place in tragedy, the Palais Royal unquestionably was the home of the new comedy, and the Marais had an uncertain position without a fixed audience or *répertoire*.

In the course of time several new companies had appeared, but they had soon disappeared again. During the season of 1661-62 the chronicler Loret enumerates no less than six contemporary theatres in Paris. Besides the three we know, there were a Spanish company, which was not very popular ; the Italian troupe, which after a short sojourn in London had returned to its favourite resort, the French capital, and continued to share the Palais Royal with Molière ; and finally, an entirely new company, the Troupe of Mademoiselle,[1] which acted in a tennis-court in the Faubourg Saint Germain. Its principal actor was a certain Dorimon, who has left several proofs of having been a bad dramatic author, but also of having had all his plays performed by the company to which he belonged. Like Molière, as far as we know, he had been a successful provincial actor; but if he expected to have a similar career to that of his great contemporary, his hope was not realised. The Troupe of Mademoiselle soon disappeared from Paris, and at the same time from theatrical history.

Somewhat more importance, at all events more interest, attaches to another attempt which was made some years later, to form a new theatre of a peculiar kind with a company called The Little Actors of the Dauphin.

The origin of this company is strange enough, and it included in its youthful circle a few budding geniuses who were destined to become ornaments of the great French stage. It may not be out of place therefore to say a few words about it.

Its founder was a certain Raisin, originally an organist in Troyes, and the inventor of a so-called mechanical spinet, a *machine surprenante*, as Loret calls it, capable of playing by itself and at command all the pieces proposed by its owner. At the fair of Saint Germain this spinet created such an extraordinary sensation that even the King wanted to see and hear it. Raisin was summoned to the Palace, where the King and the whole Court went into ecstasies on hearing the

---

[1] *Mademoiselle*, that is Mademoiselle de Montpensier, daughter of Gaston, Duke of Orleans, uncle of Louis XIV.

ingenious and apparently miraculous instrument.   The
King ordered it to be wheeled into the Queen's room,
that Her Majesty might for once share his amusement.
But the magic piano had a most unexpected influence on
this exalted lady ; she nearly fainted with fright, and the
King gave orders to open the case of the instrument
then and there in order to reveal its mechanism.   Raisin
had to obey, and lo ! two charming little boys, the sons
of the ingenious organist, jumped out of the spinet, in
which they had been crouching and playing on a hidden
key-board according to their father's orders.   It was
high time, a contemporary author remarks, that the
boys were released from their prison, for they had been
locked up there for five or six hours.[1]

The boys were much petted at Court, but Raisin's
secret was betrayed, and his lucrative business—he is
said to have made 20,000 francs at the fair—was practically
ruined, though he kept it up for about a year longer.
Then, being naturally ingenious, he hit upon a new way
of making an income by his children.   He made them
dance and sing on a stage at the fair, and they scored
such great success that he formed a whole company of
diminutive actors, which included, besides his own two
sons and a daughter, a young boy named Michel Baron—
or Boyron, as his real name was—and which performed
real plays that were much applauded.

Young Baron was an orphan ; his father and mother,
who had both been distinguished players at the Hôtel de

---

[1] It is Grimarest (*Vie de Molière*, p. 54) who relates this little episode.
But he only speaks of the younger Raisin, Jean Baptiste, aged five, afterwards a very popular actor, as having been in the spinet.   In reality both
brothers were in it, as appears from other reports of the same event.

Bourgogne,[1] had died several years before. The fortune
they left had been spent by the uncle to whose charge
the boy had been entrusted. Then it was suggested
that he should become a member of Raisin's juvenile
company ; and it seems as if the eminent histrionic talent
of this child of the stage struck the manager at once, for
not only was the boy instantly accepted, but he soon
occupied the first place and became the principal
attraction of the little company.

Raisin, however, died, and though his widow continued the business, she did not possess his ability. She
went to the provinces, where she spent the little fortune
her husband had gained, and came back to Paris in
great difficulties. As Molière was well known for his
benevolence, she went to him and asked permission to
make use of the Palais Royal theatre for three
performances with her child-actors, who had been
allowed to adopt the name of the Dauphin. Mme. Raisin
had a great success, principally owing to young Baron
with whom the town became quite infatuated.

But a more important fact was that Molière saw him
and took an interest in him. By the training of the great
master, combined with his own extraordinary natural
talent and enthusiasm for dramatic art, he became,
during the last decades of the century, the most distinguished actor of the French stage.

This happened in 1666, when Baron was thirteen
years old. Both the brothers Raisin, when grown up,
became members of the French stage, and the younger
became a very good and popular comic actor.

[1] Comp. above p. 19.

Nevertheless the Little Actors of the Dauphin were soon dispersed, probably owing to the bad management of the widow Raisin, and after September 1666 we hear nothing more of this company, that seems to have been an imitation of the boy-companies formerly so fashionable in England, which even became dangerous rivals of Shakespeare's company.[1]

When, during the conflict with the Hôtel de Bourgogne, Molière declared that he did not intend to continue the fight, because he had other and more important work on hand, this was by no means a mere pretext for escaping from the quarrel. Since he had come to Paris his talent had been in constant fermentation, and he had now reached a point at which, as by natural law, one masterpiece was born after another.

Till the age of thirty-six he had led a merry careless life in the provinces, closely attached to the small company which stood under his leadership, and with the Béjart family as his only intimate associates. This was perhaps in one sense the happiest, gayest and freest period of his life. But, we know, it is not gaiety and happiness which create great poets. This period, at any rate, was the least fertile of his career as an author. Some very insignificant farces and a few neatly versified and well-constructed plays formed the only result of the first fourteen years of his theatrical career.

But scarcely did he find himself in Paris, when the atmosphere of the great city seemed to fertilise his talent into rich and luxurious growth, though at the same time

[1] Comp. vol. iii. *The Shakespearean Period in England*, pp. 39 ff.

undermining his bright spirits and physical health, and destroying the domestic peace which he had enjoyed during his easy-going, patriarchal life in the provinces.

In those days Paris was even far more than it is to-day the absolute intellectual centre of the civilised world, and Molière had the good fortune to be associated with the best of his class. The Béjart family may have been excellent and genial people, of whom Molière was very fond, and whose faithful friend he continued to be as long as he lived. But they were plain and practical professionals, not people of superior intellect, from whose companionship he could draw higher inspiration.

In the metropolis Molière found a much more fertilising set of influences. First of all he was in favour at Court and had intercourse with all the influential families, who, during the first period of the reign of Louis XIV. nearly all took an interest in art and literature, to a degree and an extent of which the sport-loving aristocracy of our own day—to whom a motor-race is infinitely more attractive than all the art in the world —can scarcely form an idea. And the great world with which he came in contact here opened a much wider field to his dramatic productions than his former life had done, and afforded a wealth of comic material for his observation, of which he fearlessly availed himself.

But of even more importance to his development was his friendship with the most distinguished and highly gifted men of his own sphere. During this period he lived on terms of the greatest intimacy with Boileau, Jean Racine, La Fontaine, Chapelle and the painter Pierre

Mignard.   Molière and the four authors met regularly
three times a week and formed a kind of unconventional
academy, the members of which discussed questions of
art and literature with a freedom of good-fellowship and
a boldness of paradox, which rendered their discussions
more valuable than the solemn dissertations of the
official Academy.

Boileau lived in the old Rue du Colombier, now Rue
Jacob, on the left bank of the Seine, in the genuine
Quartier Latin.   And here, in the rooms of the pungent
critic and the witty satirist, the good-natured, absent-
minded La Fontaine, the fiery but somewhat heartless
Racine (fig. 33), the ever humorous and ever thirsty
Chapelle, and Molière—on the stage the ardent, inspiring
genius, in his intercourse with younger friends comparatively quiet and acting as sober mediator in their
frequently violent debates[1]—met regularly three evenings in the week.   *Le Contemplateur*, Molière was
called by Boileau, who swayed the conversation
with his powerful voice and in his own self-
sufficient manner, chaffing La Fontaine, who, by reason
of his astonishing absent-mindedness, was slow to
follow the sudden changes in the discussion,[2] and

[1] La Fontaine alone (born in 1621) was a little older than Molière ; all the
others were several years younger.

[2] Once the little circle had entered on a discussion on "asides," and
La Fontaine attacked them very eagerly.   "It is perfect nonsense," he said,
"what does it mean? the audience is to hear what an actor who stands close
by is supposed not to be able to hear."   After which, as usual, he expatiated
on the subject, forgetting everything else.   Boileau observed aloud : "Isn't
he a rascal, this La Fontaine, a thorough villain !" continuing these "asides"
for a while without being heard by La Fontaine, until Molière and the others
burst out laughing.   Then he asked the reason of their mirth, and when told
by what means Boileau had refuted his long arguments, he good-naturedly
joined in the laughter.

preaching morals to Chapelle, who in return used all his cunning to make his severe mentor drunk.

Boileau, had the greatest admiration for Molière's talent, and the latter doubtless learned much from the solid classical knowledge and unbiassed intelligence of his friend. They were all fond of Molière on account of his open, affectionate character and the charm of his manner to all with whom he was in sympathy. With most of these friends these affectionate relations lasted for life. These cheerful evenings of witty intercourse with his intimates, that had begun in Rue Colombier, were continued in a remote little house at Auteuil, where Molière found a refuge from domestic torments and professional vexations.

One only of these friends broke away from the circle, and most probably a feminine intrigue was at the bottom of this rupture, which separated the two greatest dramatists of the century.

On December 4th, 1665, Racine's tragedy, *Alexandre*, was played at the Palais Royal by the company of Molière. There were six performances to good houses. Then, on the eighteenth of the same month, the *Régistre* of La Grange has one of those little notes which render this methodical actor's account-book a most valuable daily record, especially where important events are concerned. We read that " On the same day the company was surprised to see that the same play, *Alexandre*, had been performed at the Hôtel de Bourgogne. As this had been done in conspiracy with M. Racine, the company was of opinion that no author's share was due to the said M. Racine, who had behaved so badly as to give his tragedy

to other actors and to teach them to play it.   The said
author's shares [probably two] were redistributed, and
each of the twelve actors received his portion."

Racine's tragedy was acted three times more with
decreasing proceeds and then withdrawn from the
répertoire.

Racine's behaviour on this as on other occasions is
inexcusable.   It has been said that he thought the performance at Molière's theatre too feeble, and therefore
gave his tragedy to the Hôtel de Bourgogne.   But even
if this had been the case, Racine's surreptitious proceeding is quite unpardonable as a business transaction
and, particularly, as a breach of good-fellowship.   It was
downright treachery and could not be justified even by
the actual state of things.   For *Alexandre* was by no
means a failure at the Palais Royal theatre, as has been
maintained by several contemporary and subsequent
authors.   La Grange's figures speak very distinctly to
the contrary.   The first four performances yielded very
considerable proceeds : 1294 francs, 1262 francs, 943 and
1165 francs 10 sous respectively.   And theatrical
criticism, which was now in the hands of a certain
Robinet, was rather inclined to prefer the performance
at the Palais Royal to that at the Hôtel de Bourgogne.
On Molière's stage, La Grange, who was very popular,
played Alexandre, and La Thorillière (fig. 35), a clever
and highly esteemed actor, who had belonged to the company since 1662, was Porus.   It is possible that these two
were overshadowed by Floridor and Montfleury, who
with their great authority as tragedians played the same
parts at the Hôtel.   On the other hand we may suppose

that the young and brilliant Mlle. Molière as Cléophile,[1] and the much admired Mlle. du Parc, "shining like Diana, both by the magnificence of her dress and by her altogether enchanting appearance," in the part of Axiane, were quite on a par with Mlle. d'Ennebault and Mlle. des Oeillets in the same parts, at the Hôtel.[2]

Moreover, if we wish to see Racine's conduct to Molière in its proper light, we must bear in mind that the tragic author, who afterwards won such great fame, was at the time of which we are speaking scarcely more than a pupil of the great master. *Alexandre* was his second play, and Molière had readily accepted it as well as his first, *La Thébaïde*, though neither of them was of great dramatic power.

But the character of Racine shows several traces of the same ingratitude and cold selfishness, not least when, a year later, he lured Mlle. du Parc, the leading tragic actress of the Palais Royal, away from the stage of his former friend to an engagement at the Hôtel de Bourgogne. Possibly the clue to the otherwise inexplicable rupture between the two great men must be sought here.

Young Racine was greatly captivated by the mature charms of Mlle. du Parc, and the actress who was prudish as a rule, and had lost her husband, Gros René, in 1664, seems to have favoured the poet's courtship more than the advances of Corneille and Molière in former times.

---

[1] O justes Dieux qu'elle a d'appas,
   Et qui pourroit ne l'aimer pas !
(Just gods, what charms are hers ! and who could fail to love her) the poetic reporter Robinet exclaims about her in this part.
[2] Robinet's *Lettres en vers*, 20th December 1665, and 3rd January 1666.

The swiftly rising star of the talented Mlle. Molière may possibly have been an eyesore to the leading lady, who was no longer in the prime of youth ; and since, of course, it was out of the question to shake the position of the master's wife, she may have found it answer her purpose to attach herself to Racine, and with him to leave Molière.

This, however, is only a conjecture, but it is quite certain that Racine was very much in love with the beautiful du Parc, and that he had pictured her as the heroine of his future tragedies. But his plans were frustrated, for the year after leaving Molière the admired actress died at the early age of thirty-five.

If Racine proved a bad friend to Molière, others were all the more faithful, and Boileau in particular, though much younger,[1] had considerable influence over him. He may be supposed, especially, to have urged him on to higher and higher tasks. At all events it was during the period when his intercourse with Boileau and the other friends was most intimate, that Molière created his most profound and furthest reaching plays : *Tartufe*, *Don Juan* and *Le Misanthrope*.

XII

"Tartufe"—The Object of its Satire—Cabal of the Bigots—Obstinate Struggle over "Tartufe"—"Don Juan"—Courage of Molière in the Face of the Bigots.

MOLIÈRE had already shown his superiority to other playwrights by the brilliant and humorous satire with

---

[1] Boileau was born in 1636, and was therefore fourteen years younger than Molière.

33

34

35

33—Jean Racine.   35—La Thorillière.

34—Scenes from *La Princesse d'Elide*.

which he attacked the fashionable follies of his time. He showed courage enough to satirise the literary ladies and the aristocratic *petits-maîtres*. But many times bolder was the task he had undertaken in Tartufe.

This inimitable comedy was not directed against religious hypocrisy in general, or it would never have created the violent sensation and the furious opposition which were raised by it. Just as *Les Précieuses ridicules* was not intended as a satire on ordinary feminine affectation, but on the society of the Hôtel de Rambouillet in particular, the shaft in *Tartufe* was aimed at a certain religious clique known to all and feared by many, and far more dangerous and objectionable than the literary clique of the Hôtel de Rambouillet.

Since 1627, there had existed in France a religious society, called "The Society of the Holy Sacrament." It was not a sect properly so called, but an association of men and women, who, on the basis of the Roman Church, worked for moral purity and strict observation of religious ordinances, a kind of mission, which was founded originally with the best intentions, and counted many persons of high repute among its members, but which had gradually become a scourge to its fellow-creatures by insolent interference in other people's affairs, by espionage and delation, till it terrified the weak-minded and all who had reason for concealment. And, as with all similar so-called "holy" societies, this community had become a safe harbour for a number of rascals of the worst description, to whom religious hypocrisy and eager condemnation of others were the most comfortable cloak for their own vices and knaveries.

It was against this mischievous party, which was recruited from all classes of society, that Molière directed the satire in his *Tartufe*.[1]

Molière had undertaken the task of portraying this religious hypocrisy in all its phases : the cut and dried bigotry of old age in the incomparable Mme. Pernelle, who torments those about her and exposes herself to ridicule by constantly meddling with their mode of life, quite forgetting that she herself has been young and fond of amusement and fine clothes ; her son Orgon, whose bigotry has not yet reached the climax of incurable stupidity, which distinguishes the old lady.   Orgon is the blind fanatic who rushes into bigotry with the same intemperance as into its opposite when he finds himself deceived ; he is the natural victim of Tartufe, the impostor in the grand style, who practises hypocrisy not only in order to obtain good food and wine and all the other worldly benefits for which he craves, but because he finds a sort of voluptuous delight in deception.   Hypocrisy to him is a bold and dangerous sport, which affords pleasure in itself.   In this he differs from the bland M. Loyal, who practises bigotry in order to further his own nasty little trade.

The " Devotees " made much use of alms-giving as a reward to their obedient proselytes, and of numerous arbitrary imprisonments on vague accusations against persons who differed from their views.   One of their chief distinctive marks was their censure of the luxurious

---

[1] This has not been known hitherto, and guesses have been made both at Jesuitism and Jansenism.   But M. Raoul Allier, in his book *La Cabale des Dévots*, has proved to a certainty at whom the satire was aimed, and that Molière's contemporaries were quite aware of the fact.

habits and fashions in dress, which among other things prescribed very low, square-cut bodices for women, leaving part of the breast uncovered.

Thus, when Tartufe, attired like a Puritan, makes his long and carefully prepared entry in the third act, speaking of the prisoners among whom he is going to distribute alms, and is scandalised at Dorine's low dress,[1] no contemporary spectator could fail to see for whom the allusions were meant, and what in our day appears merely a witty scene and a well-drawn general type of a hypocrite, in those days must necessarily have been recognised as a daring and stinging satire on a powerful religious movement.

Molière was quite aware of the boldness of his satire, for he felt his way a little before presenting it in public, but he scarcely expected such violent opposition as that with which his play was received, nor imagined that it would take so long to overcome it sufficiently to have this masterpiece of his performed in his own theatre.

On May 12th, 1664, the first three acts were played before Louis XIV. at a series of court performances at

---

[1] *Tartufe* : " Si l'on vient pour me voir, je vais aux prisonniers,
       Des aumônes que j'ai partager les deniers . . . "
then to Dorine :
       "Ah ! mon dieu, je vous prie,
       Avant que de parler, prenez-moi ce mouchoir."
Dorine :   " Comment ? "
Tartufe :   " Couvrez ce sein que je ne saurais voir.
       Par des pareils objets les âmes sont blessées.
                                                    Tartufe, iii. 2.
(*T*. If any one comes to see me, say I have gone to the prisoners to distribute the alms I have received . . . (to Dorine) Ah ! for the sake of heaven, pray take this handkerchief before you speak to me—*D*. What for ?— *T*. To cover that bosom which I cannot bear to see. Such a sight is injurious to the soul.)

Versailles, and not till *five years later* did the great poet succeed at last in including *Tartufe* in his regular *répertoire*.

We know little of the effect produced by the first fragmentary performance, but there can be no doubt that it left a strong impression, though the principal character only made his appearance in the third act. Tartufe, as we mentioned above,[1] was played by Du Croisy, while Molière himself undertook the part of Orgon, which in a way was a more difficult and less grateful task.   Madeleine Béjart must have been excellent as the healthy, sturdy Dorine, and for the exceedingly subtle character of Elmire we can scarcely imagine a more attractive, piquant and witty performer than Mlle. Molière.

That its scenic and artistic effect was great, we cannot have the slightest doubt.   The King, however, dared not allow his favourite author to perform his play in public, though we may be sure that its caustic satire tickled and amused him.

Louis XIV. himself, at this gay and exuberant period of his life, was a decided antagonist of the "Society of the Holy Sacrament," or as it was nicknamed in secret "The holy Cabal."   But religious bigotry was so powerful, that he, absolute monarch though he was, dared not give permission to act a play in which bigotry was derided.   No more than five days after its appearance at Versailles the King forbade its public representation.   In the houses of great nobles who did not belong to the "Cabal," *Tartufe* was per-

----

[1] pp. 76 f.

formed now and then during the following months (in its complete form of five acts for the first time on November 29th, 1664) and its contents became so well known that a priest, a member of the "Cabal," Pierre Roullé, Doctor of Theology of the Sorbonne and Vicar of St Barthélemy, felt prompted to publish a pamphlet against Molière, in which his "holy" zeal goes so far as to demand that the author and his work shall be burned—literally burned on the pile—as heretical. But since the zealous priest had at that time committed some offence against the dignity of his Majesty, he received a stern rebuke from the highest quarters, and a few months after humbled himself before the throne with an apology worthy of a Tartufe.

In reply to this first onslaught, which in its violence totally missed its mark, Molière composed his first *Placet*, as it was called, which was addressed to the King.[1]

In this little epistle Molière pleads his cause in the most emphatic way, and far from humbling himself, makes many cutting remarks about the "holy Cabal." He complains in very strong terms of the prohibition of his play. "The Tartufes," he says, "have been in-genious enough in secret to obtain favour with your Majesty, in other words, the originals have succeeded in suppressing the copy, however innocent it is, and however much it has been found to resemble its prototypes." But since he is now accused of the most hideous things, nay, threatened with the stake and

[1] This and the two following *Placets* are prefixed to *Tartufe* in all editions of Molière.

with eternal damnation by a priest who does not even know the piece, he implores to be allowed to redeem his reputation in the only dignified manner, by a public exhibition of his play, so as to show people that it does not contain the blasphemous things alleged, and that it attacks only hypocrisy, not religion.

But this eloquent defence remained without effect. For the time Molière had to leave *Tartufe* where it was and to keep his theatre afloat by taking up other subjects.   By this time the public did not want to see anything but his own plays ; for instance, *La Thébaïde*, Racine's first tragedy, which was brought on the stage just at that period, yielded no proceeds at all.   Years of feverish activity began for Molière, and at the same time his mind was embittered by domestic griefs.   His relations with his capricious and coquettish wife became worse and worse, and his little son Louis died the day after the first performance of his comedy-ballet *La Princesse d'Elide* (fig. 34), which, in spite of its brilliant *mise-en-scène*, was no great success.

But Molière was not to be vanquished.   As early as the following February (1665), his great new play was ready.   The subject of it, which he had chosen in compliance with the desire of his comrades, who thought it would be sure of popularity, was the old Spanish tale of the unscrupulous seducer, *Don Juan or the Feast with the Statue.   Don Juan*, it is true, had in various forms gone the round of nearly all the Parisian stages, the last performance having been given at the Palais Royal by the Italians, who had reaped great success with their version of the subject.[1]   But it was thought that Molière with his great talents would be able to make something more and better out of the old subject than his predecessors.

And rightly so.   If, nevertheless, the play was not so successful as had been expected,[2] this may be accounted for partly by the fact that Molière had chosen to write his five-act comedy in prose, to which the public was not accustomed, and which it did not like (the same circumstance was detrimental to the success of *L'Avare*), and partly by the resentment kindled against it by the bigots.

Molière certainly had not forgotten the "holy Cabal."   With deliberate and very evident intent he uses Don Juan as his mouth-piece in retaliating on these "pious" enemies.   His words sparkle with caustic and bitter contempt of the rascals whose intrigues he has been unable to conquer, so they do not sound very appropriate in the mouth of the careless seducer, and it is Molière himself whom we seem to hear, when Don Juan speaks his mind thus : "Hypocrisy is a fashionable vice, and all fashionable vices pass for virtues.   The profession

---

[1] I may refer the reader to my analysis of the Italian imbroglio in vol. ii. *Middle Ages and Renaissance*, pp. 232 ff.   The Hôtel had had its *Le Festin de Pierre, ou le fils criminel* (*The Supper of the Stone Guest or the Guilty Son*) in 1659.   Its author was de Villiers, who himself played the valet Philippin (in Molière's, Sganarelle).   The Troupe of Mademoiselle brought with it from the provinces its *Festin de Pierre* by Dorimond, which had been performed in Lyons in 1658.   The Marais theatre did not follow suit till the close of 1669 or the beginning of 1670, when Rosimond's play, *Le Nouveau Festin de Pierre, ou l'Athée foudroyé* (*The new Feast with the Statue, or The Atheist struck by Lightning*) was performed.

[2] Yet it was performed fifteen times running at the very close of the season (from February 15th to March 20th, 1665), and the first ten times with very high average proceeds.   But it was not revived till many years later.

of hypocrisy has wonderful advantages.   The imposture
of this art is always respected, and though it be detected,
no one dares to speak against it.   Men are censured for
all other vices, and every one is at liberty to attack them
openly ; hypocrisy is a privileged vice, which, with its
own hand, shuts every one's mouth, and peacefully enjoys a sovereign impunity.   By means of shams a close
fellowship is formed amongst all people of the same set :
he who offends one, brings them all down upon him, and
even those whom everyone knows to act in good faith
in the matter, and whom we know to be really sincere,
these people, I say, are always the dupes of the others,
they run heedlessly into the snare of the humbugs, and
blindly support those who ape their actions.   How many
do you think I know who by this stratagem have dex-
terously patched up the disorders of their youth, who
have put on, as a shelter, the cloak of religion, and who
under this venerated guise, have permission to be the
most wicked fellows on earth?   It signifies nothing
that their intrigues and they themselves are known to be
what they are ; they are not, for all that, less credited
in society ; and a certain lowly bending of the head, a
humble sigh, and a pair of upturned eyes, justify, before
all the world, all they may do.   It is under this convenient shelter I intend to take refuge and to secure my
affairs.   I will not abandon my cherished habits, but I
shall take care to conceal them, and divert myself with
as little noise as possible.   If it should chance that I am
discovered, I shall, without raising a finger, find the
whole cabal looking after my interests, and I shall be
defended by it against, and in spite of everybody.   In

short, this is the true way to do whatever I please with impunity. I shall set myself up as a censor of the actions of others. I shall judge ill of all and have a good opinion of myself alone. I will never forgive anyone who has offended me however slightly, and I will quietly keep an undying hatred. I will act as avenger in the interests of heaven and, with this convenient pretext, I will persecute my enemies, I will accuse them of impiety, and I will let loose against them those indiscreet zealots, who, without knowing for what reason, will raise an outcry against them, will load them with abuse and will openly damn them on their own authority. It is thus we must profit by the foibles of mankind : a wise man adapts himself to the vices of his age." [1]

In that speech we are far from the natural thoughts of the Spanish libertine, but deep in the struggle against, the " Holy Cabal," which is all but mentioned by name, and in the defence of Tartufe. It did not remain unanswered. A certain doctor, B. A. de Rochemont, felt prompted to attack Don Juan with great violence, and to invoke the assistance of the King and the law against this blasphemous play. We can form an idea of the tone of his pamphlet [2] when we hear that he acknowledges some talent in Molière as a farce-player, but not otherwise, and that even as farce-player he places him below Gaultier Garguille, Turlupin, Gros Guillaume, Jodelet, etc., admitting however, that " now and then he can be pleasant and amusing in his *genre*."

In this style the greatest dramatic writer of his time

[1] *Le Festin de Pierre*, V. 2.
[2] *Observations sur une Comédie de Molière, intitulée Le Festin de Pierre*, par B. A. de Rochemont, Paris, 1665.

could still be described! Molière, however, had become hardened to attacks and could not be lured into controversy. Two anonymous adherents undertook to defend him, and one of them proved pithily and wittily that if the "holy Cabal" had been so scandalised at *Don Juan*, it was because they were afraid of *Tartufe*. Everything depended on preventing the public performance of this play.

In the following year, however, the Queen Dowager Anne of Spain, mother of Louis XIV., died. She had been one of the chief supporters of bigotry, and the King, who had long looked askance at all this mock saintliness, now made up his mind to dissolve the "Society of the Holy Sacrament," Molière at once took advantage of the King's favourable disposition to obtain his Majesty's verbal permission to have his *Tartufe* performed on the stage.

Meanwhile Louis XIV. joined the army in Flanders, and Molière made a few alterations in his play, left out the literal quotations from the Bible, which had been originally put into the mouth of his hypocrite,[1] and from the stern Puritan which he had been originally, converted him into a nobleman, like other gentlemen in society, dressed in "a small hat, long wig, a broad collar, a sword and a lace-covered coat."[2]   Not only the chief figure, but

---

[1] For instance, when Orgon has disinherited his son for abusing the hypocrite, Tartufe exclaims :—

> "O ciel ! pardonne lui la douleur qu' il me donne."
>
> (O heaven ! forgive him the grief he causes me.)

But in the original, which is otherwise unknown to us, he said :—

> "O ciel ! pardonnez-moi, comme je lui pardonne."
>
> (O heaven ! forgive him, even as I forgive him.)

[2] Molière himself, in his second *Placet* to the King, informs us of this toning-down of the principal character.

the whole play was disguised, and on August 5th, 1667, it appeared on the programme under the title of *L'Imposteur.*

In spite of the unfavourable season, in the heat of mid-summer, the theatre, of course, was over-crowded.[1]   But on the following day an officer of justice was sent from the mayor of Paris, M. de la Moignon, a willing instrument of the " Cabal," with orders to forbid any further per-formance of the play.   It even seems as if Molière had been in danger of imprisonment, and had escaped from the hatred of the Bigots only by referring to the verbal permission of the King to bring out this play.[2]

In face of this brutal interdict of the mayor the company was powerless, as the King was away with the army and had other matters to think of than theatrical affairs.   Molière could think of nothing better than to send a messenger to the monarch to try, if possible, to obtain his confirmation of the verbal promise, or at least protection against the venomous rage of the Tartufes.   Since 1665 his company had been under the direct patronage of the King, and no longer under that of Monsieur.   The King himself had desired to become its patron, and ever after-wards it was called " The King's Troupe."[3]

[1] According to La Grange's *Régistre*, the receipts were 1890 francs, whereas the two previous productions (*L'Ecole des Maris* and *La Veuve à la Mode*) only realised 87 francs, and no day in the month of July reached 300 francs.

[2] In his second *Placet* Molière himself says : " My play had scarcely appeared, when it was struck down by a power which we are bound to respect ; and all I could do in this encounter *to escape out of this violent storm* was to say that your Majesty had had the kindness to allow the per-formance, and that I did not think any other permission was needed, since it was your Majesty alone who had forbidden it."

[3] The company of the Hôtel de Bourgogne was called " The Royal Troupe " or " The sole Royal Actors."

Molière accordingly wrote a report to Louis XIV., the *Second Placet concerning Tartufe*, as it is called, in which he speaks his mind without the slightest reserve. He writes for instance : " However they [the Bigots] wish to make people believe that they are fighting the cause of God, it is by no means offences against Him that put them into a rage ; this they have proved sufficiently by tolerating without a murmur comedies that have been performed many times in public. These plays only attacked piety and religion, for which they care very little indeed. But my play attacks and exposes their own persons, and that they cannot bear.[1] They cannot forgive me for having unmasked their impostures in the eyes of the whole world." And he adds with much dignity and firmness : " I am awaiting in deep respect the decision which your Majesty will deign to pronounce in this affair. But one thing is certain, Sire, that if the Tartufes gain the upper hand, I must give up all thought of writing comedies."

With this bold and manly letter the two trusted actors, La Grange and La Thorillière (fig. 35), started for the army to meet the King, who was lying before Lille in Flanders. He received them very well and sent a message to Molière to the effect, that after his return to Paris he would have the play revised, after which they would be allowed to act it.

During the absence of the actors, which lasted for about seven weeks, the Palais Royal was closed, and

---

[1] In his later preface to the first edition of *Tartufe* (1669), Molière gives this same remark an anecdotal form, and a very pointed application to the little comedy of *Scaramouche ermite* then being played by the Italian company, which contained a good deal of coarse pleasantry.

ill with over-fatigue and vexation, Molière retired to his country house at Auteuil.

XIII

Molière's Power of work—His Matrimonial Troubles—"Le Misanthrope"
—"George Dandin"—The Resistance of the Cabal is overcome by
Molière, and "Tartufe" appears on the stage—Composition of the
Companies—Début of Baron on the Stage of Molière.

THESE last years of struggle had been too much for Molière, whose health had never been very robust. He had accomplished a marvellous amount of work. Besides *Tartufe* and *Don Juan*, *Le Misanthrope* had been performed during this period. It was the finest and most perfectly finished of all his masterpieces, and produced a twofold deep and personal effect by having its title *rôle*, Alceste, played by Molière himself, while his young and coquettish wife personated the brilliant but cold Célimène.

This comedy did not arouse the tempestuous, uproarious applause which rewarded some of Molière's less distinguished works. Still, it was acted twenty-one times running,[1] to a fairly numerous, though quickly

[1] Not thirty-four times consecutively, as stated by Mahrenholtz in his well-known manual *Molière's Leben und Werke.* As this German biographer of Molière is highly esteemed in his own country, and is also much relied upon by our own [Danish] students of Molière, it may not be out of place to call attention to the fact, that the statements concerning theatrical history of this author, who in other respects is very learned, are not always so trustworthy as might be expected from the assurance with which they are made and applied. The single page which treats of "the External History of *Le Misanthrope*" (p. 223), contains a good number of mistakes, owing to the fact that the author has no first-hand knowledge of the *Régistre* of La Grange. The first performance of *Le Misanthrope* did *not* take place on June 4th, 1664, but in 1666 ; it ran *not* for thirty-four consecutive performances, but for twenty-one

diminishing audience, and shortly afterwards it was revived and acted with the equally new farce *Le Médecin malgré lui*, which gave it a fresh start for a short run. The critics—Boileau, the expert, Robinet, the superficial, and de Visé, the inimical[1] — were unanimous in praising this piece more than any other of Molière's; and in Paris it constantly maintains its place as the finest and most typically classic comedy, while foreign theatres, as a rule, keep at a respectful distance from it.

While giving himself up with intense energy to these poetic productions, Molière had been constantly called upon to write a number of festive plays for court entertainments at Saint Germain and Versailles. Between the close of 1665 and the beginning of 1667 alone he wrote : *L'Amour Médecin* (comedy-ballet) *Mélicerte* (heroic pastoral), *La Pastorale comique* and *Le Sicilien ou L'Amour Peintre* (comedy-ballet), pieces which had all to be written and studied in the greatest haste. *L'Amour Médecin*, which is certainly a feeble play, though it has excellent points, was produced in the course of five days, and it stands to reason that such feverish activity as this, when Molière had to be author,

(thirty-four times during the whole year); the combined performance of *Le Misanthrope* and *Le Médecin malgré lui* brought the proceeds *not* to 773 livres 10 sous, but to 973 livres 10 sous ; these two plays were *not* performed together only once, but five times running, and each time to a much larger audience than the last occasions on which *Le Misanthrope* was acted alone. These details may seem very unimportant, but as the German author himself attaches importance to his erroneous figures and draws conclusions from them, it seems right to warn other students of his manual against trusting his authority too implicitly.

[1] In the previous year de Visé had had a piece (*La mère coquette*) produced at the Palais Royal, which accounts sufficiently for the critical *volte-face* of this poet-journalist.

manager, instructor and actor in his own person, was bound to tell upon his health.

But what told upon him most of all, mentally and physically, was the vexations and persecutions of the "holy" set, and his domestic worries.

Molière's relations with his wife had now come to such a pass, that they lived apart and only met at the theatre. This might so far have been less painful to both parties, if the husband had not cherished a deep and unquenchable love for the charming young actress. We need not believe all the unsavoury stories circulated about her by contemporary writers of gossip,[1] according to which she was not much better than a courtesan, who allowed herself to be "protected" by the most infamous libertines of the time. Most of these stories have been proved to be false, but it is no use either, like some modern authors, to represent Armande as a pure and innocent victim. That *rôle* suited her least of all, and she never even pretended to adopt that attitude.

Though we must be very cautious about identifying the fictitious characters of a dramatic author with persons in real life, and converting the creations of his fancy into actual and exciting romances, we cannot help tracing in the comedies of Molière his unrequited love and adoration of his bewitching and coquettish wife. Possibly his contemporaries were led to draw from fiction too strong conclusions concerning fact, by constantly seeing the two together on the stage, Molière as the jealous, deceived,

---

[1] The worst of them are collected in the libellous pamphlet already mentioned, *La fameuse Comédienne*, published anonymously in 1688. The author has never been discovered, and the attempts of several students of Molière to guess his or her name have led to no authentic result.

elderly husband or lover, his wife as the cold, sneering, coquettish or frivolous young woman. The public often too childishly transfer what they see on the stage to everyday life.

On the other hand, it cannot be considered a mere chance that Molière should constantly return to these relations between a man who is considerably older than the young beguiling woman, of whom he is jealous and suspicious, yet with whom he is hopelessly in love, and that it seems impossible for him to take a bright and cheerful view of the combination. He laughs at it always, but there is despair behind his laughter.

During the earliest period of his married life he still sides with the woman. Agnes in *L'Ecole des Femmes* is innocent in her love for the young man; she does not mean to deceive anybody, and Arnolphe fares so ill only because, with the self-consciousness and conceit of mature manhood, he thinks he can command the young girl's love by preaching to her about it, instead of winning it by placing himself on a level with her. But Arnolphe is not Molière, who was very far from being a conceited pedant; and Armande, the free child of the stage, had neither received the strict education of Agnes, nor had she her sweet temper. In *L'Ecole des Femmes*, which must have been written during Molière's honeymoon,[1] it is as if he congratulated himself on not having behaved so stupidly as Arnolphe, but at the same time as if he dimly felt what might happen, *if— !*

Le Misanthrope, which is more personal in feeling

---

[1] Molière and Armande were married on February 20th, and the first performance of *L'Ecole des Femmes* took place on December 26th, 1662.

36

37

36—Molière in mature age.   37—Scenes from *George Dandin*.

than any other play of Molière's, and was written during the "pious" intrigues against *Tartufe* and prompted by violent indignation at the disloyalty and smooth selfishness of high society, struck a very different note. Agnes, the naïve young *ingénue* has become a brilliant lady of the world.   Célimène does not play with love as with a kitten; to her it has become a complicated and risky game, on which she stakes her superficial intelligence and bright wit.   And Alceste does not reveal the foolish self-assertion of Arnolphe in his relation with the woman.   In his hatred of "the world," that is, the false world of affectation, hypocrisy and conceit, he is strong enough.   This hatred of all shams, whether in literature, religion, science or social intercourse, was the very nerve of all Molière's satire.   But in his love Alceste is weak.

"How is it that you, who mortally detest the morals of our time, can put up with what you find of them in this woman?   Are faults no longer faults in so beloved an object?   Do you not see them, or do you excuse them?"

So asks his sensible friend Philinte, and Alceste replies:—

"No, my love for this young widow certainly does not close my eyes to her faults, and in spite of the warm feelings with which she succeeds in inspiring me, I am the first to see them and condemn them.   But, nevertheless, whatever I do, I must confess my weakness; she has the skill to please me.   In vain I see her faults, in vain I blame her for them; in spite of all, she makes me love her.   Her charm is stronger than I, and I feel sure that my love will be able to purge her soul of the vices of our time." [1]

Célimène, however, contents herself with flirting, and Alceste still argues with her.   In *George Dandin* (fig. 37) the deepest bitterness is concealed under grim humour and farcical jokes.   If Célimène was a flirt, Angélique is an impudent, deceitful woman.   If in Alceste we meet with spite and misanthropy, in *George Dandin* we have dull resignation abandoning all resistance to his wife's unfaithfulness.   Modern spectators find some difficulty in laughing at this peculiar farce, in which Molière, in forced merriment and self-contempt, allows the unfaithful wife time after time to triumph over her miserable husband, and in the eyes of the audience permits both the right and the laughter to be on her side.   Dandin's final speech sounds all but cheerful ; it runs as follows : " No, I give it up !   I see no way out of it.   When a man has married a bad woman as I have, the best thing he can do is to go and throw himself head first into the water."

It was no doubt some consolation to Molière's bitter feelings that he was at last allowed to revive the performance of *Tartufe*.

The intrigues of the " Cabal " had been very detrimental to his theatre.   Its income had diminished considerably [2] since the good years with *L'Ecole des Maris*, *L'Ecole des Femmes*, etc., though Molière had written play after play, and among them such master-

---

[1] *Le Misanthrope*, i. 1.

[2] The season of 1665-66 yielded only 2243 francs a share ; 1666-67, 3352 francs, and 1667-68, 2608 francs, though in that year the company had only eleven shares ; whereas the season 1663-64, with fourteen shares, had risen as high as 4534 francs per share.

pieces as *Le Misanthrope, Don Juan, L'Avare* and *Amphitryon.*

At last, on February 5th, 1669, after five years of quiet, but bitter and persistent struggle, Molière gained the upper hand over the bigots, and *Tartufe* made its victorious and unimpeded entry on the stage. La Grange notes the event with specially ornate writing in his account-book ; the proceeds of the first performance were enormous (2860 francs, which would equal in value about 15,000 francs at the present day)—the highest figure ever reached in Molière's time. The piece was played forty-three times between February and June, and that season a share amounted to no less than 5477 francs 3 sous.

Of course all those years of waiting and the intrigues against the play had strained expectation to the utmost, and now the people rushed in crowds to the Palais Royal, exposing themselves to the most fearful crush to see the much disputed piece. " I swear to you in the name of all that is true," the chronicler Robinet writes in his report, " that curiosity, which like nature abhors a vacuum, here, as elsewhere, left no space unfilled. Many ran the risk of being stifled in the press ; cries such as : " I am choked ! I am dying ! O, Tartufe, must I pay with my life for my wish to see you ? " were heard incessantly."

And, better still, the interest in the splendid play was maintained, and Molière's company enjoyed prosperity again, yet without eclipsing its old rival, the Hôtel de Bourgogne, which, strangely enough, at the same time, happened to have almost as great and continuous a success with a play by Montfleury the younger : *La Femme juge et partie* ; the author's sister, the popular Mlle. d'Ennebault, gaining much admiration in the title *rôle*, especially in her scenes with Raymond Poisson as Bernadille.

Thus both the leading theatres had a lucrative season. On the whole, after the decease of the elder Montfleury, who had died, as it was said, of *Andromaque* in 1667, the antagonism between the two playhouses was not so strong as before.

The staffs were essentially unchanged. Molière had lost the two du Parcs who, as we have mentioned, had both died, the husband Gros René in 1664 and his beautiful and talented wife in 1668. Joseph Béjart, Molière's eldest brother-in-law, had died long before, and Louis, the younger, had by this time retired from the company with an annual pension of 1000 francs. This was the first occasion on which Molière's company paid a pension, following the example of the Hôtel de Bourgogne. Brécourt had transferred his services to the Hôtel in 1664. He was a very clever second-rate actor, but a wild, restless character, a great gambler and much addicted to wine and women.[1] His move to the rival theatre however, was probably not due to a rupture with Molière, for after the death of his great colleague, Brécourt, who was a tolerably fertile, though not very talented dramatic author, wrote a kind of apotheosis of his former chief, entitled *L'ombre de Molière* (*The Shade of Molière*).

[1] He was noted for his extraordinary pallor, and if the second valet in *Les Précieuses ridicules* is even nowadays represented as an unnaturally pale youth, it is a survival from the time of Brécourt, who played this part to the Mascarille of Molière.

Molière succeeded in acquiring some, though not quite adequate, compensation for the actors he had lost. According to the *Registre* of La Grange, from the beginning of the season of 1670-71, the company of the Palais Royal consisted of the following members :—

Messrs de Molière.	Mlles. Madeleine Béjart.
,, de la Grange.	,, Molière.
,, de la Thorillière.	,, de Brie.
,, Hubert,	,, Hervé.
,, du Croisy.	,, Beauval.
,, de Brie.	
,, Baron.	
,, Beauval.	

The new members were Beauval and his wife and Baron. Immediately after the beginning of the season, after Easter, that is, Molière must have seen that the company was of inadequate strength, consisting as it did of only six actors (including himself) and four actresses. He wrote therefore to young Michel Boyron, generally called Baron, who at the time was acting in a provincial company at Dijon. It will be remembered that Molière had taken a warm and active interest in the infant prodigy some years previously, when he was acting in the company of La Raisin. He saw in him a coming great actor, took him into his house, and provided for his education as a man and as an actor. But Mme. Molière did not regard the boy in the same light; probably at a very early age he already showed his tendency to conceit, which afterwards developed to an incredible degree. She was hard upon him for his cocksure manners, perhaps also for the favour in which he stood with Molière,[1] and on one occasion she lost patience with him and gave him a beating. After this the high-spirited boy felt that he could stay no longer in Molière's house ; he went to the provinces and acted there for some years.

Now, in 1670, he was glad to return to his old master and benefactor. Molière must have seen at once that the young actor was specially qualified for tragedy, for in the very first year he entrusted him with the part of Domitien in Pierre Corneille's *Tite et Bérénice*, a play which he had bought of the old poet for a large sum (2000 francs, equal to some 10,000 francs nowadays) though he could not expect any great profits from it, especially since the same subject was treated simultaneously by Racine, whose play was to be performed at the Hôtel de Bourgogne, the tragic stage *par excellence*. If, in spite of all, *Bérénice* maintained its place on the stage of Molière better than most tragedies (it ran for twenty-one performances with very good average proceeds), this was no doubt in some degree due to the charming young tragedian and his acting with Mlle. Molière.[2]

[1] The author of *La fameuse Comédienne* explains Molière's predilection for the handsome boy as a depraved amorous inclination ; but though his lampoon is not directly aimed at Molière, but only at his wife, we cannot give the slightest credit to its scandals, which in most instances have been proved to be distortions of fact.

[2] To his performance of this part is attached a little episode, which gives an amusing picture of some of the great men of the time. In Cizeron Rival's *Récréations littéraires* of 1765 we read as follows : "M. Despréaux [Boileau] generally distinguished between two kinds of nonsense, simple nonsense and double nonsense ; the former expression being applied to things understood by the author, but not by the readers, the latter designating passages which were understood neither by the author nor by his readers. . . . As an instance he quoted these four lines of the great Corneille's *Tite et Bérénice* :—

38—Michel Baron.

Baron was engaged at once with a whole share, an extremely high remuneration for a young man of seventeen. In Molière's own plays he did not obtain a prominent position at once. He played Cupid in the spectacular piece *Psyché*, Octave in *Les Fourberies de Scapin* and Ariste in *Les Femmes savantes*; but after the death of Molière he obtained an absolutely first-class position as lover and tragic hero; in fact he became the representative actor of the close of the century (fig. 38).

Of much less significance were the Beauvals, whom Molière engaged a few months later, and who had belonged to the same company as Baron. We have briefly mentioned this couple before,[1] and there is not much more to say about them. Molière probably meant the sturdy *soubrette*, Mlle. Beauval (fig. 39) to replace Madeleine Béjart, who was now well advanced in age, and after her death Mlle. Beauval "created" one of the best soubrettes drawn by Molière, Toinette in *Le Malade imaginaire*. Her husband was a very insignificant actor,

> " Faut-il mourir Madame ? et, si proche du terme ?
> Votre illustre inconstance est-elle encor si ferme,
> Que les restes d'un feu que j'avais cru si fort
> Puissent dans quatre jours se promettre ma mort ?"

" Baron, the famous actor, was to play Domitien in this tragedy, and while he was studying the part, these lines puzzled him somewhat by their obscurity. He went to Molière, in whose house he lived, and asked him to explain them. After reading them Molière admitted that he did not understand them either. "But, wait a little," he said to Baron, "M. Corneille is coming to supper here this evening and then you can ask him to explain them." As soon as Corneille arrived, young Baron fell upon his neck, as he used to do, for he was very fond of him. Then he asked him to explain the four lines, saying that he could not understand them. After meditating on them awhile, Corneille said : "I don't quite understand them either. But you speak them nevertheless. Those who don't understand them will admire them all the more.."

[1] See above, p. 122.

and received only half a share as his remuneration.   But he was an indispensable appendage to his wife, who was so ignorant that she could scarcely read and could not write at all.   She could only study her parts when they were in his handwriting.

XIV

Lulli and Molière—Court Entertainments and Farces—*Les Femmes savantes* and the Personal Attacks contained in it—Last Play of Molière—His Death and the Behaviour of the Clergy at his Burial.

AFTER the long controversy over *Tartufe* and the final and complete victory of Molière, the general irritation of the theatres seemed to calm down.   In his joy at the victory which had brought him honour, wealth and peace, and in his gratitude to the King who had supported him to the best of his ability in the dangerous conflict with the " Cabal," it seemed as if for some time Molière wished to devote his talents exclusively to the amusement of the monarch.

He wrote a series of pieces which count among the weakest of his productions.

To a loyal subject it would seem a doubtful compliment, that great poets, who wish to adapt themselves particularly to the taste of crowned heads, should generally offer them the most shallow and childish productions of their minds ; but since this experiment constantly proves successful, we must conclude that the poets know what they are about.

If Molière had written nothing but such plays as *M.*

39

40

39—Mademoiselle Beauval.   40—Jean Baptiste Lulli.

de Pourceaugnac with its "syringe-brandishing" doctors, the affected amours of *Les Amantes magnifiques*, *Le Bourgeois Gentilhomme* with its Turkish clowneries, the spectacular *Psyché*, *Les Fourberies de Scapin* with its ominous sack scene, *La Comtesse d'Escarbagnas*, *Le Ballet des Ballets*, or *La Pastorale comique*, we should certainly have seen his great comic talent and splendid technique, but of all the superior qualities which in our eyes constitute the great poet, his deep knowledge of the human heart, his clear sharp satire and his manly love, this long list of farces and other entertainments shows no vestige.

Some of them are merely frames for the musical and dancing intermezzos, which amused Louis XIV. so much that he sometimes joined in them himself. Thus it was with *M. de Pourceaugnac*, the grotesque *divertissements* of which formed the real attraction of the play, especially the famous dance in which the doctors gambol round Pourceaugnac waving their syringes while persuasively singing the following words in Italian :—

> Piglia-lo sù,
> Signor Monsu,
> Piglia-lo, piglia-lo, piglia-lo sù.[1]

For these entertainments Molière had an excellent collaborator in the celebrated composer Jean Baptiste Lulli (fig. 40) an astute Florentine, who, partly by his great musical talent and partly by his sharp wits and easy conscience, had made his way upward from kitchen-

---

[1] "Take it [the syringe], be quick, Signor Monsieur, take it, take it, take it quick!"

boy to an entirely independent and privileged position as Superintendent of the Royal Music.

There can scarcely have been any deep or heart-felt friendship between Molière and Lulli : for such relations the character of the intriguing and grasping Italian stood too far beneath that of Molière. But their professional connection was very close at one time, and the frolics and wild pranks—poetical and musical—invented by "the two great Baptistes" as they were called, delighted the King, the Court and the public (fig. 41).

In *M. de Pourceaugnac*, in which Molière himself, profiting by the knowledge he had acquired in his younger days of the dialects of southern France, gave an exceedingly comic picture of the stupid Provençal nobleman who is taken in by the Parisians, Lulli took part not only as composer, but also as actor, playing the musician disguised as a doctor, Signor Chiachiarone, who pursues M. de Pourceaugnac with the syringe. The tomfooleries of Lulli and his ludicrous facial play and gesticulations were famous at Court, and it was irresistibly tickling and ridiculous to the public of those times to see the two Baptistes, the great poet and the great composer, playing their fantastic pranks.

In *Le Bourgeois Gentilhomme*, again, which like *Les Amants Magnifiques*, had been written to order, on a subject suggested by the King himself, Lulli was an eager collaborator and fellow-actor. This play, which under its crust of childish nonsense and tinsel conceals pearls of the most genuine comic power, had an enormous success, first at Court, and afterwards at the

Palais Royal, where it was performed alternately with Corneille's *Tite et Bérénice*.[1]

The long spectacular play *Psyché* also enjoyed a lasting success, though nowadays we find it very dull reading. Louis XIV. had ordered it of Molière and Lulli for the purpose of exhibiting a scene of Hades which was stored in the King's lumber-room, and was otherwise useless, and a special theatre was built in the Louvre, which was used for this one play only.[2] Molière had to apply for help to old Pierre Corneille, with whom at that time he was on very friendly terms, and to Quinault, who wrote all the words for the music.

Handsome young Baron and Molière's wife shone as Cupid and Psyche, which of course afforded quite sufficient grounds for accusing them of too intimate relations with each other.

Though the character of Baron was by no means ideal, and though we have reason to think that Mlle. Molière was no model of innocence, it must be stated that there is not the slightest evidence to show that Baron was guilty of such treachery to his master and friend.

The story in *La fameuse Comédienne*, which forms the basis of all later reports concerning this supposed intrigue, is so obviously fictitious, that we fail to understand how anybody can place the slightest reliance on it as a source of information. Baron enjoyed Molière's friendship to the last, and was with him in his hour of

[1] Comp. p. 202 f.
[2] Not till 1716 was this theatre, which had been built at great expense by the Italian Vigarani, again made use of for court ballets.

death.   But this is an additional instance of the tendency
in the public to transfer the illusions of the stage to real
life.

At great expense *Psyché* was moved from the Court
Theatre to Molière's own stage, where it became an
event of importance, by no means on account of its
artistic value, but because of the magnificence dis-
played on this occasion by the Palais Royal Company.

As a rule, the mounting of a play in those times was
a very cheap affair ; there was no variety of decoration
or scenery : a colonnade, a room, a wood—that was all ;
so no great risk was incurred in staging a play.   But
according to La Grange, who seems overawed by the
boldness of Molière's business speculations, here was a
play which cost the enormous sum of 4359 francs, 1 sou,
besides requiring at each performance an extra expense
of more than 300 francs, for dancers, singers, machinists,
etc.   In other words, Molière had entered on the path
of speculation in gorgeous displays of scenery, which
afterwards became very common, and which in our time
makes theatrical management on a grand scale a very
dangerous and not very artistic occupation.

Molière's speculation, however, proved successful.
His theatre throve splendidly.   The last year's proceeds
yielded shares of between 4000 and 5000 francs.   For
the time fortune smiled on Molière.   He was on better
terms with his wife ; they were living together again ;
Molière furnished a house in the Rue Richelieu with
extravagant splendour, and a year later (on August 15th,
1672) his wife gave birth to a son.   His enemies were
silenced ; the King's favour was greater than ever.

In short, a little breath and gleam of happiness seemed
to be falling to Molière's share after his many bitter
struggles and trials.

The Muses only wept, and so did Boileau.   To his
severe friend all the farcical productions in which
Molière had revelled for some years were a pestilence.
The play which scandalised him most, by the bye,
but which has been judged with the greatest leniency
by posterity, *Les Fourberies de Scapin*, is the only one
which holds its place on all stages where Molière is acted,
while the other works of the same period are either
utterly dead, or only revived as curiosities at very rare
intervals.

Scapin, which certainly found no great favour with
the contemporary public, in the eyes of Boileau was
quite unworthy of Molière's genius.   To this somewhat pedantic critic the fact that certain old coarse
tricks, such as that with the bag, were introduced, was
quite enough to condemn the whole merry and well-
constructed play as mere jugglery, and he exclaims in his
grief :—

Dans ce sac ridicule ou Scapin s'enveloppe
Je ne reconnais plus l'auteur du Misanthrope.[1]

What Boileau could not understand seems clear to us
nowadays.   After the trying years of domestic misfortunes, a hard struggle for life and furious persecution by various enemies, it was a relief for Molière
to shake off all bitterness, enmity and depression in

---

[1] Boileau: *Art poétique, chant III.* "In the ridiculous sack in which
Scapin envelops himself I cannot recognise the author of *The Misanthrope.*

peals of pure laughter, in unrestrained and unsatirical mirth.

The things he created in this frame of mind certainly had not the value of *Tartufe* or *Le Misanthrope*, which were drawn with his heart's blood. Still, we cannot consider *Monsieur de Pourceaugnac, Le Bourgeois Gentilhomme* or *Les Fourberies de Scapin* as unworthy of him ; and in many sparks of genuine comic power we distinctly recognise the author of *Le Misanthrope*, though he has thrown off his ceremonial attire.

Another thing which Boileau could never understand was Molière's unwillingness to give up acting and to devote himself exclusively to authorship. He frequently urged him to do so, but Molière invariably replied that it was a point of honour with him to continue acting. In the eyes of Boileau there was little honour in blackening one's face with the moustache of Scaramouche, and presenting one's back to all the blows to which a comedian is exposed. It remained a perfect enigma to the critic that the man whom he considered as the greatest genius and the greatest dramatist of his time, could be mad enough to seek honour by acting.

In this view posterity perhaps agrees with Boileau, and only one who himself has lovingly cultivated the histrionic art will understand that Molière may have derived as much joy from representing as from inventing the children of his fancy.

He was, moreover, the best and the most popular comic actor of his company, and both his theatre and his plays would have suffered if he had withdrawn from acting. The public, we find, are frequently at a loss

41—A Court performance at Versailles.

to understand what it is that retains an actor, who is proficient in some other art as well, in a profession which they regard as far from attractive.

In the case of Molière there can be no doubt that the desire to make his own theatre the first and best in Paris—and thereby in the world—also attached him to it as an actor. It was a matter of honour, nay, of passion, with him. And on the raising of his theatre to a position which would do honour to himself and his comrades, he staked all his powers as manager, author and actor, and, in doing so, sacrificed what was of higher value in the eyes of the world : the seal of the Academy on his dramatic authorship,[1] civil honour and the blessing of the Church ; in the end he literally sacrificed his life to sustain his theatre in a momentary emergency.

But if Boileau and other severe critics among Molière's friends were afraid that his talent would be altogether lost in court entertainments and popular farces, their fears were without foundation.

His mind was resting, but it was not exhausted. This is clearly shown by the play which—feeling, perhaps, that he had descended too far below his proper level—he next presented to the public Though *Les Femmes savantes*, which was produced at the Palais Royal on March 11th, 1672, does not come up to *Tartufe* or *Le Misanthrope*, either in dramatic form or in deep knowledge of the human mind, it is a definite step

---

[1] Molière had been promised the membership of the French Academy, if he gave up his profession as an actor, but he refused. Not till more than a century after his death was he made a member *in effigie*. See p. 142 n. 1.

forward on the road which had led to the production
of those two masterpieces.

Les Femmes savantes was not written to the order of
a King nor for a particular festivity, but simply for his
own theatre, and it proved to be even more attractive
than the great spectacular plays, full of music and dances
and all sorts of surprises in scenery.

We may conclude, perhaps, that Boileau, who had
disapproved of so much of his later work, had at last
prevailed upon Molière to carry out an idea which for
years had occupied his mind.

The principal theme of the play—a satire on the
emancipation of woman and her claims to pursue the
same studies as man—appears a little feeble nowadays,
partly because the progress of time has shown Molière
to have been wrong in his arguments, and partly because
the emancipation has in course of time produced real
types of much more grotesque power than those which
the old comedian considered as strong caricature.

But the subordinate subject, the grasping, vain and
pedantic scholars who imposed upon foolish ladies with
their pretensions to erudition, seems to have become,
in the working out of the plan, the author's principal
consideration.

For a long time, almost since his return to Paris,
he had kept an eye on the conceited *beaux-esprits*,
who had looked down upon him, the actor, the modest
farce-player. Their affectations, their artificial style,
their jealousy, both of each other and of the actors, had
irritated and amused him. Now and then he had dealt
them a little blow in his plays   But by this time his

scorn and amusement had been artistically transmuted
into a fine and cutting satire, and Trissotin and Vadius
have become types of the ludicrous pedants who use
their paltry wits to turn the heads of hysterical elderly
women, and are a horror to all real men.

His contemporaries, however, were justified in reproach-
ing Molière with having been a little too Aristophanic in
his descriptions of the two learned men.   We remember
two poems in *Les Femmes savantes* which Trissotin reads
aloud to the great delight of the ladies : a " Sonnet to
the Princess Uranie on her fever " and an " Epigram on
an amaranth-coloured Coach."   These poems were quoted
literally from a well-known wit of the time, the Abbé
Cotin, Member of the Academy and first court-preacher,
in whose *Oeuvres galantes* they may still be found.

It was impossible not to identify at a glance the
common and ludicrous Trissotin with the Abbé Cotin.
However, as there was no resemblance in their outward
circumstances, Molière might in a way be justified in declar-
ing two days before the performance that he had not
intentionally alluded to living persons.[1]   Still, the allu-
sion was too plain.[2]

---

[1] As we read in the *Mercure de France*, a periodical which was quite new at
the time and was edited by Donneau de Visé.

[2] In biographies of Molière it is generally stated that at the first performances Molière called his character Tricotin, nay, that he secretly possessed
himself of one of the Abbé's cast-off garments in which he made La
Thorillière, the first performer of the part, appear on the stage.   However,
though both assertions are derived from contemporary authorities, they
seem very improbable.   Long before *Les Femmes savantes* appeared on the
stage, Mme. de Sévigné wrote to her daughter about the very amusing
play, calling it *Trissotin*, a title which it also bore in the play-bill.   And
as far as the garment is concerned, it would seem quite absurd for Molière
to make the young *bel-esprit*, who courts the charming Henriette, appear in
the robe of an elderly cleric.

Molière indeed had an old score to settle with the Abbé Cotin, both on his own account and that of his profession. The old poet had been imprudent enough to pick a quarrel with Boileau, and to include his friend Molière in the attack. He had written the following insolent passage about actors : "What can you answer to people whom the laws, even heathen laws, call 'infamous'? What can you say to persons to whom nothing can be said worse than their own designations?"[1]

Cotin, however, had to experience the truth of Hamlet's words: "After your death you were better have a bad epitaph, than their ill report while you live." The sneers of Boileau he had been able to bear ; under Molière's attacks he broke down completely. For shame and fear of mockery he scarcely ventured out; his *rôle* as wit in the great houses was at an end. But his epitaph was none the better for that. After his death the following not unwitty lines were written about him :—

> " Savez-vous en quoi Cotin
> Diffère de Trissotin ?——
> Cotin a fini ses jours,
> Trissotin vivra toujours.[2]

Ménage who was generally pointed out as the original of Vadius, came off more easily, but he also bore the satire much better. When Mme. de Rambouillet asked : " How is this, M. Ménage, will you allow this impudent Molière to ridicule us in this way ?" he calmly

[1] In *La Critique désintéressée sur les satires du temps*, a pamphlet written against Boileau Despréaux, or, as Cotin thought it witty to call him, " sieur des Vipereaux."

[2] " Do you know what difference there is between Cotin and Trissotin? Cotin's days are at an end ; Trissotin will live for ever."

replied, "Madame, I have seen the play; it is excellent, there is nothing to object to and nothing to criticise."[1]

In connection with *Les Femmes savantes* we must mention another little peculiarity. According to the *Mercure de France* of 1723, which contains the whole of the original cast, Molière made his own servant Martine act the amusing soubrette Martine in the play. This statement has been accepted as authentic and repeated by many biographers of Molière, who have identified the otherwise unknown Martine with the more celebrated la Forêt,[2] the old servant to whom, as the legend goes, Molière used to read his plays before they appeared on the stage, in order to observe the immediate effect they produced.

As it happens, however, we are able to state that at the time in question Molière had no servant of the name of Martine. He had his old la Forêt, whose real name was Renée Vannier, and one other called Catherine.

But it is altogether absurd to believe in such a myth. Molière attached too much importance to technique in dramatic art to think for one moment of introducing crude reality into a part which required more than simply a comic appearance. There can scarcely be any doubt that Martine was played by Mlle. Beauval, who filled the part in 1685, and who had just been engaged for this branch; in the following year she played Toinette in *Le Malade imaginaire*.

---

[1] Quoted (from *Carpentariana*, p. 48) by the brothers Parfaict in their *Histoire du Théâtre Français*, vol. xi. p. 215.

[2] See, for instance, Mahrenholtz, who, however, as we showed above, is not very accurate in his statements on matters of theatrical history.—*Molière's Leben und Werke*, p. 278.

The other parts were distributed as follows : Molière himself played the weak good-natured Chrysalde ; Philaminthe, his learned wife, was in the hands of Hubert, who was very popular in the parts of comic women. La Thorillière and du Croisy represented the two poets Trissotin and Vadius; La Grange was Clitandre the lover, and Baron the wise Ariste, the *raisonneur* of the play, a part for which he seems to have been very young. Mlle. Molière was the captivating, rather disdainful young female lover, while her elder sister, formerly called Mlle. Hervé, now married as Mlle. Villaubrun, was the hysterical love-sick Bélise, and Mlle. de Brie the "learned" Armande.

It will be observed that the name of Madeleine Béjart is not in the cast. For some time her health had been declining ; in January (1672) the theatre had been closed for a week on account of her illness ; and in the absence of the company, who were acting *La Comtesse d'Escarbagnac* at the Court of Saint Germain, Molière's old and faithful friend died, after having bequeathed all she possessed to Armande, which of course confirmed people in their belief that Mlle. Molière was her daughter.

No doubt, the death of his old friend and companion, who had stood by him ever since the first steps of his theatrical career, was a great loss to Molière, and we may be sure that he felt it deeply, though he was prevented from making any outward display of grief by pressure of work, in the preparation of his new important play, *Les Femmes savantes*, which was acted three weeks after the death of his friend.

Altogether, his short-lived happiness was on the

wane. In the summer of the same year his last born little son died, and at the same time the poet, who was in bad health and overworked, had to struggle against numerous annoyances, especially those caused by Lulli. The musician, who was very grasping and fond of intrigue, had great influence over Louis XIV., who could not do without his help at the court festivities, for which he provided the music and in various ways showed great activity. But Lulli, feeling how indispensable he was, took advantage of his position to acquire a number of privileges, which were very detrimental to other theatrical people who had to work with him, and wanted music for their performances. The latest advantage he had obtained was a monopoly of the production of operas, a privilege which had hitherto been in other hands; and he became the founder and manager of the "Royal Academy of Music," that is the opera-house.[1] He succeeded in getting most absurd clauses added to this privilege; for instance, the right to reprint and perform all texts to which he had written music, the consequence of which was that he could collect scenes out of Molière's plays, combine them into a sort of pot-pourri and, without the author's permission, perform them on his own operatic stage.

Molière, of course, was displeased with this as with many other of Lulli's encroachments, and he and his companions protested against them. But it was no use; the Florentine was too persevering, and though Molière was liked by the King, Lulli stood higher in the royal

[1] The great Opera in Paris still bears the official title of the "National Academy of Music," dating from the privilege mentioned above, with the substitution of "National" for "Royal."

favour.   Naturally enough, in the long run, the King and Court found more pleasure in operas and ballets than in the daring satires of Molière.

The consequence was that Molière did not wish Lulli to compose the music for his new comedy-ballet, *Le Malade imaginaire*, which was originally intended for a court festival, but entrusted the work to the musician Charpentier.   So, naturally, this play, which with all its dances and songs was the very thing for a court entertainment, did not make its first appearance at Versailles or Saint-Germain—this of course, Lulli would take good care to prevent—but at the Palais Royal, where it might have entirely dispensed with all the costly display.

All these annoyances, and most of all the fear of losing the King's favour, told upon Molière's health which, as it was, had always been delicate.   His spirits were affected ; he became hypochondriacal and lost his interest in life.   We read in Grimarest that during this period he said one day to his wife, in the presence of Baron : [1] "As long as my life was an equal mixture of sorrow and joy, I felt happy, but now being so overwhelmed with troubles that I cannot expect a single moment of pleasure and satisfaction, I see clearly, I must give in ; I can no longer stand all the pain and all the annoyance, which do not leave me one moment's peace.   But," he added musingly, "how a man must suffer before he dies !   At all events I feel certain that I shall soon have done with it." [2]

Le Malade imaginaire appears to us now to be one

[1] It was probably Baron who repeated the words to the old biographer.
[2] Grimarest : *Vie de M. de Molière*, Amsterdam, 1705, pp. 180 f.

of the best of Molière's farces, one of the freshest and
certainly one of the most full of vitality. It is found
in the *répertoire* of every theatre where Molière is acted,
and its quaint and witty humour is an everlasting source
of pleasure.

But to the spectator who knows the life of Molière,
the mirth is tinged with a sadness unwarranted by the
play itself, but due to the remembrance of the background of mental and physical suffering, on which the
bright picture was drawn.

Can we imagine a more extraordinary swan-song
from a poet whose mind and body were tormented to
death? A comedy which plays the most wanton pranks
with illness and death and all their attributes; which
mocks medical science and its representatives of all shades
and degrees; which by no gesture or word reveals the
slightest vestige of sympathy with suffering and disease!
A comedy which seems to be written by a man in the
most robust health, who holds the principle that good or
bad health is a matter of choice, entirely depends upon
the patient, who has only to throw the remedies into the
gutter and the doctors down the stairs!

If the life and death of Molière were enveloped in
mist or obscurity, no doubt some ingenious commentator
would have concluded and proved convincingly that this
play was written at a particularly happy period of his
life, during which he had thrown his sorrows and his
medicine overboard together. And he would have been
much astonished on hearing the truth—that the man
who wrote it knew that death was near, and felt life a
burden.

Nobody who studies Molière's art and character can help being attracted by both ; but what perhaps appeals most deeply to our sympathy and affection is his rare gift of making his personal feelings and thoughts serve his art without forcing his intimacy upon us, and turning his sufferings and trials to mercenary use.

Le Malade imaginaire (fig. 42) certainly is not one of the greatest masterpieces of the human mind, not even one of the finest of Molière's own works, but it is a remarkable instance of his superior capacity for extracting the pure elements of satire and comedy from his varied and bitter experiences.

It was performed for the first time on February 10th, 1673, before a very numerous and enthusiastic audience. Molière himself, of course, played Argan, the principal part. His wife and La Grange were splendid as the lovers, and even many years later, the grace and delicate expression with which they played the difficult musical scene stood as a model of fine dramatic art. The Beauval family was numerously represented ; Mlle. Beauval played Toinette, her husband, Thomas Diafoirus, a part for which Molière had considered him particularly qualified,[1] and their little daughter Louison.

Molière's caustic satire on the medical profession does not seem to have much scandalised his contemporaries. In our days, when physicians are always accustomed to see themselves presented on the stage as the noblest, most disinterested lovers or supernaturally witty *raisonneurs*, such an attack would no doubt call forth indignant protest. But the medical profession in those times was

[1] See above p. 122.

scarcely looked upon with such great respect as it is now ; and moreover, we have reason to think that this satire was not quite so seriously meant as several of the others.

At any rate, Molière was on very friendly terms with Mauvillain, his own medical adviser, for whose benefit he even used his influence with Louis XIV.

On this occasion the King asked Molière, who had repeatedly sneered bitterly at medical science,[1] how he got on with his own physician. The poet replied : "Very well indeed; he prescribes remedies, I do not take them—and I recover."

This last assertion, however, was anything but true. His health had gone on declining, and now, while acting *Le Malade imaginaire*, he was really as ill as possible. His closest relatives and friends were very anxious about him ; at the third representation of the new play he was not expected to be able to act, and on the morning of the fourth day of performance he was in such a state of suffering that his wife and Baron besought him to give it up.

But he was anxious not to upset the extremely lucrative performance and thus entail a great loss on the company and all the people employed. So he went to the theatre.

With great difficulty he dragged himself through the long part, and when, in the third act, he was lying in his easy chair feigning to be dead, it was agonising to his companions to notice how closely he indeed resembled a dead man. In the scene, subsequent to the play proper,

---

Compare *e.g. L Medecin malgré lui, L'Amour médecin, L'Avare* and *Moniseur de Pourceaugnac*

in which the degree of M.D. is conferred, he had still greater difficulty in keeping up, and while pronouncing his first *Juro*, the spectators noticed that he was seized with convulsions, which he attempted to hide by a forced outburst of laughter.

Nevertheless he succeeded in getting to the end, thus avoiding to break off the performance.   But when at last he had done, and, half dead from overexertion, was sitting in his dressing-gown in his tiring-room, the first words he said to young Baron, who was by his side, were : "Was it all right ?   How did they like the play?"   The words sum up the whole of the theatrical character.

Very ill indeed he was taken to his house in the Rue de Richelieu, a few steps from the theatre, where he was at once put to bed.   The cough that had been long and spasmodically suppressed, now broke forth violently with copious vomiting of blood.   The parish priest was sent for, but he refused to come to the ungodly artist who had presented *Tartufe* on the stage.

Two sisters of charity to whom Molière had shown hospitality, were living in the house; in their arms the great poet expired about ten o'clock in the evening. In his *Registre* (fig. 43) La Grange makes a note of the death of his great friend and master, which, for all its brevity, is strangely touching, among its surroundings of dry figures.   As a sign of death, he has painted a black lozenge against February 17th, 1673, on which day the proceeds of the performance are stated to have amounted to 1219 francs, and the note runs as follows : "On this same day after the play, at about ten o'clock in the evening, M. de Molière died in his home, Rue

1673

Dimanche 29 Janvier Maris Infidelles 599:10ʃ 33:

Mardy 31ᵐᵉ Maris Infidelles · · · 179:10ʃ 5:5ʃ

Vendredy 3 feuvrier Trissotin · 298: 11

Mardy 7ᵐᵉ Repentieux — Dimanche 5 Idem · · · · 388: 18:10ʃ

Piece Nouuelle et dernière de Mʳ de Moliere — Vendredy 10ᵐᵉ 1ʳᵉ Representation du malade Jmaginaire · · · 1992 71:14ʃ

Dimanche 12 Malade Jmag.ʳᵉ 1459: 55:

Mardy 14ᵐᵉ mal. Jmag. · 1879:10ʃ 80:

Du Vendredy 17 · · · 1219 39:

Ce mesme Jour apres la Comedie Sur les 10 heures du Soir Monsieur de Moliere mourust dans sa maison Rue de Richelieu, ayant Joué le roolle dud. malade Jmaginaire fort Jncommode d'vn Rhume eflucksion Sur la poictrine qui luy Causoit Vne grande toux de Sorte que dans les grans Efforts qu'il fist pour cracher il se rompit vne veyne dans le Corps et ne Vescut pas demye heure ou trois quarts Dheure Depuis lad. veyne Rompüe Et Son Corps Est Enterré a St Joseph ayde de la parroisse St Eustache. Il y a vne tombe Esleuée d'vn pied hors de terre.

Dans le desordre Ou la troupe Se trouua apres cette perte irreparable le Roy eust dessein de Joindre les acteurs qui la composient aux Comediens de l'hostel de bourgogne

43—Page of La Grange's *Registre*, with the entry of the death of Molière.

de Richelieu, after having acted the part of the said Malade imaginaire, strongly incommoded by a cold and a fluction on the chest which caused him a violent fit of coughing, so that in the great efforts he made to spit he burst a vein in his body, and did not live half or three quarters of an hour after the said vessel burst. His body is buried in St Joseph, chapel of ease to the parish of St Eustache. There is a tomb raised one foot above the ground."

But La Grange omits to relate the incredible scandal that preceded the burial of his body in St Joseph. The Parisian clergy refused a decent burial to the greatest poet of the century.

Their pretext was that as an actor he was excluded from the Sacraments of the Church,[1] having not "abjured" his profession before his death, as it was customary for people of the theatre to do on their death-bed. But the real reason was, of course, that *Tartufe* had hit the flock too hard ; and his presumption was now to be avenged by the army of the devout.

[1] According to a ritual order of 1654, the Holy Sacrament was denied to "persons who are manifestly unworthy, such as outlaws, excommunicated and infamous persons, *e.g.*, harlots, whoremongers, actors, usurers, sorcerers." Christian burial was denied to "Heathens, Jews and all Infidels, Heretics . . . and those that are under the Interdict of the Church . . . open and notorious sinners, who have died impenitent." In the latter paragraph actors are not specially mentioned, but the words : "open and notorious sinners, who have died impenitent," included the categories mentioned in the first clause as excluded from the Holy Sacrament. In practice the order was followed in the case of actors, only, however, in so far as they were required to show penitence, *i.e.* to promise that they would abjure acting (a vow, it must be stated, which was readily broken in case of unexpected recovery) and declare that they repented having followed such a profession. It was this act of penitence that had been denied to Molière by the parish priest's refusal to come to his deathbed. Whether Molière would have renounced his art and submitted to the priests, is another question.

It must be admitted that if Molière's wife had been unworthy of her husband during his lifetime, at his death she seems to have felt what she owed to his memory and his honour.

The refusal of a decent burial to Molière by the Archbishop of Paris, François de Harlay—a notorious libertine, by the bye, whose amorous escapades were a scandal and a laughing-stock all over Paris—naturally roused great anger among the friends of the deceased. Chapelle wrote an epigram which, brief as it was, burned like red-hot iron.　It ran thus :—

> Puisqu' à Paris on dénie
> La terre après le trépas
> A ceux qui pendant leur vie,
> Ont joué la comédie,
> Pourquoi ne jette-t-on pas
> Les bigots à la voirie?
> Ils sont dans le même cas.[1]

Mme. Molière at once applied direct to Louis XIV., requesting his interference.[2]　Though the King was, and

[1] Since Paris denies a burial-ground to those who have played comedy during their life time, why are not bigots thrown into the dung-hole?　They are in the same case.

[2] There are several early anecdotes connected with this appeal. Madame Molière is said to have offended the King by making the following imprudent remark : "If my husband was a criminal, your Majesty has at least approved of his crimes."　It is most improbable that Mlle. Molière, who was not stupid, should have behaved so maladroitly, and that the King would have helped her if she had.　Another story makes the King say to the parish priest that he ought to bury Molière.　The priest pleading that the usual order forbade the burial of an actor in consecrated ground, the King asked : "How far down is the ground consecrated?"—"Four feet deep, your Majesty," "Well," replied the King, "bury him six feet deep, and say no more about it."　It is quite unnecessary to point out the absurdity of this anecdote.　That Louis XIV. should have been so easy going in an ecclesiastical matter is entirely out of the question

44

42

44—Michel Baron in his last period. **42**—Scenes from *Le Malade Imaginaire*.

was bound to be, very prudent in church matters, he prevailed on the Archbishop to repeal his decision. Molière was accordingly allowed burial in consecrated ground, though with the smallest possible amount of ecclesiastical honours. The ceremony was only permitted to take place in the evening, and the body was not to be presented in the church ; not more than two ecclesiastics were to accompany the hearse to the churchyard, and no service was to be held.

Molière's wife had a right to the complaint which became her constant lamentation after her husband's death : " They deny a grave to the man to whom Greece would have raised altars ! "

In the darkness of night, by torchlight, without the slightest pomp, as if by stealth, the greatest poet of the country was carried to his last resting-place, while an immense crowd gathered outside the house in the Rue de Richelieu, evidently under the impression that it was no ordinary man whose burial was taking place.

Mme. Molière gave a thousand francs to be distributed among the poor people present, requesting them to pray for the departed.

And so it was the people who paid him the last honours, which were denied him by the Church.

XV

IT is unnecessary to state that the death of Molière was an irreparable loss to his company. This was felt by all its members, and La Grange mentions the sad event in those very words.

The company has been very severely censured for re-opening the theatre only a week after the death of its master, and for resuming after a fortnight the very play which had caused his death, with another actor in his part. Many modern biographers of Molière consider this an act of ingratitude and irreverence on their part.

But these critics do not sufficiently consider the position of the company. In Molière it lost not only its leader, its playwright and its principal actor, but also the support and confidence of the King. The first idea of Louis XIV. was that this masterless theatre could do nothing, and he conceived the plan of amalgamating the old company of Molière with that of the Hôtel de Bourgogne.

That, however, would have meant its extinction.

The great thing therefore, was to show that they were still fit for their work, and to strain their efforts to the utmost to keep afloat till the end of the season. There was only one month left, the theatres were closed during Easter, and that month had to be utilised to the best of their ability. With this end in view, Baron speedily studied the Misanthrope, and La Thorillière Argan in *Le Malade imaginaire*, the great success of which had to be sustained. And indeed, they succeeded in bringing the season to a close in a manner which financially could not have been better, as La Grange's accounts clearly prove.

The crowded houses also showed that the public of the day was not scandalised by the fact that the actors continued the performances after the death of their master.

Indeed, the end of the season showed very good profits. Each share amounted to 4585 francs 13 sous, the third highest sum obtained in any year since Molière started his theatre in Paris.

In spite of this good result, and though the danger of the realisation of the King's plan of combining the two theatres was happily averted, the position of Molière's theatre was indeed very precarious.

The season was scarcely closed, when two misfortunes fell on the Palais Royal. First of all the Hôtel de Bourgogne succeeded in acquiring four of its members, Baron and La Thorillière and the two Beauvals. Of these, Baron was decidedly a genius of the first order, and the others were players of very good abilities. In any case, their departure meant that the company could not continue its work without recruiting its staff.

At the same time an even worse thing happened. Lulli, who always had the knack of fishing in troubled waters, persuaded the King to allow him to appropriate the old Palais Royal theatre for the use of his opera, and the actors received notice to quit at once. So there they were, according to La Grange, "not only without a company, but also without a theatre."

No doubt it was La Grange himself who at this juncture undertook the management, and whose energy succeeded in keeping the remains of Molière's company on foot, thus securing the continuance of the most important of French theatres, a continuance which has lasted right up to our own time.

The first step he took was to make a contract [1] with Rosimond, the leading actor of the Marais theatre, and to secure him as a kind of substitute for Molière, At the same time the company engaged a young girl, a daughter of the actor Du Croisy, but she did not distinguish herself in any way.

Rosimond, if not a Molière, became a very useful actor. Claude la Rose, called Rosimond, was not only an excellent comic actor, who undertook nearly all Molière's parts, but a fertile and popular author as well. He had only been a few years at the Marais theatre, when he was engaged by the company of Molière, but he quickly won the first place. As an author he strikes us now as clumsy and coarse, but several of his plays had a great success; for instance, his version of the story of Don Juan, *Le nouveau Festin de Pierre, ou l'Athée foudroyé* (*The new Supper of the Stone-Guest or*

---

[1] This was done on May 3rd, 1673, according to La Grange's *Registre*. The fact deserves to be noticed, since both the brothers Parfaict in their great *Theatrical history*, and Lemazurier in his often quoted *Galerie des Acteurs français*, make his début in *Le Malade imaginaire* take place a fortnight after the death of Molière. But it is absolutely clear from La Grange, that it was La Thorillière who replaced Molière in this part, and that Rosimond was not engaged till after the close of the season; which means that he never acted in the Palais Royal, but in the new theatre that was rented by the company.

the Atheist struck by Lightning). He was, moreover, an educated man, a scholar and a great collector—he possessed the largest collection of plays to be found in Paris—and, if evil reports are to be credited, a great drunkard. When Rosimond died in 1686, the landlord of the wine-shop which he frequented is said to have exclaimed with tears in his eyes : " Now I lose 800 francs a year." Others, however, assert that this is calumny, and that he was a very sober and orderly man. Besides his coarse comic plays, strange to say, he also published an ecclesiastical work : *Vie des Saints pour tous les jours de l'année* (*Lives of the Saints for every day of the year*). If this book had not appeared under a pseudonym, it might have been expected to secure Rosimond against sharing the fate of Molière after death. But in this point also he followed the lead of his great predecessor. He died suddenly and without confession, and consequently was buried without religious ceremony in the corner of the churchyard where un-baptised children were interred.

It fell to Rosimond's lot to replace Molière, at any rate as actor ; but the company was still very defective, and as yet it had no theatre.

Soon, however, a building was found, and that an excellent one. The opera-house that had been built three years previously by the eccentric and fastidious Marquis de Sourdéac, who was himself a machinist and by a M. de Champeron, was now standing empty, as Lulli had obtained the monopoly of performing operas. This theatre, which was admirably arranged and provided with a number of the most up-to-date ' machines,' was situated in the Rue Mazarine, opposite to the Rue Guénégaud. From the latter street the theatre adopted the name "the Theatre in the Rue Guénégaud." [1]

The two aristocratic machinists wished to get rid of their theatre, as it was no longer of any use to them, and both the Marais troupe and the Molière company were eager to get it, but the latter came first. On May 23rd they had already bought Sourdéac and Champeron's Guénégaud theatre for the sum of 30,000 francs cash. Of this sum, however, only 14,000 francs were paid down— and it was Mme. Molière who advanced this money to the company—while the remaining 16,000 were to be paid by instalments of 50 francs each evening of performance. This form of payment, however, was subsequently altered so as to include Sourdéac and Champeron as shareholders in the theatre on a par with the full-share actors, an arrangement of which the actors bitterly repented afterwards. They got into constant difficulties with the two original owners. During these years La Grange's account-book bristles with furious little marginal notes against Messrs Sourdéac and Champeron. Their petty quarrels at last led to a lawsuit, which resulted in excluding the two masterful machinists from the company.

These difficulties, however, did not occur till later. For the present the theatre was acquired without any great trouble. What remained was to fill up the vacancies in the company, and here again circumstances favoured the actors of Molière's company.

---

[1] Now Nos. 42 and 44. A marble tablet on No. 42 still reminds us of the situation of the old theatre.

The Marais theatre had long been on the decline. Its situation had always proved bad, and no author or actor had been able to overcome the disinclination of the public to journey to this gloomy and dismal spot. Exactly a month after the company of Molière had acquired its new theatre, a still greater stroke of luck happened. The Marais theatre was put down by royal command, and an order was issued at the same time that the two companies, Molière's and the Marais, were to unite and to act in future in the Guénégaud theatre.

Whether this fusion took place at the instigation of La Grange, we do not know, but there can be no doubt that, if the company of Molière maintained its position during this difficult time, it was due to this skilful and energetic man. Molière's widow afforded a never failing financial support. She was, indeed, the owner of the *répertoire*, and continued to receive her share of the proceeds of her husband's plays, though she had no legal claim to it. But light-minded and unbusiness-like as she was, she willingly left the whole management to La Grange. And now, after the amalgamation of the two companies, he stood as the official manager of the whole of the numerous staff. The united company consisted of the following members :—

Actors.

From the original company of Molière :—	From the Marais :—
La Grange.	Rosimond.
de Brie	la Roque
du Croisy	d'Auvilliers

Hubert   du Pin
                                    Verneuil
                                    Guérin d'Estriché

Actresses.

Molière   d'Auvilliers
de Brie   du Pin
Aubry (Geneviève Béjart)   Ozillon
la Grange   Guyot
Angélique du Croisy

In quality the additions to the company were not very valuable. The new ladies, especially, were decidedly inferior. Mme. d'Auvilliers was a daughter of old Montfleury, and Mme. du Pin of Raymond Poisson; but though both had excellent stage-blood in their veins, neither had inherited the talent of her father. Mlle. Ozillon was impossible, and had to be dismissed on the first opportunity, and if Mme. Guyot attained some distinction, it was less by her talent than by her good looks and astuteness. At a more advanced age she became cashier to the company, and in that position cheated it systematically. This, however, was not discovered till after her death, when it was revealed through her will, in which she bequeathed all her property to her colleagues.[1]

The actors were not much better. La Roque, who

---

[1] Some modern biographers of Molière have attributed the authorship of *La fameuse Comédienne*, the lampoon on Molière's widow, to Mlle. Guyot or Judith de Nevers, as her real name was; and this conjecture is not without plausibility, though there is no means of proving it. At all events it is not so utterly unfounded as the suggestion which Mahrenholtz announces with much confidence, that the gentle Mlle. de Brie might be the author.

had held a leading position at the Marais theatre,[1] was now far on in the seventies, d'Auvilliers and du Pin were at best fit for "utilities," and Achille Varlet, called Verneuil, the brother of La Grange, was no better. The only actor who became a valuable support to the theatre was Guérin d'Estriché. He is best known to posterity by the fact that in 1677 he married Molière's widow, and this marriage, by which he became the successor of so great a man,—and moreover became happy with a wife who had made Molière suffer all the pangs of jealousy,—has most unjustly cast a shadow on his fame.

Even in his life time we read in an epigram on his wife :—

Elle avait un mari d'esprit qu'elle aimait peu :
Elle en prend un de chair, qu'elle aime d'avantage.[2]

But even if he was very inferior in every respect to Molière, the mere fact that Armande Béjart got on better with him than with her first husband is not sufficient ground for considering him an outcast of humanity.[3]

He was, according to all testimonies, a very honest man, and became a very able actor, who, even up to his eighty-first year, was exceedingly popular at the Théâtre français, especially in the parts of old men, the " *rôles de manteau*" as they were called, among which

---

[1] See above p. 89.
[2] She had a husband of wit, whom she loved but little :
She takes one of flesh, of whom she is more fond.
[3] Thus, for instance, Mahrenholtz calls him, "*ein roher Mensch von zwei-felhaften Antecedentien*" (a rough person of doubtful antecedents). At the same time this inexact historian of the theatre states him to have died in 1705, while, as a matter of fact, he lived right up to 1728 and continued acting till 1717.

L'Avare and *Le Grondeur*[1] were his most celebrated performances.

On the whole, the combined Guénégaud company was no doubt considerably inferior to that of the Hôtel de Bourgogne, its only rival at the time, and it may be supposed that La Grange's feelings were not over hopeful, when on Sunday, July 9th, 1673, he opened the spick-and-span new theatre with *Tartufe*.

And it must be confessed that the season turned out a poor one. The theatre lived, so to speak, exclusively on Molière's old plays, which, besides being to a great extent exhausted, were probably not so well acted as in the days of the master. Scarcely any new plays saw the light, and those that did were not much appreciated. Yet two of the former constant contributors to the *répertoire* of the Hôtel de Bourgogne, Antoine Montfleury and Thomas Corneille, were engaged as playwrights. The difference between the old and the new periods is best shown by some bald figures: during the last year of Molière's life each share had amounted to 4585 francs 13 sous; the first season of the Hôtel Guénégaud only yielded 1481 francs a share.

Moreover, there were plenty of internal dissensions, on which we have only imperfect information. Among them the quarrels with the two machinists, Sourdéac and Champeron, are sufficiently elucidated by the documents in the lawsuit. This affair all but led to a general revolt, as some of the actors, the two d'Auvilliers

---

[1] *Le Grondeur* by Brueys and Palaprat, a very popular play in most *répertoires*.

and the du Pins, for instance, sided with the machinists. These members were for a time excluded from the company. Details of other quarrels transpire through the marginal notes of La Grange. Thus in one place we read (in the very first season) "Mlle. de Molière refused to play."[1]—Why?—Nobody knows. In another place: "Here (Nov. 9th) Mlle. de Brie sided with Messrs d'Auvilliers and du Pin, refused to go on playing and pretended to be ill."[2] If even the gentle de Brie, the model of true femininity, showed her claws, clearly La Grange had a difficult task to grapple with, and no doubt he often exclaimed with his great master: "Queer animals, indeed, those actors!"

But though La Grange was not a genius like Molière, he possessed a tough energy, which irresistibly pursued its end, and in the long run led to quiet and order. In its action against the machinists and the refractory actors the company obtained full satisfaction. Moreover they had some real success, especially with the play which had occasioned the whole quarrel, Thomas Corneille's *Circé*.

This tragedy was a mere spectacle, and constructed expressly with a view to the good machinery possessed by the theatre of the Hôtel Guénégaud, but the mounting was very expensive, and the heavy costs had enabled the intriguing machinists to frighten part of the staff into refusing to be shareholders.

Now the opposition was crushed, *Circé* was performed on March 17th, 1675, and became an enormous attraction, yielding unheard-of takings. Donneau de

---

[1] La Grange: *Registre*, p. 151.   [2] *Ibid.* p. 163.

Visé, who himself held a share in the piece, writes in his *Mercure Galant* (January 1710): "The success of the play was so prodigious that it was played uninterruptedly from the beginning of Lent to September,[1] and the run would have been longer still, had not the interests of one single person put obstacles in the way of the singing.[2]

"It is a remarkable fact that during the first six weeks the Salle de la Comédie was full by noon, and since it was impossible to find room there, people used to pay half a *louis d'or* at the entrance to be allowed to go in, and were quite pleased when for the sum which usually secured a place in the front boxes they now got a place in the third row. I state nothing which cannot be proved by the actors' register."[3]

Thenceforth Thomas Corneille and his collaborator de Visé became the chief purveyors of successful plays to the company, and, under the steadygoing management of La Grange, the theatre worked its way onward slowly but surely. It was no longer what the Palais Royal had been in Molière's time, the radiant focus of attraction to

---

[1] This statement is not quite accurate. *Circé* was produced for the first time just at the end of the season, which it closed in nine consecutive performances, with the enormous average proceeds of 2600 francs. In the subsequent season it ran sixty-six times, but not uninterruptedly, as for a time it alternated with Le Clerc's *Iphigénie*. This is clear from the *Registre* of La Grange. The brothers Parfaicts' corrections of de Visé's statements are much more incorrect than the originals.—*Histoire du Théâtre français*, xi. p. 410, note *a*.

[2] This one single person was Lulli, to whom all the gold spun by *Circé* was an eye-sore, wherefore he prevented the actors from obtaining the help of the dancers and singers they were in need of.

[3] In spite of this solemn assurance of de Visé's, he is exaggerating a little. The great rush only lasted for the first nine performances. The rest were certainly well attended, but not by the crowds that de Visé describes.

all who took an interest in art, where the first performances were exciting events that stirred the passions, and
sometimes even roused the authorities of the State.   But
gradually it became, as it were, the broad, calm flow
of a swift and foaming stream, descending from the
highest summits.

Meanwhile the Hôtel de Bourgogne had a somewhat different career. When Baron, La Thorillière,
Mlle. Beauval and her husband joined the Royal Actors
after the death of Molière, the Hôtel possessed a
company of superior artistic power.   Michel Baron was
or became absolutely the leading actor during the first
period after Molière.

He soon acquired a very strong hold on the public,
not only by his manly beauty and by his unshakable
self-confidence, which was partly inborn and in the
course of time developed to a marvellous degree, but
also by his genuine and noble talent.

His gifts were essentially those of a tragedian, and
therefore it was not so unnatural as has been alleged,
that after the death of Molière he should join the
theatre where tragedy was the line particularly cultivated, and for which Racine, the greatest tragic author
of the time, wrote his works.   However, Baron also
acted a number of great parts in comedy, and shone
quite as much in them as in those of his real *genre*.
He played, for instance, Alceste in *Le Misanthrope*,
Jupiter in *L'Amphitryon*, Dorante in *Le Menteur* and
Moncade, the principal part in his own play *L'Homme à
bonnes fortunes*.

He came to the Hôtel de Bourgogne trained in a

school which differed very much from the style that had hitherto reigned at that theatre. His conception of the tragic style was due to the influence of Molière, but he evidently possessed a far greater capacity for carrying out the great master's principles than the teacher himself; for he was successful in just the point where Molière constantly failed, in convincing the public, that is, that a natural style of speaking is right, even in tragedy. In France he became the first victorious advocate of the cause of naturalness in the everlasting strife between the two tragic schools, the school of pompous, rhythmically chanting declamation, and that of the varied speech that breaks up the verses, and points its utterance by the meaning of the sentences.

And these principles of freedom in art he did not— as many others have done—desert as he grew older. On the contrary, he developed them more and more radically, and that under very peculiar circumstances.

His theatrical career was capricious to an extraordinary degree. After rising as high as possible in the opinion of all, not to speak of his own; after reaching at an early age the distinction of being absolutely the first actor in France, the actor who gave the French theatre its stamp, he suddenly broke off at the very zenith of his years, at the age of only thirty-eight. It is clear that he left the stage from mere caprice, according to some accounts, because his comrades would not give up their autonomy and put the whole power into his hands. However, he retired with full honours. Besides the usual pension paid him by the company, the King gave him an extra annuity of 3000 francs. He very nearly refused this latter favour, because the royal decree stated that this sum was to be paid " *au nommé Michel Boyron, dit Baron, l'un de mes comédiens.*[1]   This offended him deeply.

For all that he accepted the annuity, and for thirty years he lived apart from the theatre.   Then suddenly, in his sixty-seventh year, he informed his former comrades—or rather their successors, for only one of the old troupe, his brother-in-law, La Thorillière the younger, still remained—that he wished to return to the stage, not as a guest for a few appearances, but as a permanent member.

The extraordinary thing was that he came back, not with a weak *réchauffé* of former triumphs, but with new impulses and fresh ideas, which again revolutionised the tragic style, exposed the bombastic manner of mediocrities like Mlle. Duclos, and guided great talents, like that of Adrienne Lecouvreur, on the right path.   The " new manner" of the nearly septuagenarian Baron was the general topic of conversation, and his style was discussed, disputed and parodied, as if it had been that of a new man.

Contemporary reports on the "new manner" are interesting to read, not only because they throw light on its nature, but also because they show to what degree the interest in histrionic art had increased at that date. Whereas in the first half of the seventeenth century the existence of such an art was not acknowledged at all, and in the latter part people began to realise that the representation of human character might be considered

[1] "To the said Michel Boyron, called Baron, one of my comedians."

as an art in itself, in the eighteenth century this hitherto despised art was taken up as a subject for eager argument and philosophical discussion, and people went to the theatre not merely to see a sensational play, to meet their friends or to kill time, but also to enjoy the art of the actor for its own sake, and to draw parallels between this and that player and this and that performance.

Thus histrionic art rose to honour and dignity, and the eighteenth century became not only the age of the great philosophers, but also that of the great actors.

A well-known Italian actress, who played in Paris, has left a description at first hand of Baron's reappearance and his new style, and as this document has never yet been brought to notice by any French historian of the theatre, we think part of it ought to find a place here.

It is the celebrated Elena Riccoboni,[1] who, in a long letter to the Abbé Conti, writes as follows : —

" To the honour you have shown me in asking my opinion about the manner of M. Baron, now that he has reappeared on the stage, I reply by letter, first of all in order to prevent all the concoctions, which in such cases are produced in Paris, and the accusations of saying what I have not said, and secondly in order to be instructed by your profound knowledge in a question in which I might easily be mistaken.   I confess that when, before he had appeared on the stage, one part of the Parisian public wanted him to be hissed, the other to be violently applauded, some asserting that he would not please with his old manner, others that he would gain

---

[1] For this actress and her even more famous husband, see vol. ii. *Middle Ages and Renaissance*, pp. 304 ff.

the highest approval, I confess, I say, that I conceived the most ardent desire to hear this excellent man. But when, after the first day of his appearance before the public, I learned that he did not follow the present manner, or resume his earlier manner, but introduced an entirely new one, not hitherto known on your tragic stage, that is to say that he *speaks* and does not *declaim*, then my desire to become aquainted with him increased. At last I found for once an opportunity of leaving my occupations.

" In my opinion M. Baron, generally speaking, is an excellent actor. He always listens to his fellow-actors, a thing to which actors, as a rule, pay little heed, and his attention is accompanied by such movements of face and body as are required by the nature of the speeches to which he listens. When speaking, his talk is real conversation. For instance, in *Polyeucte*, where he speaks of the persecution of the Christians, or in *Les Horaces*, the first scene with Curatius, which is nothing but a friendly interchange of polite speeches, he conversed with the most delicate naturalness, without falling into any excesses, either of exaggeration to sublimity or of too realistic imitation.

" For the rest—be it said with all the respect due to the reputation of so great a man—I certainly always thought the style of M. Baron true and natural; but just as nature is not always beautiful, and every truth is not suitable for the stage, so at times he does not appear to me to be in harmony with the subject. It is indisputable that the tragic hero, in so far as he is a human being must not alienate himself from nature; but certainly it is

also true that the great actions and high lineage or position of tragic heroes require a naturally majestic and
dignified manner . . ."

The Italian actress now blames Baron for being
too commonplace in his movements in tragedy—a thing
for which modern tragedians of the same school are still
blamed, and she maintains that this may indeed be true
to nature, but to the nature of a citizen or shop-keeper,
not to that of a sublime hero.   However, her examples
show that her notions of the sublime in tragedy are
quite conventional, and that Baron was undoubtedly
right.   Signora Riccoboni thinks that Baron's style is in-
appropriate to tragedies of a classical character, but more
suitable for tragic dramas or more modern subjects, like
Le Cid, *Le Comte d'Essex*, etc., because in her eyes the
men of remote periods seem superior to nature, superhuman.   This is a widespread mistake, even in our own
days, and it is the cause of much superhuman, or rather
inhuman delivery employed by many actors in ancient
plays.

Signora Riccoboni thinks, however, that even
Baron himself cannot carry out his principles of true
acting.   " I have noticed," she goes on, " that M. Baron
frequently changes his bearing [*figura*] and allows himself to be carried away by the necessity of laying stress
on his verses or the hero's feelings, or of keeping up a
situation, and that on these occasions he declaims
like the others, and cries out as loud as he can.   This
necessity makes him appear as an actor with different
phases, now sublime and now commonplace, which
jars on my ear, as in the same scene and the same

actor I seem to hear a tragic Horace and a comic Dorante.

" How can it be maintained that Mithridate, in inform-ing his sons of his resolution to go to Rome and make war on its inhabitants, should speak with the same nonchalance and the same cool, everyday tone, as if he were telling them of some entirely indifferent matter?—This was how Baron did it. . . .

" M. Baron says—and with many of his spectators this is a merit—that he tries by every means to avoid the rhyme. I myself commend him for it, but I cannot admit that a tragic actor, in attempting to disguise the rhyme, ought also to do his best to efface the verse by levelling it to such a degree, and by adopting the tone of the most commonplace talk." [1]

The struggle which is ever breaking out afresh between grand declamation and natural speech, here for the first time finds its distinct and conscious expression in France, and what was generally said in praise of Baron was repeated in almost similar words of Talma about a century later.

Let us take the opinion of an acute critic about Baron —even when he was so old that he had no longer ab-solute power over his natural resources (compare fig. 44).

In his critical and literary Memoirs Charles Collé writes as follows: " Baron, Adrienne Lecouvreur and the two Quinaults, whom I have seen though I am not so very old yet,[2] gave me an idea of perfection, especially

---

[1] This letter has been published by A. Ademollo in his monograph on the Riccoboni family: *Una famiglia di comici italiani nel sec. xviii.* Ap-pendix iii., pp. 124 ff.

[2] Collé wrote this in 1750, at the age of forty. The passage occurs in his *Journal historique*, 1805, pp. 170 f.

Baron, who, if he had not occasionally lacked a little warmth, would have been the most perfect actor who could ever have existed. And indeed it must be supposed he possessed this quality—essential in an actor—when he was young. When I saw him he was already between seventy-two and seventy-five years old, and at that age he might well be forgiven for not being kindled into passion so easily as an actor of thirty. However, he made up for this drawback by an intelligence, a noble bearing and dignity, which I have seen nowhere but in him. He particularly distinguished himself in the details of a part; he possessed a naturalness which went so far as to bring the familiar style into tragedy without thereby lowering its dignity.

"He was no less superior in comedy; I have seen him play divinely in such parts as the Misanthrope, Arnolphe and Simon in *L'Andrienne*; his performance was so full of truth and naturalness that he constantly made us forget the actor, and he carried the illusion to the point of persuading one that it was a real action taking place before one's eyes.

"He never declaimed, not even in the highest tragedy; and he broke the measure of the verse so as never to fatigue you with the intolerable monotony of the Alexandrines. Fine verse, therefore, gained nothing in his mouth, and it was difficult to distinguish whether the verses he was reciting were by Racine or by la Chaussé; he never accentuated the rhythm of a verse, only the situation, the feeling which it expressed. His pauses were so long and his acting so slow, that the performance lasted half an hour longer when he took part in it.

" Before he entered the stage he used to work himself up by soliloquising or whispering to the actor entering with him, and by this means he *was* the character he represented from the very first words he uttered.

" He was fond of theatrical pomp, and when acting the rôle of an emperor or king, he always had half a score of supers dressed up in Roman costume marching in front of him. *À propos* of this, I remember that once, when he was playing the High Priest in *Athalie*, and the supers whom he had ordered to be attired as Levites did not arrive in time for a necessary piece of business, he cried at the top of his voice : ' A Levite, a Levite— What the devil! Isn't there a single —— of a Levite?' Those who were on the stage heard it and had a good laugh at his eagerness and anger. He was a fanatic in his art, and that is an important thing for getting on in it."

To those who did not see or took no interest in the extraordinary dramatic powers of Baron, he stood as a unique example of vanity, and of an arrogance bordering on megalomania. The following observation of his own is very characteristic. He said : " In every century you may meet with a Cæsar, but it requires two thousand years to produce a Baron, and since the days of Roscius I know of none but myself." We can scarcely doubt that this was his real opinion.

His incredible self-confidence, which frequently made him appear ludicrous outside the theatre, was very useful to him on the stage, where it gave him a never-failing assurance and a presence of mind which was never thrown off its balance by occasional impudent apostrophes from the pit.

Thus, for instance, when playing Agamemnon in
Iphigénie en Aulide, he chose to begin the piece quite in
an undertone. Voices from the pit cried: "Louder!
louder!" "If I said it louder," replied he, "it would be
wrong," and calmly went on as he had begun.

In his old age he still acted Rodrigo in *Le Cid*, a
part in which the following lines occur :—

> " Je suis jeune, il est vrai, mais aux âmes bien nées
> La valeur n'attend pas le nombre des années.[1]

These words were so flatly contradicted by the
actor's appearance that the pit broke out into roars of
laughter. Baron was not put out. Quite coolly he
repeated the two lines, even laying special stress on the
dangerous words :—

> "Je suis jeune, il est vrai, . . ."

And this unruffled self-assurance commanded such
respect from the audience, that they now burst out into
applause.

For all that, he could not, of course, avoid being scoffed
at on account of his age, and he shared the fate of those
who even in private life try to preserve a youthful
appearance by artificial means—he was considered much
older than he really was. Thus, when he was seventy-
three, Lesage makes his *"Diable boiteux"* say of him :[2]
"This actor is so old that not a human creature in

---

[1] I am young, it is true, but a high-born mind does not wait for
mature age to prove its valour.

[2] *Le Diable boiteux* by Lesage originally appeared in 1707, but at that
time Baron was only fifty-four years old, and not at the theatre at all ;
the passage quoted does not appear in the first edition ; it was not added
till the edition of 1726 (chap. xvi.).

Madrid can say that he saw his *début* . . . He possesses talent, and is so proud and vain of it that he thinks such a being as himself is something more than human."

In his *Gil Blas*, by the bye, the same Lesage gives an exceedingly vivid and realistic caricature of the old actor. It is not very respectful and does not by any means give him sufficient credit as an artist, but it must be borne in mind that Lesage, who mostly wrote for performances at fairs and for the Italian theatre, did not feel favourably inclined towards the " French Actors."   In a chapter (book III. chapter xi.) headed : " How the Actors lived together, and how they treated the Authors," he writes :—

" Now two actresses came in, Constance and Celinaura, and a moment after Florimonde appeared, accompanied by a man who looked like a most exquisite *señor cavallero* . . . He wore a hat turned up with a bunch of pale green feathers and very tight breeches . . . His gloves and his pocket handkerchief were lying in the hollow of his sword-hilt, and he wore his mantle with peculiar grace.

" Though he was good-looking and exceedingly well-proportioned, I at once noticed something singular about him.   That nobleman must be an original, I said to myself.   And I was not mistaken, he was indeed a man of marked individuality.

" As soon as he came into the room he opened his arms and rushed up to embrace the actresses and actors, one after the other, with even more exaggerated demonstrations than the *petits-maîtres*.   Nor was my impression changed when he began to speak.   He dwelt with fondness on every syllable, and pronounced his words in an emphatic tone with gestures and glances appropriate to the subject.

" I was inquisitive enough to ask Laura who the gentleman was.—' I pardon you,' she answered me, ' this fit of inquisitiveness, for it is impossible to see this Don Carlos Alonzo de la Ventoleria [1] for the first time without feeling the inclination that now torments you.   Now I will draw you a portrait of him from nature.   In the first place he was originally a player.   He left the theatre from caprice, and afterwards repented of it from common sense.   Did you notice his black hair ?   It is dyed as well as his eye-brows and moustache.   He is older than Saturn.   But as on his birth his parents forgot to have his name put down on the church register, he takes advantage of their negligence and pretends to be a score of years younger than he really is [2] . . . He spent the twelve first lustres of his life in dense ignorance, but in order to become a scholar he engaged a teacher who taught him to spell out Latin and Greek.   Moreover, he knows a multitude of good stories by heart, which he has repeated so often, pretending that they are of his own making, that he now really believes that he has invented them.   He intersperses his conversation with them, and it may truly be said that his mind shines at the expense of his memory.   For the rest he is said to be a great actor, and I will gladly pay him the compliment of believing it ; but I confess to you that I do not like him.   I sometimes

[1] It must be borne in mind that both in *Gil Blas* and in *Le Diable boiteux* the scene is laid in Spain ; but the portraits were not the less transparent for that.

[2] The first two volumes of *Gil Blas*, which contain this portrait of Baron, were published in 1715 ; so he was sixty-two years old at the time.

hear him recite here, and among other faults I think his pronunciation is much too affected, and his voice vibrates, all of which renders his declamation old-fashioned and ludicrous.' "

Baron's alleged ignorance is no doubt much exaggerated, though he was by no means a learned man. At any rate he was an able dramatic writer, and most of his plays were successful. The best known among them is *L'Homme à bonnes fortunes* already mentioned, in which he has described himself as the frivolous ladies' man, *La Coquette* and *L'Andrienne*.

Baron's claim to the authorship of the dramatic works which have appeared under his name has been disputed, but without any positive proof. There are innumerable examples of the fact that an excellent actor can write acceptable plays without being either a poet or a scholar, and when a man is as conceited and vainglorious as Baron, his contemporaries are inclined to deny him every good quality.

Meanwhile, in pursuing the artistic career of Baron, we have strayed far away from the period which is the principal object of our study. Baron died, tired of life, in 1729, after playing in comedy till within a few months of his death. But we have still to mention a few of the colleagues of his younger days, especially the actress who stood beside him in all the great tragedies, the celebrated heroine of the Hôtel de Bourgogne, Mlle. Champmeslé, *née* Marie Desmares.

In tragedy she gained a fame equal to Baron's, but she was no doubt far from being so prominent in her art. While Baron came to the Hôtel with something

new and with the training he had received from the most
talented dramatist of the time, Mlle. Champmeslé produced her most striking effects by her ardent tragic
temperament and her excellent stage appearance ; otherwise she followed in the old groove.

Originally a provincial actress, she came to the Marais
in 1669, where the esteemed La Roque instructed her
in the best principles of declamation.　The Hôtel de
Bourgogne, which had no first class tragic actress but
Mlle. des Oeillets, who was old and ugly, at once cast
its eyes upon the new star, and immediately engaged
her for the next season.　She was then twenty-nine
years old, a born actress (she belonged to a large family
of actors), very captivating without being a regular
beauty, and blessed with a beautiful voice, of which she
made a fine, if not a natural, use in her declamation.

Her manner, however, was approved of, not only by
the ordinary public, but also by the great authors, abo·e
all by Racine, who at once, on her first appearance in the
Hôtel, became enthusiastic about her ; a feeling which
was reciprocated, and very soon developed into a *liaison*.
She thus became *par excellence* the interpreter of Racine
and the impersonator of his heroines, after being most
carefully prepared for the performances by the author
himself, and having her tendency to oratorical and
chanting declamation further developed into mannerism.

In spite of this, her passionate temperament, which
was of genuine dramatic power, must clearly have mani-
fested itself somehow, or it would have been impossible
for her to produce such a strong impression, even on
minds that had no inclination for oratorical pomp, as, for

instance, Mme. de Sévigné. This lady writes very vividly and enthusiastically about her " daughter-in-law," as she calls her, because her son had been the actress's lover. " I thought Racine's play [1] beautiful ; we went to see it. My daughter-in-law appeared to me the most miraculously good actress I have ever seen. She stands a hundred thousand miles above des Oeillets. And I myself, who am considered fairly good on the stage, I am not fit to light the candles where she acts. At close quarters she is ugly, and I do not wonder that my son felt somewhat choky in her presence, but when reciting verses, she is bewitching."

On another occasion (April 1st, 1672) she writes : " Mlle. Champmeslé is something so extraordinary that you have never seen anything like it in your life. It is the actress, not the play, people go to see. I went to see *Ariane* [2] for the sole sake of Mlle. Champmeslé. This comedy is washy, and the actors damnable ; but when Mlle. Champmeslé enters, you hear a murmur, all are carried away, and you shed tears at her despair."

These strong statements by Mme. de Sévigné, who was easily roused to enthusiasm, are only one voice among the many of Mlle. Champmeslé's admirers. What we constantly find praised by her eulogists is her voice, that wonderful voice which at one moment could be so sweet and melting that it moved you to tears, and the next so powerful and sonorous that, when the doors

---

[1] *Bajazet*, it was performed for the first time at the Hôtel de Bourgogne, on January 5th, 1672. Mme. de Sévigné's letter is dated January 15th of the same year.

[2] A tragedy by Thomas Corneille, performed for the first time on March 4th, 1672, at the Hôtel de Bourgogne.

of the boxes at the back of the house were open, her declamation was said to have been heard in the Café Procope.[1]

"You will admit," says the author of *Entretiens galants*, "that Mlle. Champmeslé would not please you so much, if she had a less pleasant voice. But she shows so much art in the use of it, and she accommodates its modulations so well to nature, that her heart really seems to be full of the passion which is only in her mouth."

In one way Mlle. Champmeslé formed a school, in so far as the chanting declamation, in which the principal stress was laid on the training of the voice, became a good tradition in the first half of the eighteenth century. Her niece, Mlle. Desmares, and her pupil, Mlle. Duclos, adopted and cultivated her principles of voice-training, in which the former succeeded because she had real talent, while Mlle. Duclos became a forbidding example of false and hollow declamation. To this day we can trace in the French tragic actresses—in Sarah Bernhardt for instance—the old technique, with the chanting, insinuating *voix touchante* and the violently over-strained and high-pitched utterance.

From certain facts which have been mentioned casually, the reader will possibly have received the impression that the moral life of Mlle. Champmeslé was not quite so beautiful as her voice, and this impression is by no means wrong.

M. du Tralage, whose manuscript notes we have quoted repeatedly, made two lists, on one of which he

[1] The Café Procope was a well-known resort of actors and writers. It stood opposite to the Theatre in the Rue Guénégaud, of which Mlle. Champmeslé afterwards became a member.

put down the names of the actors and actresses who led a virtuous life, and on the other the names of those whose lives were by no means blameless. Among the former he mentions, for instance, Molière, La Grange and his wife, and Floridor. But among the sinners—and the worst of them—we find the names of " Sieur Baron, great gambler and general satyr in relation to beautiful women ; the wife of Molière, who has been repeatedly 'protected' by influential men, and who was separated from her husband ; Sieur Champmeslé and his wife, who are separated from each other by their debauches. The wife was enceinte by her lover, while the servant girl was in the same case by Sieur Champmeslé. Their amorous adventures would fill a large book."[1]

The immorality of her life was a well-known fact, and while her art was exalted in enthusiastic songs, malicious epigrams swarmed like gnats about her private life.

Her husband, Charles Chevillet, called Champmeslé, by no means came up to her as actor, at least not at this period at the Hôtel de Bourgogne, where he was over-shadowed by the exceedingly capable La Thorillière, the old comrade of Molière in the branch which they both cultivated, *i.e.* kings in tragedy and broad comedy parts. Champmeslé, however, had a style of his own. A decided epicurean in his private life, fond of champagne and handsome women, fat, good-looking and polished in manner, he was the prototype of the *père noble*, with a touch of depravity and *bonhomie de grand*

---

[1] *Notes et Documents, etc. par Jean Nicolas du Tralage*, published by le Bibliophile Jacob, 1880, pp. 14 f.

seigneur, who is still one of the types of the French theatre.   Moreover, he was an educated man, of pleasant manners, and though born in the modest home of a tradesman's family (his father was a dealer in ribbons on the Pont-au-Change) he possessed not only a delicate taste for luxury, but a correct artistic sense, which led to his being consulted on matters of art by men of far greater distinction.   He even enjoyed the honour of collaborating with La Fontaine ; for instance in the comedy *La Coupe enchantée*.   He himself was the author of a number of plays, which are by no means without talent.[1]

The two Champmeslés, Baron and La Thorillière were the fresh additions to the Hôtel de Bourgogne, and to some extent betokened a new school.   Still a portion was left of the old staff, notably Raymond Poisson, who now, after the death of Molière, was probably the first comic actor in Paris.   The excellent Floridor was dead, and the old de Villiers was pensioned off.   In 1674 the troupe was composed as follows :—

Actors	*Actresses*
Hauteroche	Beauchâteau
La Fleur	Poisson
Raymond Poisson	d'Ennebault
Brécourt	Brécourt
Champmeslé	Champmeslé
La Thuilerie	Beauval
La Thorillière	La Thuilerie
Baron	
Beauval	

[1] V. Fournel's *Les Contemporains de Molière* contains a complete enumeration of the plays of Champmeslé.

We have made acquaintance with most of these names ; La Fleur and his son, La Thuilerie, alone have not been mentioned in our report. La Fleur was an actor of the old school of Montfleury ; he is commended also for his " feeling," and is said to have been the first who possessed what a French technical term calls *entrailles,* meaning the self-consuming method, which by exhibiting strong individual feeling carries away the spectators. He was married to a daughter of old Gros Guillaume, and by her had a son, La Thuilerie, whose theatrical career has left no deep impression. La Thuilerie's wife, who possessed no talent at all, was a daughter of Raymond Poisson.

On the whole, actors grew more and more into the way of intermarrying, and soon came to form a kind of large family. It was natural enough, therefore, that a closer connection between the companies could be thought of, and ere long there was a good opportunity of bringing about such a union.

It would seem that the troupe of the Hôtel de Bourgogne was very superior to that of the Guénégaud theatre ; the latter, nevertheless, was the more prosperous, owing to the excellent management of La Grange.

We have seen that he first enticed Thomas Corneille from the Hôtel, and this was a most important conquest, for at this time Thomas Corneille was by far the most popular dramatist and the one most capable of adapting a play to the taste of the public. Plays like *Circé, L'Inconnu,* and last but not least, *La Devineresse,* a dramatisation of the case of the poisoner la Voisin, gave the Guénégaud theatre an immense start.

But La Grange made even a better move, when in 1670 he prevailed on the Champmeslés to leave the Hôtel and join the Guénégaud. His company made a sacrifice to win them by giving them, besides a whole share each, an additional annuity of a thousand francs. But this was a small consideration in comparison with the gain of such an important addition as Mlle. Champmeslé, especially as La Grange thus deprived the rival theatre of the most celebrated tragic actress in Paris.

It was indeed neither more nor less than the death-blow of the old theatre. To be sure it still had Baron, but there was now no actress fit to play with him, and this, in the branch and the *répertoire* in which he acted, was absolutely indispensable. Quarrels within its ranks and lack of firm leadership shook the old company to its foundation, and on the death of La Thorillière, on July 27th, 1680, it lost its last administrative pillar of support.[1]

It was then that the union of the enfeebled old Royal company and the prosperous company of Molière seems to have been decided upon. The plan had probably been conceived at an earlier date, and very likely La Thorillière had been an obstacle to its realisation. Both earlier and later historians of the theatre maintain that the idea of the fusion had originated with the King, and some of them even assert that it was the Royal

---

[1] " On Saturday, July 27th, 1680, M. de la Thorillière died at the Hôtel de Bourgogne, which occasioned the junction of the two companies in the following month of August."—Marginal note of the *Registre* of La Grange. (p. 235).

troupe which absorbed that of Molière.[1]   The latter assertion is absolutely wrong.   As to the former, it seems to me to follow from the *Registre* of La Grange, that the union was concluded at the desire of the companies, and that subsequently they sought the royal sanction to their proposal.   More than three weeks after the fusion was considered as settled among the actors came the first royal warrant, which ran as follows : " His Majesty, being desirous to unite the two troupes of comedians acting in Paris, has ordered me to acquaint them that it is his intention to keep in his service those whose names I have written in this memorandum, His Majesty's will being that it shall be carried out in every point; and those actors and actresses who will not acquiesce therein shall not be permitted henceforth to act in Paris.   At Charleville, the 18th August 1680.   (Signed) The Duke de Créqui."[2]   Then follow particulars of the actors and actresses who were to remain.   They were twenty-seven in all, fifteen actors [3] and twelve actresses.

[1] For instance Mahrenholtz, p. 291 and elsewhere.

[2] The document, which is reprinted from the authentic original by Bonnassies (*op. cit.* p. 56), retains this date ; but La Grange, who also gives it, has the 8th August.

[3] In the original document we read "fourteen actors," while La Grange has fifteen. The latter figure is the right one, and the difference can be explained as follows. According to the royal order, du Croisy, the first performer of Tartufe, was to be discharged with a pension. However, he sent in a petition to be allowed to remain, in which he wrote, "that the late Molière wrote several parts on purpose for him, which the actors admit ; that it cannot be denied that he is quite as capable of acting as ever, that he is only forty-six years old, that even the majority of the actors of both troupes wish him to be reinstated, for which he is to pay an annuity of 1000 francs, if the King consents thereto." Du Croisy's petition was granted, but he was only to receive half a share, whereas formerly he had had a whole share. So we must suppose that his powers had, as a fact, somewhat declined, or that possibly after the death of Molière he was unable to work by himself.

Two months later came the actual *lettre de cachet*, which somewhat more specifically gave the combined companies the monopoly of all acting in Paris in the French language.   As for the Italians, who till then had shared a theatre with the company of Molière, they now took over the Hôtel de Bourgogne.   This *lettre de cachet* was couched as follows :—

IN THE KING'S NAME.

His Majesty having thought convenient to unite the two companies of actors who have had their stations in the Hôtel de Bourgogne and in the Rue de Guénégaud in Paris, so as in future to form one company, in order to render their dramatic performances more perfect through the help of the actors and actresses whom he has admitted into the said company, His Majesty has ordered and does order that the two companies of French actors are to be united in future, so as to form only one and the same company, which company is to consist of the actors and actresses whom His Majesty has set forth above ; and in order to give them the opportunity of improving more and more, it is the will of His said Majesty that the said company shall have the sole right of performing plays in Paris, and that all other French actors shall be forbidden to settle in the said city of Paris and its suburbs, except by the express order of His said Majesty.   His Majesty enjoins M. de la Reynie, Lieutenant-General of the Police, to see that the present order is carried out.

Given at Versailles, the 21st day in the month of October 1680.

LOUIS.   COLBERT.

However, on August 25th of the same year the two companies had already begun to act together, so that the company of the Guénégaud theatre simply admitted the *personnel* of the Hôtel de Bourgogne as shareholders, without otherwise interrupting or changing its performances or its *répertoire*. That the amalgamation was looked upon with interest by the public is obvious from the fact that the same programme, *Phèdre* and *Les Carrosses d'Orleans*,[1] which on the 23rd August, two days before the event, had put 680 francs into the treasury, on the 25th produced more than double that amount, viz., 1424 francs, 5 sous.[2]

The present Comédie Française, that is the French National Theatre, dates its origin from the year 1680. It would seem more natural to have chosen 1658, the year when Molière returned to Paris victorious, for not only is it a fact that it was Molière's theatre which assimilated the two others (which fully justifies the present company of the Théâtre Français in calling itself a direct descendant of the troupe of Molière) but, what is more, it was Molière who impressed the stamp of his greatness on the French Theatre; it was his genius which sustained it and gave it its peculiar national character, and it is his memory which even now makes us look up to his House with veneration, though it may not in every respect be managed so well as at the time when he himself reigned in it. An anniversary of the foundation of the French National Theatre ought never therefore to have been chosen outside the life-time of Molière.

---

[1] A new little play by Champmeslé.
[2] La Grange, *Registre*, pp. 236 and 242.

However the newly amalgamated company was far from forsaking its deceased master. His old enemies, indeed, made their entry into his house, but they came as vanquished, not as conquerors, and they willingly consented to co-operate in the plays at which they had formerly looked askance, but which continued to form the nucleus of the *répertoire*.

But though, financially, the newly privileged French Theatre prospered admirably, it must be said that, in the matter of art, the close of the century marked a decadence ; and its last twenty years would have been of no great importance, if during that period all that Paris possessed in the way of theatrical art had not fought in conjunction under the one proud banner—Molière.

BIBLIOGRAPHY

Ademollo, Ag. : Una famiglia di comici italiani nel secolo decimottavo. Firenze, 1885.

Allier, Raoul : La Cabale des Dévots (1627-1666). Paris, 1902.

Baluffe, Auguste : Molière inconnu. Sa vie. Vol. I., 1622-1646. Paris, 1886.

Bapst, Germain : Essai sur l'Histoire du Théâtre. Paris, 1893.

Baron, Michel : Théâtre de Monsieur Baron, 3 vols. Amsterdam, 1736.

Bonnassies, Jules : La Comédie-Française. Histoire administrative (1658-1757). Paris, 1874.

Bouquet, F. : La Troupe de Molière et les deux Corneille à Rouen en 1658. Paris, 1880.

Cailhava d'Estendoux, J. F. : Etudes sur Molière, ou Observations sur la vie, les moeurs, les ouvrages de cet auteur, et sur la manière de jouer ses pièces, etc. Paris, an. X. (1802).

Campardon, Emile : Documents inédits sur J. B. Poquelin Molière. Paris, 1871.

———— : Nouvelles pièces sur Molière et sur quelques Comédiens de sa troupe. Paris, 1876.

———— : Les Comédiens du Roi de la Troupe française pendant les deux derniers siècles. Paris, 1879.

Celler, Ludovic : Les Décors, les Costumes et la Mise en scène au XVII siècle, 1615-1680. Paris, 1869.

Chappuzeau, S. : Le Théâtre françois divisé en trois livres. Lyons, 1674. (Reprint by the Bibliophile Jacob. Brussels, 1867.)

Collé, Charles : Journal historique ou mémoires critiques et littéraires. Paris, 1805.

Corneille, Pierre : Œuvres, I.-VII. (Ed. Grands Ecrivains de la France).

Despois, Eugène : Le Théâtre français sous Louis XIV. Paris, 1874.

———— and *Paul Mesnard* : Œuvres de Molière, 9 vols. (Grands Ecrivains de la France).

Fameuse Comédienne, La : ou Histoire de la Guérin auparavant femme et veuve de Molière. Reprint, etc. by J. Bonnassies. Paris, 1870.

Fournel, Victor : Les Contemporains de Molière, recueil de comédies, rares ou peu connues, jouées de 1650 à 1680, 3 vols. Paris, 1863-1875.

———— : Curiosités théâtrales, anciennes et modernes, françaises et étrangères. Paris, 1859.

Grimarest : La Vie de Mr. de Molière. Amsterdam, 1705.

Hillemacher, Frédéric : Galerie historique de la Troupe de Molière. Lyon, 1861.

Jal, A. : Dictionnaire critique de biographie et d'histoire. Paris, 1872.

Jullien, Adolphe : Histoire du Costume au Théâtre depuis les origines du théâtre en France jusqu'à nos jours. Paris, 1880.

———— : Les Spectateurs sur le théâtre. Paris, 1875.

Jusserand, J. J. : Shakespeare in France under the Ancien Régime. London, 1899.

Lacroix, Paul : Iconographie Moliéresque. Paris, 1876.

La Fontaine : Les Amours de Psyché et de Cupidon. Paris, 1810.

Larroumet, Gustave : La Comédie de Molière, l'Auteur et le Milieu. Paris, 1893.

Lemazurier, P. D. : Galerie historique des Acteurs du Théâtre français depuis 1600 jusqu'à nos jours. Paris, 1810.

Léris, A. de : Dictionnaire portatif historique et littéraire des Théâtres. Paris, 1763.

Lesage : Histoire de Gil Blas de Santillane, 2 vols. Paris, 1835.

────── : Le Diable boiteux, 2 vols. Paris, 1878.

Loiseleur, Jules : Les Points obscurs de la Vie de Molière. Paris, 1877.

Mahrenholtz, R. : Molières Leben und Werke vom Standpunkt der heutigen Forschung. Heilbronn, 1881.

Mesnard, Paul : Notice biographique sur Molière (vol. x. des Œuvres de Molière, éd. Grands Ecrivains de la France). Paris, 1889.

Moland, Louis : Molière et la Comédie italienne. Paris, 1867.

────── : Molière, sa vie et ses ouvrages. Paris, 1887.

Monval, Georges : Chronologie Moliéresque. Paris, 1897.

────── : Le Moliériste, revue mensuelle, I.-X. Paris, 1879-1889.

Mouhy, Chevalier de : Abrégé de l'Histoire du Théâtre françois, 3 vols. Paris, 1780.

Parfaict frères : Histoire du Théâtre françois depuis son origine jusqu'à présent, 15 vols. Paris, 1754.

Pougin, Arthur : Acteurs et Actrices d'Autrefois. Paris, n. d.

Racine, Jean : Oeuvres, 4 vols. (Edit. Grands Ecrivains de la France).

Reynaud, Charles : Musée rétrospectif de la classe 18, Théâtre, à l'Exposition universelle de 1900 à Paris.

Rigal, Eugène : Le Théâtre français avant la période classique. Paris, 1901.

Sauval, Henri : Histoire et recherches des antiquités de la ville de Paris. Paris, 1724, 3 vols.

Scarron : Le Romant Comique. Paris, 1662.

Schweitzer, Heinrich : Molière und seine Bühne. Molière Museum, Wiesbaden, 1881-1884.

Soleirol : Molière et sa Troupe. Paris, 1858.

Tallemant des Réaux : Les Historiettes. 3rd edition, by Monmerqúe and P. Paris, 9 vols. Paris, 1854-1860.

Taschereau, J. : Histoire de la Vie et des Ouvrages de P. Corneille. Paris, 1854.

────── : Histoire de la Vie et des Ouvrages de Molière. 3rd edition. Paris, 1844.

Thierry, Edouard : Registre de la Grange (1658-1685) précédé d'un notice biographique. Paris, 1876.

Tralage, Jean Nicolas du : Notes et Documents sur l'histoire des Théâtres de Paris au XVII siècle. Edited by the Bibliophile Jacob. Paris, 1880.

INDEX

Sourdéac, Marquis de, 229-230, 234-235.
Spanish acting, 4 ; companies, 170.
Spinet, the, 171-172.
Stage, seats on, 100-104.
Subsidies, royal, 29-30, 79.

TABARIN, see Salomon, Jean.
Tallemant, see Réaux, Tallemant des.
Talma, 243.
Tennis-Courts, at Berthault, 15 ; at Fontaine, 17 ; Hôtel de Nesle, 37, 43, 47 ; on tour, 51 ; in Faubourg St Germain, 171.
Theatre, the :—
Disturbances, 10-11, 91-93, 96, 100 et seq. ; construction, 100, 104 ; seats on stage, 100-104 ; scenery, 104 ; orchestra, 106-107 ; pit, 106-108 ; boxes, 107-108 ; greenroom, 109 ; lobby, 109 ; rehearsals, 111, 115, 116.
Théâtre français, 75, 77, 82 note[1], 106, 134, 233.
Thierry, Edouard, 75.
Thorillière, La :—
Molière and, 119 note[1], 192, 201, 227, 228 note[1] ; in "Alexandre," 178 ; in "Les Femmes savantes," 213 note[2], 216 ; in Hôtel de Bourgogne, 227, 254, 256.
Thuilerie, la, 254, 255.
——, Mlle., 254, 255.
Tickets, free, question of, 91, 92-94.
Ticket-seller, 94, 96.
Torelli, 138.
Tralage, M. du, 252-253.
Travelling companies, 80-81.
Treasurer, office of, 86, 87.
Troupe de Mademoiselle, 171, 187 note[1].
Troupe de Monsieur :—
Molière's company titled, 66 ; members, 67 note[1] ; loyalty to Molière, 138.

"Troupes de Campagne," 81.
Tuileries, 138.
Turlupin, 6 and note[1], 25 and note[3], 189.

URLIS, Etienne des, see Brécourt, Mlle.

VALLIOT, Mlle., 29.
Vannier, René, see Forêt, la.
Varlet, Chas., see Grange, La.
Venier or Vernier, Marie, see Laporte, Mlle.
Verneuil, 232, 233.
Versailles, 153 note[1], 184, 194, 218.
Vigarani, Signor, 137-138, 207 note[2].
Villaubrun, see Béjart, Geneviève.
Villequin, Edme, see Brie, de.
Villiers, de (Philippin) :—
Hôtel de Bourgogne, at, 24, 29, 127 ; and Molière, 68 note[2], 156 ; plays of, 116 note[2], 187 note[1] ; account of, 127 ; "La Vengeance des Marquis" attributed to, 155 note[3], 166-167.
Vinot, 76.
Visé, Donneau de :—
Molière, on, 67-69, 71 note[1], 159, 213 note[1] ; "La Devineresse," 94 and note[1] ; on Floridor, 133-134 ; on "L'Ecole des Femmes," 144-145 ; "Zélinde," 149-151, 154 note[1] ; age of, 152 note[1] ; "La Vengeance des Marquis" attributed to, 166-167 ; "La mère Coquette," 194 note[1] ; on "Circé," 236 and note[3].
Vivonne, Catherine de, see Rambouillet, Marquise de.
Voice-training, 252.
Voisin, 94 note[1].
Voltaire, 101.

WALLER, A. R., 28 note[2].